MEN *Seeking* MEN

Other Books by Michael Lassell

Poems for Lost and Un-lost Boys
Decade Dance
The Hard Way
A Flame for the Touch That Matters

Edited by
The Name of Love: Classic Gay Love Poems
Eros in Boystown: Contemporary Gay Poems About Sex
Two Hearts Desire: Gay Couples on Their Love
(with Lawrence Schimel)

Adventures in Gay Personals

MEN
Seeking
MEN

edited by Michael Lassell

Painted Leaf Press
New York City

Printed in Canada.

Cover design by Bill Sullivan.
Text design by Brian Brunius.
Special thanks to Jesse Dorris.

Published by Painted Leaf Press, 308 W. 40th St., NY, NY, 10018.

Library of Congress Cataloging-in-Publication Data

Men seeking men : adventures in gay personals / edited by
    Michael Lassell.
            p.   cm.
    ISBN 1-891305-02-6 (alk. paper)
    1. Gay men--United States--Social life and customs. 2. Gay men--United States--Sexual behavior. 3. Personals--United States.
    4. Dating (Social customs)--United States. I. Lassell, Michael, 1947-
HQ76.2.U5.M47   1998
306.76'62'0973--DC21
                                                            98-27646
                                                            CIP

This book is dedicated to
anyone who has been brave enough
to pursue desire...
and especially to those gay men
whose stories are included here, pioneers
of the heart's frontiers, for having the
courage to risk ridicule and
censure by writing about
their lives with
honesty,
poignancy, and
humor.

ACKNOWLEDGMENTS

First, I want to thank Bill Sullivan, whose idea this book was, for giving me the chance to make it happen, and the writers, almost all of whom came up with new work written specifically for *Men Seeking Men*. Thanks go to those few gay/lesbian city newspapers who ran our Call for Submissions and thus brought to my attention writers I would not otherwise ever have found out about. I want to thank my friend and sometime co-editor Lawrence Schimel for recommending David Harrison and Barry Lowe in particular. Thanks, too, to the men of Painted Leaf Press who produced *Men Seeking Men:* Brian Brunius, Griffin Hansbury, and Jesse Dorris.

I should note that "Getting Personal" by David Harrison was first published under the title of "The Personals" in *Pomosexuals: Challenging Assumptions About Gender and Sexuality,* edited by Carol Queen and Lawrence Schimel (Cleis Press, 1997), and that portions of James Joseph Arnold's "American On-line" appeared in somewhat different form in *Frontiers,* the L.A.-based newspaper that has published so much of my own work over the years. Neil Plakcy's "Hard Disk Not Found" appeared in different form in *Computoredge* and *The Miami Herald.* All are reprinted here by permission of the authors.

I'd also like to thank Richard Labonté and the crew(s) at A Different Light in New York, Los Angeles, and San Francisco, all of them hometowns at one time or another in my life, and—as always—the shining boys of my golden youth whose joys inform every breath I take, though they are no longer here to share the life I learned to live in their company. I will never forget them.

MEN *Seeking* MEN

TABLE OF CONTENTS

Introduction by Michael Lassell —————————— 3

Adventurous Italian ——————————————— 13
    by J.R.G. de Marco

?WM ——————————————————————— 18
    by Glenn Mills

Hard Disk Not Found ——————————— 29
    by Neil Plakcy

American On-line —————————————— 33
    by James Joseph Arnold

Friendship, Possibly More ——————— 37
    by Wayne Hoffman

Whipped Cream and Cherries ————— 41
    by Achim Nowak

Exit 40 —————————————————————— 48
    by Fred Bernstein

Public News ————————————————— 51
    by Erasmo Guerra

Lessons ——————————————————— 60
    by Jameson Currier

What I Wanted, What I Needed ——— 72
    by Nels P. Highberg

Dad ———————————————————————— 77
    by Patrick Arthur Dakin

Archaeologics ————————————— 80
    by Achim Nowak

Rebel ——————————————————————— 88
    by Tom Reilly

DHEA, Testosterone, Minoxidil, Fruition, and Eye Zone — 91
    by David Sanders

Missing Paul ————————————————— 100
    by Marc J. Heft

Berlin Connection —————————————— **108**
   by Owen Levy

Lie ————————————————————— **115**
   by Eric Latzky

Past Perfect ——————————————— **118**
   by Jessie McHallon Hall

Piss Elegant ——————————————— **128**
   by Barry Lowe

Personals ————————————————— **132**
   by Robert E. Penn

The Earth Moved ————————————— **135**
   by Roy Cameron

Dominant Sexual Animal —————————— **139**
   by Doug Harrison

None of the Above ———————————— **146**
   by J'son M. Lee

Impending Sex ——————————————— **162**
   by Lawrence Schimel

Jim the Virgin ——————————————— **168**
   by D. Spoiler, pseud.

Shit Happens ——————————————— **173**
   by Tim Driscoll

Play Party ————————————————— **183**
   by Doug Harrison

Flame ————————————————————— **197**
   by Tom Bacchus

Getting Personal —————————————— **205**
   by David Harrison

To Be Loved ———————————————— **212**
   by David Pratt

About the Authors ——————————————— **223**

About the Editor ——————————————— **233**

INTRODUCTION

by Michael Lassell

From the minute Painted Leaf Press's publisher, Bill Sullivan, first broached the idea to me of a collection of gay men's real-life experiences with personal ads, I was intrigued. We were having lunch in an 8th Avenue dive in New York City (publishing is *so* glamorous), talking about the cover for my latest book of poetry, *A Flame for the Touch That Matters,* which Bill was publishing. After agreeing on a concept, he brought up the book you have in your hands as a possibility for a next project together. We shared some of our own experiences trying to find love in the pages of queer and mainstream publications and repeated the stories friends had told us. I was sure I would not have the time to do yet another anthology (my fifth), but there you are—or here, I guess, because the schedule worked out just fine.

My own experience with advertising for boys dates from about five years ago, when friends began telling me of the successful liaisons they had effected by placing personals in the pages of the *Village Voice,* New York City's rather too venerable left-leaning arts weekly (or art-savvy political journal, depending on your point of view). I had been living in the city for about five years, all of it single after breaking up with my long-term lover in Los Angeles and moving back home. I had not found love in the places I had been looking, so I decided to boldly go where so many had gone before me. I took an ad.

I decided to tell the truth in the ad, a practice I came to learn that is not universal. I worded my ad carefully, stating that I was over 40 (I was about 45 at the time, but chose to believe folks who said I looked 38). I noted that I weighed 180 pounds, which was at the time true enough, since I'd been dieting and exercising like the good little third-generation obsessive/compulsive my parents raised. I represented myself as bear-like, hirsute, a poet by vocation and by nature, and (not beating around the bush) a top. I included the fact that I was in recovery, did not drink, use drugs, or smoke; that I was looking for dating situations with the possibility of a long-term relationship; and that I hoped to find a younger, smaller, employed, and homosexual male human being who cared more about spirituality than six-pack abs or circuit parties.

My seven lines of not more than 35 characters each were composed with the scalpel-like precision of a skilled neurosurgeon. Given that it is a *prose* form, the personal ad ranks in difficulty somewhere between a haiku and a villanelle. I was satisfied that my little one-inch of newsprint represented my accurate enough self both wittily and with some modicum of soul.

Dozens... nay, *scores* of New York men (and one woman) responded by leaving voice messages in my "mailbox."

I was flattered by the number.

I was appalled by what I heard. (Almost as appalled as I was when I got the phone bill a month later.)

"Hello, Michael... I loved your ad. I am 60 years old, weigh 400 pounds, smoke and drink, and don't know anything about writing or the arts, but I'd love to meet you..." is not an exaggeration.

"Hello, Michael... I loved your ad. I am a bisexual male..."

Click.

Okay, I admit it. I'm a bigot. I hung up every time I heard that one.

"Hi, Michael... I loved your ad. I've never had a homosexual experience before, but I'd really like to have one with you. I'm 24, and good-looking, according to my wife... oh, I'm straight, by the way. I'm looking to connect sexually in the afternoons while she's at work. Oh, and, I'm a paraplegic, so you should probably know that, too."

"You're making that up!" hooted Bill Sullivan from across the table when I told him the story over our 8th Avenue lunch of overcooked hamburgers and coalescing gelid french fries.

No, I did not make that one up.

I didn't make up the one about the priest who wanted to have sex in St. Patrick's Cathedral... oh, wait a minute. I *did* make that one up.

I declined people who were only after sex and people who said that they'd like to meet, but only if there were to be no sex involved.

I also declined to answer the responses of men who could barely speak English. Not because I have anything against any race, color, or country of origin (in fact, I *prefer* people who have not been bullied and tortured through childhood in the inexpressive Caucasian American middle-class, the one I grew up in). However, I *am* a writer. Communication is my business. Connection is my goal, my aim, my raison d'être. I just couldn't feature dating (with the possibility of a long-term relationship) people I could not understand on the telephone. This is probably making me sound like Jerry Seinfeld—not that there's anything wrong with that—but I was looking for a boyfriend, not a lubricious receptor for carnal lust. Okay, I was looking for the ready and willing orifice, too. I just wanted it attached to a decent, real, honest human being who shared some of my wide range of interests.

I chose some of the vaguely appropriate folk and started to schedule dates.

My first was a doctor, who happened to have been born in the Philippines. Well, my ex was part Filipino, so maybe that was a good omen.

Besides, he was a *doctor,* I thought. I might be actually be dating someone who earned more than I did for the first time in my life.

He was lovely. Not ravishingly attractive, but smart. He had a sense of humor. We had dinner at a neighborhoody Italian restaurant, and he—*we*—seemed simpatico. I asked him back to my apartment, a studio where socializing is not really feasible unless it involves condoms and lubricant.

We had sex. It wasn't the best sex I've ever had in my life. It wasn't the worst. I came; he didn't. Not for lack of trying. We agreed to meet again.

At first he accepted my calls but was busy changing hospitals.

Then I had a vacation.

Then he didn't return my phone calls.

The end.

My next first date turned out to be someone I already knew from my gym, and a weird little lad I'd always thought he was, too. He was very, very quiet at the gym, which I wrote off to shyness. He was quiet at dinner, too. Not that I mind talking exhaustively about myself, but I do require some sign of life behind the eyes. End of another story.

Next came a man from up the Hudson. He came to town on a rainy Saturday.

"Well, what would you like to do?" I asked.

"I don't know. What would you like to do?"

"You want to see a movie?"

"I don't know. Do you want to see a movie?"

"Sure. What would you like to see?"

"I don't know. What would you like to see?"

Well, you get the picture. Now, there's nothing I like better than being in control. I like being agreed with and catered to as much as anyone. But I like my dates to have a personality, too, and enough sense of self to have an opinion and to express it. I mean, it's one thing to be a bottom and another to be a doormat.

Then there was the boy who blathered *nonstop* about Judy and Liza and Barbra and every other pointless thing under the vicarious Hollywood sun, including who told what friend of the hairdresser of a cousin of a neighbor that each and every male actor in The Industry was a big fag, including Burt Reynolds (with Dom DeLuise, of course). Burt, you old chubby chaser, you!

"Oh, I'm talking too much," he said, filling a minuscule pause in his celebrity gush fest.

"Oh, *no*," I said, "it's keeping me awake."

"You want to go to your place?" he asked after dinner.

"Not tonight," I said. "I have to get up early." (So much for the promise I had made to myself to be rigorously honest.)

But really, can you say to a perfectly nice, reasonably appropriate if somewhat deluded (and bleached-blond) young man, "I'm sorry but I don't want to see you again" and offer no explanation whatsoever? Well, apparently, I came to discover, you can—or other people can.

He walked me home.

"Okay," I said on my corner. "Good-night. Gotta go."

"Well, I hope to see you again soon," he said.

"Good-night," I said.

I hadn't even gotten undressed when the phone rang. Guess who.

"I just wanted to make sure you understood that I really like you a lot, and I think there's a lot of potential between the two of us, and I hope you'll call me real soon."

Can you guess if I did?

(And I told Mr. Therapist—oops, excuse me, *Dr.* Therapist—that if he suggested to me that I was sabotaging myself by not going out again with the tragic-lady-singer fanatic just because he wanted to go out with me, then I would sabotage his Jungishness where it hurt him most, in the pocketbook.)

Next I had some lovely conversations on the telephone with a 6'3" African-American 30-year-old who worked as a toll-taker on the New Jersey Turnpike. He wasn't "smaller," he wasn't a doctor or a great talker, but he was "younger," and he sounded sweet, straightforward, blissfully non-neurotic. We made a date.

He stood me up.

I schlepped up to the Upper East Side. Always a mistake in my estimation, and this was no exception. (The apartment was a block from the movie theater where I had seen a film with another failed match, which was not a good omen.) The young man who answered the door was attractive, articulate, personable. He worked in an interior design showroom and, thankfully, had a very tasteful apartment that said he knew who he was and wasn't ashamed of it. His dog and I hit it off instantly. It was clear, however, from the minute our eyes met, that he had no interest in me, an intuition later confirmed when I called him for a second date and he said, there just wasn't any "spark."

Now, the notion of "spark" is an interesting one. It has to do with instant sexual attraction. I have had it often with people I've met at parties or seen on the street. I have had two long-term relationships with men who caused sparks to fly behind the fly of my jeans the first time I saw them, the first one in a bar in San Francisco, the second in a bar in L.A. Talk about your California dreamin'! The first spark was assisted by alcohol; the second was a sober spark. I followed the sparks like a surfer the waves.

Now, it was part of my point in taking a personal ad and meeting all these lovely single gay men to begin acting like a responsible adult instead of a horny adolescent, to get to know someone gradually whether or not there was any "spark," to let attraction grow with affection, to find the beauty in the intimacy before sex (okay, during sex, too). It is this "spark" thing,

I have come to believe, that is responsible for there being so many single gay men.

In fact, when the manuscripts started coming in as submissions to this anthology, there were more than a few that stated rather unapologetically, that the writer had gone to whatever place had been assigned for a first meeting and knew instantly that the waiting candidate was too old, too fat, or too ugly (all one word in common gay parlance: *oldfatandugly)* or that there was just no spark. Of course, people who lie about their age, size, or magnitude of attractiveness on a scale from a Calvin Klein model to, say, Jesse Helms (just to name the ugliest person I can think of at the moment) invite instant rejection for not being who they say they are, and they really *should* be chatting with their therapists about self-sabotage. The fact is that loneliness causes the kind of desperation that leads to lying because the values of the community are so... hmmm... shallow enough for a gnat to wade it?

For the record, I'm as romantic as the next person, and I believe that it is possible to *love* someone on first sight (as opposed to or in addition to being swept away on a rush of desire). But I think it is a *minority* phenomenon (also, you run the risk of falling on first sight in love with someone who isn't falling back, which has also happened to me). Naturally one wants to be attracted to one's boyfriend. However, the knee-jerk rejection response that seems built into the patellae of way too many pansies seems to me the reason so many of us are lonely, so many of us feel rejected. I am finding—and editing this anthology confirmed—that a dismaying number of us have substituted the notion of desiring someone with the notion of loving them, and of feeling desired for feeling loved, appreciated, accepted. In other words, having been rejected by our parents, our churches, our government, etc., etc., we have internalized homophobia to such an extent that we have codified "being desired" as the be all and end all of gay identity. And our market-driving "community" publications tend to perpetrate this problem by shoving an image down our throats, both in the advertising they allow to run and in the editorial content produced for us, that we have no value, no identity beyond inflated pecs and the purchasing power of our discretionary income.

My authentic life experience—as opposed to my "Someday my prince will come" fantasy life—is that I am either immediately, chemically attracted to someone, no matter how inappropriate or unavailable they are, or—in the alternative—come to find myself attracted to people I already know as some intellectual, emotional, or spiritual intimacy grows between us. I believe in honoring instant, chemical attraction. Certainly some of the best sex I have ever had has been of the spontaneous spark variety. I also believe that gay men who fail to pursue appropriate relationships because there isn't an immediate "I want you!" firecracker going off in their heads, hearts, or heinies are often (not always, but often) using the missing spark to hide behind.

But then, I am a child of the '60s and '70s. I believe that intimacy between people is what gives rise to morality as well as to camaraderie and love. Imagine my surprise when an old friend from San Francisco suggested to me one day in the mid-'90s that it was his experience that many gay men actually did not believe in intimacy as a goal. "You know," my wise friend Roy said, "this is a shocking thing to say, but a lot of gay men are not interested in intimacy. Intimacy is not what they are looking for. They're scared to death of intimacy, so they do sex instead."

It *was* a shocking thing to consider. It had in fact, never *occurred* to me that there were people who did not want intimacy in their lives (even though from time to time Dr. Therapist suggests that I am one of them, to which I am forced to point out that *fear of intimacy* based on wretched life experiences and *refusing intimacy* are two different things). Well, my friend Roy actually met his lover through the personals (his story is included in this book), so I wasn't quite ready to give up.

Jim was an artist. He was 38 at the time we met, I believe. We had dissimilar backgrounds but a lot of things in common. When we first met, he seemed attractive, decent, intelligent, compassionate. He was not "my type" (which is small, dark, smooth, and androgynous); I did not have to restrain myself from jumping all over him. However, he had all the qualities I would like to have in greater abundance than I do, and I liked him very much.

We'd meet for movies and meals, the usual gay-men-getting-to-know-one-another activities. We both liked films with literary content, but we could go for something loud and popular, too. Choosing a film was never difficult, even though we both had ideas about what movies were worth the time and money. We both had opinions, but negotiating didn't seem to intimidate us.

At one point I went to a show of his art.

Thank God, I remember thinking, *his art is good.* There is nothing worse than being around someone who is not good at what they do but think they are.

I gave him one of my books. He said he liked it.

Then over some meal or other, he told me he did not want to pursue a romantic relationship, even though I was someone he wanted in his life.

I took that, of course, as a rejection. When I have said it to others, it was meant as a rejection, albeit a soft-peddled one. It's a lot easier to reject an escaped lunatic with a loaded gun in a bar, I have found in my rather over-eventual life as an out fag, than it is to turn down a sweet soul you just don't think you can share your life with. It is, in fact, easier for me to be rejected than to reject another person.

Now, the fact is, I wanted a boyfriend, not more friends, and while I try to stay open to anything life presents, if Jim was not interested in being my boyfriend, there just was no compelling reason to see him much anymore, given the rejection that would always hover between us, and eventually we stopped making contact.

About a year later, deep into my own deeply self-destructive obsession with a young man who did not want to be my lover, I was sitting on the Brooklyn Bridge on a lunch break from jury duty, and Jim jogged by. He looked at me; I looked at him. I found him terribly desirable in his little nylon running shorts and rock-hard flexed thighs, hot-footing it toward Manhattan. I don't know what he thought. Or if he recognized me, or made the connection. Because we haven't spoken since. But I think of Jim as the one who got away.

Over the last five years, I've given up dating altogether. I'm 51 now (that's "early 40s" in ad-speak), and my waist size is still a smaller number than my age, but not by much. Most of my good friends are dead, and I'm not really feeling glamorous or optimistic about settling down to a contented golden age. An increasing number of young men seem to warm up to me as a daddy, but most of the time I think my real task in life is either to accept being single gracefully (if not happily), or to rekindle my relationship with my sweet ex (who unfortunately lives 3000 miles away: Economy is destiny).

Occasionally someone will IM in when I'm on-line (even though my AOL profile is quite, quite honest) and flirt. I flirt back, if it seems appropriate. I keep up quite a serious correspondence with some of these people, although I've met only one of them, a man named Marc, who is funny and sweet and smart and loves to go to the movies, which we do almost every week. And though he isn't the least inclined to pursue a romantic relationship, he has certainly been a happy addition to my life, which is better for the time I spend with him.

The stories that comprise this book represent an enormous variety of experience with personal ads, both in print and on-line. Some are stories of first-timers, some are tales of finding true love. A few are sagas of peak erotic experiences; more than a few are hilarious, sometimes both hilarious and steamy at the same time. Of the 30 stories that follow, some are written by professional, or at least experienced writers; others are by neophytes, appearing in print for the first time in these pages. Some of the writers were known to me (one for over 20 years); others I have never met. Some are seasoned sexual outlaws; others are veritable virgins. At least one is by a FTM transsexual. (I didn't ask, and only one identified as such, but who knows?)

All of them represent attempts to find connection—physical, emotional, spiritual, or some combination of these. "Only connect," was the advice of E.M. Forster, one of our tribe's grandfather scribes. And it speaks to the courage of all the men who contributed to this book that each of them tried to connect. I am in their debt for everything I have learned in the course of this anthologizing process, because all of the interactions between me and the authors were connections, too, of a sort; all represent new relationships or new levels of relationships; each story was the occasion for me to connect with another queer man, something I don't do nearly enough of.

I am, in fact, greatly heartened by the stories in this book. They suggest to me that intimacy still exists as a goal among gay men—some gay men in any case. We are, I was reminded while working on this book, more than the ads and fashion spreads of our own so-called press. Perhaps because I have not personally had any luck connecting with a soul mate, I had forgotten that many of us are still searching for things in each other that can enrich our individual lives while building the kind of values that have been scarce in our own community. I have, to some significant extent, stopped thinking of gay men in the late '90s as "them," and have come back to thinking of the far-flung faygelehs of the earth as "us." Of course, a lot of *us* have a long way to go before self-respect is held in greater regard than zero percent body fat and a drug-fueled circuit party stops being the ne plus ultra of queer existence.

A wonderful, crazy, complex friend of mine who became a well-known writer named Paul Monette, once told me that he knew that being in love was not the only way to find happiness, either as a human being or as a gay man. It was just the only way for *him.* I agree with him, especially now that I've been living alone for over ten years. And I salute the men whose stories appear on the following pages, for their successes in finding and maintaining love, and for their fortitude, persistence, and festive gay valor in the pursuit. *They* have the spark!

New York City

July 15, 1998

ADVENTUROUS ITALIAN

J.R.G. de Marco

I shivered as I walked. I kept thinking I had to be crazy to meet a guy I didn't know. In his apartment. On his terms. He could be a serial killer, and my liver might be his next meal. The possibilities frightened and excited me. I wondered if he'd be thinking the same things, since he only had my ad to go on:

Adventurous Italian
*GWM seeking to explore new worlds
and try things I haven't. Me: 5'6", br/br, 22,
clean shaven, well endowed, eager.
ISO someone around my age,
attractive and experienced,
redheads a plus, your own place
a must. Write care of PGN Box...*

It was honest, even if it was a little spare. We had also talked on the phone—not that doing that guarantees anything. So, I worried as I walked. The closer I got, the less adventurous I felt. Trudging through the slushy, snowy Philadelphia streets, I kept asking myself why I was doing this. Why this guy? Why not the accountant with a nine-inch dick? Why not the actor who said his favorite sexual thing was sixty-nine? No, it had to be this one, who claimed to be a mechanic and had a voice that screamed *"sex!"* Why did I want a mechanic, even if he was a couple of years older than me, blond, tall, muscular but not too much, and who enjoyed sex more than anything else?

The slush was like ice in a bucket around my shoes, and my toes were frozen, but my feet moved as if they knew the way. I neared the brownstone where he had his apartment, and my jaw began to quiver so much that my teeth clacked like a cartoon character. Gingerly taking the steps, trying not to slip on the ice, I felt as if I were climbing to the gallows.

When I found his name on the list, I pressed the buzzer. A moment later, the door latch made a razzing sound, and I tentatively pushed my way in. The curtain of warmth enveloped me like a security blanket. An old tune floated down the stairs from some apartment. I looked around at peeling paint and worn wooden floors and thought it felt cozy and lived-in. Not having my own place, it seemed like everything I longed for. Then I remembered why I was there.

An uncontrollable shiver shook my left leg as I placed a foot on the stair. His apartment was on the second floor at the rear. I knew he was waiting, but I didn't want him to see me quivering like a new bride. I took a few deep breaths and climbed the steps slowly. Each creak of the old wood seemed to cheer my progress or signal a warning. I wouldn't know which until I reached his door.

I found his apartment, 2E, and knocked so lightly that I could hardly hear it. But he must have been standing just behind the door, because it opened almost before my knuckles left the wood.

He was everything he had promised, maybe more. I could feel the shivers coming on again, so I tensed my jaw to keep my teeth from chattering. Of course, I couldn't speak that way. He smiled and opened the door wide. I smiled back stiffly then quickly averted my eyes, fearing that this would all be a disaster, that I'd be a failure at sex, and he would laugh, tell his friends, and shame me in front of a community I hadn't even joined yet.

If only I'd had sex with someone before this, so I'd at least *seem* experienced, so I'd know what to do with his body. I wanted to bolt and run out the door, but he had shut it behind me and was inviting me to sit in a macramé chair. I sat, figuring there was no room for him to sit next to me—which would prevent the inevitable for a while.

The lamps in the long, narrow efficiency apartment gave everything a soft yellow glow. The place smelled clean and fresh, not what I thought a mechanic's home would smell like.

"Joe, right?" He held out a hand. The fingernails weren't dirty as I'd expected.

"R-right," I stammered. "And you're Kyle. Nice to meet you." I stared at him and noticed his perfect skin and green eyes.

He wore a short terry-cloth bathrobe, which was tantalizing. Moving to his bed, not far from my chair, he slipped off the robe, displaying a body that belonged in a museum, then dropped to the bed, covering himself carelessly with a sheet. I stared, not knowing what to say, and tried smiling.

"Take off your coat and stay a while." His voice was soft and smooth and sexy.

I felt a muscle in my right leg jump like a plucked guitar string as I pulled off my gray overcoat and unwound the woolen scarf from my neck. Balling them up, I plopped both on my lap in a lumpy parody of a chastity belt.

We looked at each other for a moment, saying nothing. He appeared about my age but far more self-confident and calm. Which made me feel inadequate and small and comfortable all at the same time. His skin had that pink tone that some blonds have and that I wanted to smell and lick and consume. Breaking the silence, he said, "I liked your ad. I like adventure, but I told you that in my letter."

I gulped and nodded. Even if I could think of a response, I couldn't speak, because my mouth felt glued shut.

"What kind of adventure were you looking for?" he asked, then moved, causing the sheet covering his crotch to fall away. I could see his pink dick, semi-hard and looking like the most delicious thing I had ever seen in my life. I wanted it, and I was afraid of it. The muscle in my right leg kept hopping. My dick did some hopping of its own buried underneath my coat and scarf. It got harder, and I felt more frightened. I didn't know if I could control it. What if I came on the spot? What if I couldn't come?

He just stared at me. It was a kind stare. He wasn't mocking me, and he didn't seem amused by my inability to respond.

"You could put that coat somewhere else and be more comfortable, you know," he said. He moved a leg, and his generous balls, dark pink and heavy-looking, moved, too.

"It's... it's okay," I managed to croak out. "I ca... "

"This is your first time, right?" His tone was soothing.

"No... uh... yeah... I mean... yeah," I conceded.

"It's okay. Don't worry," he pushed himself to a sitting position, his legs still wide open, his cock long and inviting.

"I'm gay," I explained, hoping that would help. "I just haven't..."

"You haven't met anyone else from your ad? I'm the first?"

"Uh... yeah. The first. I liked the way you descri... I mean, I liked the way you sounded in the letter." My hard-on refused to go away. The coat was my only protection.

"This is a real adventure, then. Your first time." He dropped a hand to his thigh, but without touching his dick.

Suddenly his cock became the only thing in the world. It seemed to zoom out toward me, the eye of it staring at me, urging me to do something before it was too late. It was all I could see. I felt a bead of sweat trickle down my back. He didn't move his hand. It lay just next to his cock—close, but not touching. I wanted to be that hand.

Instead, I sat in the macramé chair hiding my woody, my eyes bugging out—or it felt like they were. I wondered what would happen next. He wasn't making any moves, and I sure as hell didn't know what to do.

The next thing I knew my mouth was moving, and words were coming out. "I... I guess I better get going..."

"You've gotta go?" There was sadness in his voice. I wanted to run over and hug him, but I was frozen to the damned chair.

"Yeah... well, you know. I live with my parents and they kinda expect me for dinner..."

"It's only three o'clock," he said.

"Well, I have a couple of errands to run before I get home. The library... You know how it is. I have a paper to write for a class. I'm in grad school and..." I trailed off.

"Yeah, well, I guess so." He pushed himself off the bed, stretched his golden-pink body. I wanted him, I just didn't know what to do. He bent down to pick up his robe, and I saw the most beautiful ass I had ever seen before, or have seen since.

All of a sudden, he was covered in the robe and walking me to the door.

"You know the address. You can come back anytime." He smiled. I wanted to faint.

"Did anyone ever tell you how cute and sexy you are?" he asked and stroked my cheek with a warm finger. I could feel the heat rise in my face.

"I'll call. Promise."

I stood outside his door, coat in my arms, remembering the sight of him, wanting to kick myself. I kept thinking how perfect he had been, how gentle and quiet, how he never tried to force anything—probably because he saw how nervous I was.

Feeling as if I had lost something, I turned to the door and traced the brass 2E with my finger. It was smooth and golden. Like him.

"Shit," I whispered to the air as I wrapped the scarf back around my neck. "I wish he had tried something," I mumbled into the folds of the blue wool. Leaning against what I thought was the wall, I exhaled my frustration. Was life going to be like this all the time?

Just then, I felt the wall fall away. Instantly I realized that I had been leaning on the door, and he was opening it. I fell backward onto the floor and sprawled there, looking up at him. He said nothing as he bent down to pick me up. Helping me to my feet, he planted a kiss on my lips and wrapped his arms around me.

The library, the paper, and dinner would have to wait.

?WM

Glenn Mills

I've always been ballsy in a cowardly sort of way. This chicken-shit tendency in me is responsible for a long list of Most Embarrassing (even Shameful) Moments that preceded my coming out. In high school I picked a fight with a guy two years younger than me who just happened to be both the town "fag" and the only guy of the 150 in Richland who was skinnier than me. And until he kicked my ass, he also happened to be the only guy at whom I caught myself constantly staring.

In college I used my skill in hitting road signs with beer bottles from a moving vehicle to win cheers from my friends as we raced by the only queer bar in Southern Baptist southwest Missouri. From the safety of a crowded pickup truck a block away, I could drop a bomb on the two steps behind the handful of people as they tried to sneak into the unmarked bar and watch them duck as if they were being shot at. After college, on business trips with my first job in an oil company management-training program—motivated by Jagermeister and my frat-boy co-workers—I became a generous tipper in titty bars across the Rocky Mountain Region. In Green River, Wyoming, one Wednesday, a stripper named Tuesday pulled, without using her hands, ten ones from between my teeth as I lay on the stage between her stiletto heels. When she offered me a private demonstration of how she used certain muscles, I was appropriately disappointed as the guys dragged me out of the bar so we could help lay pipe at six a.m.

I had always been motivated most by fear. Fear of being caught staring, fear of protesting the cruelty of the normal majority over the ashamed few, fear of having a different appetite than the heterosexual men with whom I shared expense-account meals. This motivation made me susceptible to taking dares to keep from disappointing those who accepted me and to prove that I deserved acceptance. The last and biggest such dare came shortly after I came out.

In the first year I lived in Kansas City, I attached myself completely to the two friends I had from college. As I watched Brian desperately trying to make partner in an accounting firm and Jed consumed with falling in love with Paula, my cultivated enthusiasm for the courtship rituals at Friday's happy hour shriveled up and died. I got my own tiny apartment and spent the next year reading Kafka's notebooks and listening to the Smiths. I sat on the beige carpeted floor in the dark and chain-smoked while staring up at parties that took over the balconies of the high-rise behind my building.

One Sunday afternoon, I accidentally discovered Michael Chabon's book, *The Mysteries of Pittsburgh.* I stayed up all night and called in sick the next morning to finish reading it. By Monday afternoon, the fear that had conditioned me to be the most eager-to-please puppy dog had changed. Whatever animal instinct that the fear curbed was now closer to tearing free from its leash. I suddenly knew and accepted what I was inside, and the safe kennel that I had readily helped construct felt more like a cage. But twenty-five years of practice were not forgotten overnight. I spent another six months crouching in the dark and chewing on the leash before my best friend moved to Kansas City and helped free me completely.

Telling Millie was made easier by her open acceptance of her own bisexuality. We had never discussed it as a subject of its own. Before her move to Kansas City from Washington, D.C., I pointedly steered any conversation we had away from sex and toward anything else—how messed up our families were, how neurotic we were over nail-biting and intestinal gas, how boring most people were. When I told her, on her third day in town, at the bottom of our fourth pitcher of beer, I grabbed onto the hope that she could understand and explained my year of self-imposed solitary and Chabon's book. Then I told her I could no longer deny a sexual attraction to men, that I had accepted that I must be bisexual. The relief I felt made the implicit lie of an existing sexual attraction to women dissolve to nothing, and we never discussed it again.

My hyper-vigilant concern for careful representation of who I was had not been entirely a curse. Such minute attention to detail had been a gift when it came to writing cover letters and going to job interviews, and it had earned me the role of resume consultant with most of my friends. Soon after Millie's arrival, she and I set about getting her a job by using the computer at my office at night. As she marked up the Sunday paper and printed off each targeted resume, I pretended to work while I wallowed around between relief and frustration. My suggestions for phrasing her skills in the best possible light were interrupted with the questions and fears that settled in with my revelation.

I knew no one who was gay, and I was only beginning to realize that the stares I received in my apartment building, or in the bars of Westport, were communicating more than some judgment of what a freak I looked like because of my wild curly hair and geeky black glasses, or because I looked too young to be wearing a suit and tie to work. Sure, *I* now knew, and it was no longer a secret, but now what?

Millie first met my concerns with an obvious suggestion—the direct approach.

"The next time a cute boy is looking at you, try saying 'Hi, my name's Glenn.'"

For her, it worked. For me, it was impossible—there were two risks I couldn't take. What if the guy wasn't gay? What if he was but was only looking because he couldn't decide if I looked like Elvis Costello or Buddy Holly? Her response was that I might be able to get lucky in some video booth at an adult bookstore. Instead of telling her I already knew about Ray's Play Pen and Erotic City, I laughed and said I wasn't about to try to kiss some creepy old man I couldn't see through a glory hole.

Her next suggestion was also made as a joke, because she just knew I would never do it. She explained that in D.C. she had a couple of friends who regularly met people for social and/or sexual relationships through personal ads. She reasoned that it made as much sense as meeting someone in a bar, and said that life in D.C. was so scheduled and rushed and focused on appearances, that a personal ad could be a filter to get through the crowd before one even had to decide on physical attraction.

"Besides, for someone like you who is too embarrassed to just tell someone your name in person, maybe it would be more like getting a job. They apply on paper, and then there's a phone interview first. By the time you would actually see the person, maybe you could say your name."

That night, I studied the personal ads in the *Pitch,* Kansas City's entertainment paper. I had regularly read them and often told myself I might respond to one if it stuck out as different from the five to ten ads in the Men Seeking Men section each week. But they were always the same. I could pick any ad and match its generic data to any one of twenty guys who walked by from one bar or restaurant to another on Westport Road. Did every man in a button-down shirt call himself "preppy"? Did every guy whose gut didn't hang over his belt think he had a "swimmer's build"? How many of the guys walking by with their girlfriends in tow thought of themselves as "straight acting"?

The next night, while Millie worked on my computer, I went through four pages of paper playing with different phrases and factoids about myself. I was imagining the kinds of things I would want to know about someone before I would ever respond to an ad. Any ad I to which I was going to respond would have to be a sort of puzzle, not an impossible one, but one whose solution would reveal something unique about the guy writing it. Having the ability to solve the puzzle would mean that I, as a respondent, had something very particular in common with the ad's writer. I figured all the physical stuff would only matter when I finally faced the guy.

In composing my own ad, I considered mentioning how much I liked to cook, but decided to rule it out because I didn't want anyone to think I wanted a domestic arrangement. I thought about avoiding any mention of sex, because I didn't want to give the impression, no matter how true, that I was desperately horny. And I felt I would have to find a way to draw the attention of guys in a similar place as I was with regard to their sexuality.

When Millie was ready for me to shut down the computer, I presented her with my little composition:

?WM

*26, professional. New explorer seeks
other "?"-ing male eager to search the
deepest recesses of mind, body, and thrift stores
while learning "The Mysteries of Pittsburgh."*

Spiritual slacker enjoys theater, small films, cycling,
tennis, get-naked canoe trips, and
Thursday nights at Javagaia.

The half-joke I made about running it the following week was met, before she even read it, with, "Yeah. Right. Sure you are. And I start my new job tomorrow."

By the time she finished reading it, I had decided, in silence, that I would run the ad. Knowing there was a protective veil of anonymity around it let me put aside the fear of actual contact with anyone who might respond. No one who read it would know me anyway. Besides, I would not have to return a single call if anyone did respond, right?

I missed the next week's deadline, so I had almost two weeks to ponder what might happen. During that time, I had two opportunities to try the direct approach in meeting someone and failed at both. I began to believe that if I didn't experience real contact with another man soon that my creativity in the kitchen would be exhausted by searching my refrigerator for new ways to masturbate. I became obsessed with the images from my growing porn collection not for dicks or chest muscles or rounded butts, but for lips—sneering, pouting, wet, parted, puckered lips. I was dying to know what a kiss from an unshaven face felt like. Nothing in my vegetable crisper offered itself, and I knew of the dangers of raw meat. As chilled air poured around my bare feet, I imagined the electric meter orbiting at light speed, and all I could see was some meter reader pulling on his lip as he puzzled over what might be going on in Apartment 209.

I had planned to meet Millie at Javagaia the day the *Pitch* came out to begin our usual Thursday hanging out. I arrived early, grabbed a copy, and got coffee. I was terrified and somehow imagined they might not print it. But the question was answered while I waited for my drink. One of the guys working the counter was raving about the ad to a customer he knew. It wasn't like a spotlight flashed on me, but I suffered a wave of panic that went away when I figured that maybe they were just jazzed about the publicity the coffeehouse received in the ad. That conclusion didn't last long though when the customer said, "I wonder what he looks like sprawled out naked in a canoe?"

This would have been the point where Millie would have said, "Well, why don't you ask him?" and pointed at me. Luckily I was early, and alone. So I just stood there and tried to keep the capillaries in my face from exploding while the barista said, "I don't know, but I bet he's hot." Already the ad had been useful. It had helped answer a question that Millie and I spent weeks debating about the cute little coffee boy.

The ad ended up being one of the most popular the *Pitch* had published. I stopped counting responses after a few days of retrieving the voice-mail messages left me with a total of 37. And I learned quickly that no amount of care I took in the wording would have prevented half of the respondents from calling. There were guys who called to invite me to join their "private, clothing optional, outdoor clubs," whatever that meant. There were old men who were eager to use their "experience" to teach me anything I could possibly want to know. And there were even a couple new age types who thought Javagaia was either a temple or a commune. But none of those responses affected me much. I was glad I'd never knowingly have to face them. I wrote down the number of the first guy (I think he was the third or fourth call) who actually spoke some understanding of the more cryptic aspects of the ad, and he was the only person I called.

In his voice mail message, Andrew said quite a few things that connected with me, even things that had nothing to do with what I had revealed in the ad. He said that Javagaia was one of his favorite places in town and that he was glad it opened because he had missed such places since moving to Kansas City from D.C. a year before (the first connection—since Millie had lived there and I had visited her a couple times). He mentioned that he was originally from Colorado (the second connection, since I had lived in Denver before I accepted the job that moved me back to Missouri). He told me he worked as an artistic director in a children's theater (the third connection, again not explicitly stated in the ad, but I had been taking acting lessons as my only hobby for two years—hoping to pull myself out of my shell but instead, learning how to be more convincing about whatever shell I chose to wear).

But it was his mentioning what a great book he thought Michael Chabon had written that pulled me in. He ended the message with some by-the-way, in-case-you're-wondering, data about his physical appearance—something I never remembered about his height and weight, hair and eye color.

He left me both a home and work number. I decided to call him from my office at lunch when everyone would be gone. I thought I would get some indication of the weirdo factor if he behaved strangely on the phone. A woman answered the phone, using the name of the theater, and when I asked for Andrew, she called him to the phone saying, "It's some boy."

Once I got him on the phone, we began talking easily from the common facts I'd already learned. We discussed D.C. and Denver and acting. We talked about thrift-store bargains—my specialty was finding Krups kitchen appliances, and his was finding props and costumes for his shows. And we both had strange recycled furniture in our apartments. I told him I would soon be using the benefits of my recent promotion to move into a converted loft in the City Market. Coincidentally, he lived in a loft near the building where I had signed a lease. He had recently moved to a larger space because the view in his old apartment was limited to an alley and part of the Missouri River. When he described his previous apartment and the old barber chair he owned, I realized I had actually been in the apartment before he moved when I first started looking at the lofts.

We decided to have lunch in the City Market. I made a safety plan to meet friends at five o'clock but determined that—unless he was a monster—anything goes. When I met him, I was most struck with how much he looked like Peter Frampton (the first rock star I developed a crush on—to impress an uncle six years older than me). He told me how his friend Brian presented the ad to him, and Brian said it wasn't his type, but he thought Andrew might be interested. I showed him the empty apartment that was waiting for me to move into the following month. We went back to his apartment, and soon silence set in. He checked his watch, and asked what I wanted to do, stammering out the words.

I responded with the corniest thing ever to come out of my mouth: "Um, anything. I guess. I'm completely in your hands." I'm completely in your hands. It was corny, but within ten minutes it became true.

I know kissing him couldn't have lasted more than two minutes, but it was the slowest, most completely satisfying two minutes I had ever experienced. He complimented me on the perfection of my teeth. From the kiss we moved through four hours of pure animal sex. He told me he couldn't believe I had never done any of this. He expressed amazement at the length and curve of my dick, though I knew he was only being nice—since his wasn't so much shorter than mine but was as big around as my thin wrists. He removed his finger from between my legs to applaud my first orgasm when I apologized for drenching the velvet curtain that served as his closet door four feet away. Staining the curtain was followed by making three other messes around the room—one on the carpet, and two on opposite ends of his bed. He was enthusiastic and patient, and though I consider myself attentive during sex now, I still can't recall his getting off.

I finally left, an hour late to meet my friends. I was completely devoid of tension in any muscle in my body, a satisfied, tired soreness in places that had never tingled before—even after whole weekends spent abusing myself alone with my latest stash of magazines purchased in a safely foreign suburb of Kansas City. I left knowing I would be seeing Andrew again as soon as I possibly could.

I did see him. The next night. And every night for a month. And almost every night for the next six months. He introduced me to his friends. I met the Kansas City theater crowd and began to realize that people found me attractive. I met his friends David and Gary at a play a week or so after our first day together. I caught them staring at my mouth and, once or twice, at my crotch. It was only after establishing a friendship with David on my own that I learned why they had stared.

I made it clear to Andrew that I couldn't imagine the concept of a boyfriend. But that didn't matter—within a month he imagined the concept for both of us, and began giving me little gifts to celebrate monthly anniversaries. He took me on a weekend trip to a gay bed and breakfast. He cried when I gave him a boxed set of ABBA CD's.

I began to feel close enough to David to talk about what was happening, that I had fun with Andrew, but I just couldn't be his boyfriend, and maybe it was time to change our relationship. I let David know that I appreciated how kind and patient Andrew had been, and that it was beginning to feel like I was just using Andrew while he, as he said himself, was falling in love with me. I was still trying to negotiate how I felt about dancing with men, how uncomfortable I felt in the presence of effeminate men and irreverent drag queens. And if the idea of "boyfriend" was still foreign, I couldn't even let myself imagine what it meant to fall in love. I told David that Andrew deserved better after being so good to me.

It was at this point that David told me why he and Gary had been surveying me on our first meeting. At that time they didn't even know my name. All they knew was that I was "that guy with the perfect teeth and really long dick who came four times and shot across the room." They didn't know that we had met through my ad until a week after I met them. This info didn't really affect me much. After getting to know Andrew, I figured in some strange way he was only trying to ensure that others got the impression that there wasn't much riding on a relationship with me at the time. And like many things that had the power to embarrass me, it was true.

David's other revelation made me feel like a fool almost as completely as getting my ass kicked by the town pansy in high school. As we talked about my ad, and how I ended up meeting Andrew, David corrected the story Andrew had told me. Yes, his friend Brian had presented Andrew with the ad, but he had not suggested that it seemed more Andrew's type. He presented it for Andrew to read, and asked Andrew whether he thought Brian should respond. When Andrew saw the ad, he told Brian that he had already called about it, and thought it would be weird if they both responded. And that's both how Andrew found out about the ad, and how he prevented at least one competitor. But what about *The Mysteries of Pittsburgh?* David told me that Andrew admitted to Brian that he hadn't actually read the book, and so Brian told him about it.

Finding out these little truths wrecked me a little at the time. I felt so stupid for being defrauded. Now I see it as a certain flattery that someone could be so determined to meet me. But what I held onto at the time, and what I still hold onto are the facts— we did have a lot of common connecting points that made it possible for me to dance around some neurotic tendencies that might have kept me from ever being able to touch another man. He was the first man with whom I had complete sex—in the daylight, with all our clothes off, in the flesh. And he was the first man I ever kissed.

I also expressed to David that I still felt like I didn't know anyone other than him. I had met a lot of people, but had nothing in common with the theater types who saw me as a novelty—an innocent, hyper-responsible company man and fledgling fag. He said I didn't have anything to worry about—there would be guys lining up just waiting for me when they found out I was single, when Andrew was no longer constantly parading me around. I doubted that that would be the case, because I still couldn't approach a strange guy in a gay bar, much less on the street. I openly stared, and smiled, but I still couldn't open my mouth.

Shortly after this discussion, Andrew and I talked about my intention to meet some people on my own (though I had no plan in mind as to how). He said he understood, though he wished it were otherwise. I didn't tell anyone about the second ad I wrote:

WM

*26, not political but not afraid, seeks similar
male with similar character flaws for low-key
hanging out and bent weekend fun.
Physically active corporate prostitute enjoys
thrift store mining, tennis, hacky sac, Kafka,
the renaissance of Disco, and occasional trips
outside of My Own Private Idaho.*

Re-reading the text now, I see the changes between the two ads. The question mark was gone, though I still wouldn't enthusiastically call myself gay. *The My Own Private Idaho* remark was supposed to be indicative of some contempt for people so comfortable with whatever little clique to which they belonged. In particular, I had in mind the theater crowd that seemed to forget who I was whenever Andrew wasn't around. And the words "but not afraid" have a certain irony because, though I was dwelling on the progress toward self-acceptance I had made in six months, I see now that much of my long-learned fears still hung around my neck.

The ad was published on the day of one of my last real dates with Andrew. When I arrived at Gary's house, David greeted me with the paper, and cornered me with the second ad. He couldn't believe I had not considered that someone might recognize the writing—"Come on, the last time there was an ad in here anything like this was the first ad you ran." But I hadn't. I didn't see myself as having any particular style. I was just being me. I'm just now beginning to learn that the two things can be synonymous.

The response to this ad was completely different. It won Ad of the Week and earned me a big boxed, headlined second printing along with a T-shirt from a classic rock station I never listened to. But in my voice-mail greeting, I made sure to piss off most of the people like those whose calls I didn't return from the first ad. I lectured against anyone who would call himself "straight-acting" by explaining that the phrase implied a pointed effort at fakeness or hypocritical behavior. Then I turned around and said I wasn't interested in anyone who was effeminate or interested in teaching me something. I didn't claim I now had nothing to learn, but I did know that I could teach myself. As a result of my philosophizing, I received only a handful of responses. And this time I chose the one who didn't seem so eager to express our commonality. He told me he was also a "corporate prostitute" and that he wasn't political either, and that was it.

Mark and I were together for over two years. In that time I made gay friends of my own. And when he earned a promotion that moved him to Philadelphia, I chose to stay in Kansas City rather than move to a strange city where I would be his "roommate" if anyone called. With a network of friends and the complete realization (if not understanding as to why) that men found me attractive, I learned how to flirt in person. And though I still have a long way to go, I've learned a lot about the difference between a conditioned pseudo-courage that comes from cowardice and having the balls to show the world how afraid I can sometimes be.

HARD DISK NOT FOUND

Neil Plakcy

He answered my personal ad, which I'd headlined "Computer Jock."

"What did you mean by that?" he asked during our first phone conversation.

"I know my way around a hard drive," I told him, a little immodestly. "I'm not afraid to take the case off and fiddle with the modem or the com port. And I never read the instruction manuals that come with software. I'd rather just figure it out myself."

It must have been the right answer. We talked about our families and our busy lives in Miami, and then we agreed to meet at a café on Lincoln Road in South Beach.

There, under the soft lights, we talked more about ourselves. He had a large cast of characters in his life and a Dilbert situation at work—the usual tangle of petty jealousies and office infighting—all of which I tried to keep straight.

But I had a hard time paying attention. The problem was his eyes: They were simply beautiful, mesmerizing, coy—maybe holding a secret. I found I couldn't keep from smiling when I looked at him.

Somehow the conversation settled on computers. He seemed fascinated by them. He wanted to hear about hardware malfunctions and software bugs. He teased me that if we dated, my computer might be jealous.

Then he mentioned, quite casually, almost an afterthought: "I have a laptop. But I'm not sure it even works."

"I can take a look at it for you," I volunteered.

"That would be nice."

Eventually, we spent a night together at his town house in Kendall, a lovely place full of artwork and antiques. Kisses on the sofa led to lovemaking in the bedroom. At that particular moment, the last thing on my mind was computers.

But as he lay beside me, slowly threading his fingers through the hair on my chest, he gazed at me with those mesmerizing eyes and said softly, almost in a whisper, "Would you look at my laptop?"

Next thing I knew I was out of his bed and perched on a hard stool in the kitchen. He brought the laptop out, and I plugged it in and watched as the liquid crystal screen came to life. It cycled through its memory check and then displayed some bad news: HARD DISK NOT FOUND.

"You've got a problem with your CMOS," I said.

"My sea moss?"

"The hardware setup," I said. "I can fix it."

My fingertips flew over the keyboard as he gazed worshipfully over my shoulder.

"If you can fix my computer, I'll love you forever," he promised.

It took a couple of tries to get the hardware configuration right. Finally, I got everything working, and I logged into Windows. A perfect repair.

He kissed my cheek, taking my hand in his.

"Ready to go back to bed?" he asked.

Foolishly, I hesitated. "Let's just check one last thing," I said.

I exited Windows and turned the computer off. Then I switched it on again. The screen illuminated the same old bad news: HARD DISK NOT FOUND.

I went back into the CMOS and found that none of the settings I'd changed had been retained when I turned the power off. I tried it all once more. HARD DISK NOT FOUND, the computer hooted at me.

"This is more than I can fix, " I finally said.

He looked sadly at the plastic case. "I thought it was dead anyway," he said. "But there for a moment, watching you..." He shrugged. "Oh, well."

Then he yawned. And then he said those deadly words, familiar to all who have loved mightily and lost pathetically: "Boy, it's late. And I have to get up early."

I collected my clothes and kissed him good night. "Next week is really busy for me," he said. "I'll call you."

When he hadn't called by Saturday, I called him and left a message on his machine. It took two more unanswered messages over the next two weeks to convince me I wouldn't be seeing him again.

I told my friend Steve all about it. He's one of the few computer guys I know who had been able to work through the dating game, finding a boyfriend he could love and cherish.

"I tried everything I could," I said. "And it still didn't work out."

"The battery had probably been drained so far it couldn't come back," he said. "Sometimes you just have to give up on them."

I suppose he meant the laptop.

AMERICAN ON-LINE

James Joseph Arnold

In the spring of 1996, I was laid off from my job of eight years as a PR guy for a big Hollywood movie studio. With the nice severance package the powers-that-be provided, I took some great advice and set forth on a walkabout, which at 41 years of age in 1996 America took the form of a three-month road trip around the United States.

I wanted to meet other gay men everywhere I went, and being a high-tech kind of guy, I took my laptop computer with me and placed ads on Usenet Groups and on America Online, looking for local guys to provide me with companionship, sex, information, encouragement, or all of the above. That's basically what the note said, and it also listed the cities I planned to pass through.

Jeff (Fort Lauderdale, Florida)

I'm staying in South Beach and getting hornier by the hour! The men here are unbelievably hot. It's like "Water, water everywhere and not a drop to drink"—at least for me. I can't seem to connect with any of the tan, buff, snotty little gods patrolling Collins and Ocean avenues. Finally, not able to take one more minute of the vintage air conditioner blasting my ears, I get out of the Claremont Hotel, speed over the causeway, and hook a right on to I-95 heading north.

Fort Lauderdale is just north of Miami, so it takes only minutes to get there. Initially, it reminds me of a small resort town, like Palm Springs, only with an ocean. (I know, it's a big difference.)

But fuck the water for a minute. In my shorts, my dick leaks. The reason for this is that I have been chatting on-line with a guy who lives here. He's been teasing me, promising some sexual paradise. I can't think of anything else.

His real name is Jeff, though he has an appropriately risqué handle on AOL. Jeff and I have been talking for a couple of days now about getting together when I reach Ft. Lauderdale. I race into a grocery store parking lot as soon as I see the pay phone. Fuck! No change. My fanny-pack disguises my hard-on as I go in and buy a banana so I can get a quarter for the phone. I peel and start eating it as I fumble for his number. Of course, I don't taste banana; I taste dick. I find the number, phone Jeff. He's there, waiting for my call.

Jeff gives great direction and, as luck would have it, he lives right in the neighborhood. Thank God for small towns! I'm at his house in a matter of minutes. Jeff has the kind of body I really go for: He's an ex-gymnast—short, smooth, muscular, tattooed, cocky and kind of slutty. I swoon. I ask about the thick bandage wrapped around his thigh as he pulls my shorts off.

Nonchalantly, he tells me he has been stabbed in the leg saving his old neighbor lady from some crack dealers. Suddenly, this little tryst takes on the new, exciting, and frankly sexual dimension of possible danger.

Anyway, we have sex standing up, since Jeff tells me any kind of weight or pressure on his bandaged leg hurts him. It's quick and we come on each other's thighs. I'm out of Jeff's house before the crack dealers have a chance to extract any revenge, but what has transpired is just what the doctor ordered.

Steve (Pittsburgh, Pennsylvania)

I think that northwestern Pennsylvania has to be the road-kill capital of America: More dead deer carcasses line the highway than I've ever seen before, and it's at once sad and also frightening—these are not small animals.

It's a Friday night and I'm to meet Steve, an Internet friend I first met on AOL. We had cybersex. He played the top; I was his willing bottom. Since then, we've had several slightly deeper conversations (no pun intended). At ten years my junior, Steve has a multitude of boyfriend and school/career issues I'm more than happy to offer some solicited advice on.

But right now I'm trying to navigate my way through some dark and rainy Pittsburgh industrial streets, trying to find the establishment where Steve is working behind the bar tonight. I end up at Two Rivers Stadium twice before finding the old brick building hiding beneath a bridge.

I know at once it's him when I walk in, and he knows immediately who I am. Thank God for computer graphics technology! He's funny—makes a big deal out of his thinning hair by removing his baseball cap, as if I could care. Steve is a thirty-year-old aerobics instructor with a smile that could melt all the ice in all the drinks he serves up to these gay men of Pittsburgh. I can't stay a long while in any bar, and we make plans to spend Saturday together.

He picks me up at the motel, and I feel immediately at ease. Our friendship shifts seamlessly from a cyber to a real one without missing a beat, and I have to admit I'm flattered with this attention from a younger man.

We drive up into the hills surrounding downtown Pittsburgh, which is on a point of land where the Allegheny and Monongahela rivers meet to form the Ohio. The Allegheny is blue, the Monongahela brown. Steve explains that there is still much industry upriver on the Monongahela. From our vantage point across that river, high up on Mount Washington, he stands too close to me and points out several landmarks. My impression of this view is that Pittsburgh remains proudly working class; the predominance of modest single-family frame homes reminds me of Milwaukee, where I grew up.

During our day together, I find out a lot about Steve, his family, his problems with his dad, his dreams for the future, and his relationship woes, which are not simple. After the gym, the sightseeing, and some shopping (hiking boots for him—these boys are butch!), we get back to the motel, and I find a biker momma in the parking lot to snap a picture of us. My heart pounds as we walk back to the room. I ask him to come in.

I give him a kiss, as I have been wanting to do since I met him, though I'm really not expecting a whole lot more since I know he's involved. He keeps saying, "I shouldn't do this" through his sexy smile, and something tells me he's going to anyway. Within minutes, all our clothes are scattered, and we are on the floor. It's even better in real life than it was on the phone.

This is what I want, though I feel a bit guilty because this man has a lover. I'm the brazen hussy this time, but I honestly don't care. I hope our paths cross again in other than the electronic world. Steve's a keeper.

Phil (Somewhere in the Colorado Rockies)
Much further along on my trip west, I stop to meet Phil, who has answered my post on AOL for a Colorado liaison. Phil lives in a tiny, dusty town on the western slope of Colorado's Rockies, a far cry from the glitzy ski resorts just a few miles to the east.

I find him at the his general store on the town's deserted, parched main drag. Phil said he was 60, but I am guessing he is really closer to 70. Before I agreed to see him I had said that my sexual tastes ran to younger men, but that I'd be delighted to meet him for coffee. He's shorter than I am with a shock of white hair and a limp suggestive of some injury or illness, but he has a surprisingly strong handshake and a devilish grin. He takes me over to Mike's Burgers, where everyone in the place greets him by name, and we sit at an oilcloth-covered table.

With very little prodding, Phil launches into a major historical recitation of the high points in the area's first hundred years. Phil was born out in the country about twelve miles from where we sit. He taught school for a while back East, but when an offer came to run the town newspaper, he returned. Not only was he the editor, he set the type and did just about everything else. The paper eventually folded, so Phil opened his store sometime in the 1970s.

I ask Phil what it's like to be gay in a place like this, and he doesn't say too much but hints that he is far from being the only one. Many men in the area may consider themselves bisexual, and Phil suspects this classification makes them feel better about what they feel inside. I get the impression he's not lacking, and there's some gay social life in Grand Junction, the neighboring metropolis of forty thousand.

Phil seems a man comfortable in his own skin, something I often don't see in big-city guys. He pays for my coffee and frozen yogurt and directs me to the back roads that will take me into Utah. As I drive off, the screen door of his general store bangs shut, and Main Street's deserted once more.

Alex (Vancouver, British Columbia)
Occasionally, things happen that make you want to pinch your-

self, because you just can't believe your good luck, and you visualize God smiling above. I spend the day with Alex, who is my last date from the Internet and the last man I will meet on this trip.

We make arrangements to rendezvous at Hamburger Mary's for brunch, and when he walks in I think I'm dreaming: A smiling young Latino, he's got dark-brown, buzzed hair and a goatee, light-blue eyes like gemstones, and muscles that bulge from under his shirt (I can't keep my eyes off his shoulders and arms). So we eat, we chat, we go back to his place, conveniently located on the road between the restaurant and Stanley Park's sea wall, which he is going to show me.

Alex is a composer who produced a CD of his own last year, which he plays for me. I love listening to his music and watching him talk, using his hands to emphasize his many points. I watch his fish play in the tank, wondering if he is as attracted to me as I am to him (although when a man asks you into his house, it's a pretty good sign). After a long pleasant conversation, we start to touch, to kiss. He sits on my lap, and the clothes come off.

He takes my hand and leads me into his room, where his bed is completely covered with down pillows, and we sink into them. It's delicious. I experience some of the sweetest, most luxurious kisses in recent memory. He's a wonderful lover, a perfect combination of male animal passion and that gentleness you find in a gay man who is truly at peace with himself.

Afterwards, we really do take that walk down to Stanley Park, and I am in love with Vancouver and with Alex, if only for today. Someone offers to take a picture of us, and he puts his arm around me. We talk some more. He's very opinionated about certain things, not all of which I agree with. Still, I enjoy spending this time with a man who knows where he stands and isn't afraid to say it.

Update: It's been almost two years since I took my cross-country trip. I still keep up a 'net relationship with both Steve and Alex. I wish Jeff and Phil my best, and I'm beginning to think about traveling again.

FRIENDSHIP, POSSIBLY MORE

Wayne Hoffman

I was sweet 16, and I wanted some answers.

It had been over a year since I'd started coming out to my best friends, and after months of talking about being gay, I pretty much knew what my questions were, but I still didn't have any answers. I needed someone gay to talk to. That's when this ad, in Washington, D.C.'s alternative weekly, the *CityPaper,* caught my eye:

Bi/GWM
*Attractive undergrad, seeking same
for friendship, possibly more. It's good
having an understanding friend,
if only through letters.*

The euphemism went right over my head. "Possibly more," indeed. I wasn't up to euphemisms yet. I just wanted a friend.

I grabbed a sheet off my father's yellow legal pad and hand-wrote a letter, explaining my situation briefly: high school senior, getting ready to head to college in the fall, in the process of coming out. Then came my list of questions: How do you come out to your parents? How can you meet guys if you're too young to go to bars? Should I tell my college roommate I'm gay before we move in and risk him pre-judging me, or wait until we know each other and risk him feeling betrayed? How do I get involved in my university gay group? How soon should I come out in the fall?

I couldn't yet envision this man's most likely (and totally understandable) reactions. Too young! Too pushy! Too needy!

(Any of which would land my letter in the same wastebasket.) At 16, I had full confidence that he'd come through for me.

Scott wrote me back—thirteen pages. Three-two-one: *Contact!*

He told me a bit about himself: a WASPish upbringing (read: repressed), given to alcoholic binges, out to only his closest friends. He enclosed a family photo (cute, yes, in a blond, preppy, sweater-and-loafers kind of way). He also offered some answers to my queries.

First, he warned me against placing a personal ad of my own. "The other guys you're convinced are out there won't be able to bring themselves to answer ads," he wrote. But all was not lost in my search for love. College, he promised, would prove a liberating experience, specifically where I was heading—Tufts, with its liberal reputation. Perhaps I could find someone there.

But he wasn't much for coming out on campus. "I want to keep all doors open," he wrote. "I will not do anything that might preclude me from the privileges of being thought to be straight." He acknowledged that an openly gay friend of his felt quite differently, but still he wrote, "I advise not to advertise." Needless to say, he never joined his college organization at George Washington, or came out to his roommate, so he couldn't help me on that front.

Or parents: "A vocal *don't!*" he warned, although again he allowed that my priorities—and parents—might differ from his. (He was right on both counts.)

I mulled over his letter several times. (Oh, those simple days before voice-mail personals!) His answers weren't exactly the ones I had in mind, but here was my first gay pal. I dragged my Princess phone into the basement and called Scott that evening. We spoke for hours.

We became fast friends, and Scott was there for me through my last semester in high school. We'd talk endlessly on the phone—as long as his roommate (who "didn't know") wasn't around—and I'd tell him everything.

I called Scott immediately on the spring day I took a Metro trip to Dupont Circle with one of my friends who "knew" and sat on the fountain watching the men. (Cruising: Act One, Scene One.) Across the fountain, an older man—perhaps 30, with thinning hair, glasses, and purple gym shorts—was giving me the eye and splashing his hands in the water. He smiled, I quickly looked away, and he came over to introduce himself.

Alan.

Gulp!

"You go to school?" he asked.

"Yup, at Springbrook," I replied. He was expecting me to say Georgetown or American—not a suburban high school—and I didn't yet know to lie.

"I was just heading home. Where are you heading?" he inquired, hopeful.

"I was just heading home, too," I answered, disappointed. I was hoping he'd sit and talk to me. "I guess I'll see you around."

He watched me walk clear into the subway station, looking confused. I was through the turnstiles already when I figured out that I had blown my very first pick up.

"Where did I go wrong?" I asked Scott. I should have picked up on his signals, then maybe I'd really have had something to talk about.

But Scott didn't approve of the whole scene. He avoided Dupont Circle, wouldn't even ride his bike through the neighborhood, six blocks from his house, "because someone might see me."

I called Scott a couple of weeks later, right after I'd come out to my older sister on the telephone. She took it pretty well, I thought. Maybe I'd been worried about nothing, putting off telling my family.

Scott gave me a warning: You don't ever have to tell your family, but definitely don't do it until after you're out of college. Too risky.

I knew even then that I wasn't going to wait that long. (I didn't last another year.)

Although he was six years older and seemed to have answers to my questions, I already knew that I didn't want the kind of life Scott was living: closeted, paranoid, lonely. He dated men secretively, then made up women's names to use when talking to his friends and classmates. He never went to bars, for fear someone might spot him. The fact that he lived in Washington, D.C., with its large gay community, and attended a liberal college with an active gay student organization, was actually a detriment to him, making him have to hide all the more.

He understood that I was heading in a very different direction, though, with different motivations, and while he offered many warnings, he didn't discourage me.

We only met once, the week he graduated. I happened to be downtown with a friend one night, and called him on a lark. We stopped by his apartment, with only a half hour before the last red line subway was due to leave for Silver Spring. It was awkward—I knew we'd probably never speak again—and I can't recall anything we talked about. We never said good-bye. I don't think we even shook hands.

Within a month, I had placed my own personal ad in the *CityPaper* and fell in love with a wonderful undergrad named Larry. We met in Dupont Circle in broad daylight, and that evening, amidst a crowd of tourists, we watched the sunset over the Potomac, holding hands.

WHIPPED CREAM AND CHERRIES

Achim Nowak

It's tough being a white Puerto Rican. You're too white for the ones who want a Puerto Rican, and you're too Puerto Rican for the ones who don't. Your Puerto Rican friends ride you for trying to pass, and your white friends ride you for trying to pass. That's what Angel, my best friend—who *is* a white Puerto Rican—told me. I never wanted to sleep with Angel, but I know I want to sleep with the boy whose ad heralds him as such.

Gay White Puerto Rican Male
*28, HIV+, 6', 195 lbs., fun-loving and sincere,
looking for friendship, maybe love.*

I find the ad in *The New York Press,* a paper where not very many queer boys look to procure, and even fewer tout their positivity. And I don't think I've ever seen a white Puerto Rican advertise himself as precisely that. I'm determined to meet him. He's ten years younger than me, and I'm curious, as always, about boys his age. How did he get it? How do the young ones get infected? Boys my generation didn't know any better. We belong to the times when we all still believed being queer and proud meant you had to suck as much dick as you possibly could in a night at the baths, and the less you knew about them, the better. Stick it in as many holes as you can find, and crown the night with a final act of sweet submission, a big piece of sausage up yours.

He hobbles toward me in Tompkins Square Park, straight across the lonely square where Wigstock used to hold forth on

Labor Day. He warned me about the crutches that he must rely on as he heals a broken leg, and I am sort of relieved; it is, in a way, the easiest clue to spotting him. He hobbles toward me, an oddly handsome hulk of a man, broad-shouldered, with hair that's a dirty blond, almost as dirty blond as mine, but mine, of course, is entirely a fiction by Miss Clairol. He has a certain chunkiness to him, and is, like all chunky people I know, skilled in the art of camouflage. I immediately resort to the sort of hope I do when all is not perfect: He will look somewhat more scrumptious and firm when the clothes come off; he's out of shape because of the crutches and simply hasn't been able to get to the gym.

When he sits next to me on the bench, just a tad too near, I notice his eyes. They're light green like those of a tender young cat, and the auburn freckles that grace the valleys under his eyes only enhance the look of a gentle but ferocious little kitty. The conversation is pleasant if somewhat lacking in imagination, much like his ad, yet his eyes have the power of yearning. I know it very quickly, and I have little doubt: I want to sleep with Carlos.

I've sat with other men in other parks, looked at their handsome longing eyes, and known that I didn't wish to touch their bodies. Maybe I knew it was different with Carlos the moment I saw the crutches. There was a seductive helplessness to this act, this slow crossing of a large square of emptiness toward a man who answered his ad. And Carlos knows to stay away from the obvious and tired questions and comments, the sort that demand an answer before the event. No "Are you a top or a bottom?" No "Hum, I bet you have a really big piece inside your box." No "My pussy is yearning for a big German knockwurst" (oh, yes, *I have* heard it); no quick grab of my crotch in the park.

Carlos seems content with a certain sense of mystery, a measure of ambiguity, content with the knowledge that whatever will happen between us will be fine. He assumes that we're versatile without having to advertise it, unlike the legions of queer boys who believe that versatility is a special gift, not a basic requirement. I like the mystery of a white Puerto Rican, the not this, not that, in-between sort of mystery, just as I'm the sort of German whom strangers like to tell doesn't "seem German at all anymore," while, in the same breath, pointing out the little ways in which I'm German to the core.

I recognize this moment, right before we part: the moment when, suddenly, none of what has transpired seems real. We've both made it clear that sex will wait until the second date, but then Carlos has a sudden lapse. Just before we kiss good-bye, he gives himself away, as if he wished to hook me or required a guarantee. I wonder, is this the insecurity of a white Puerto Rican, or the insecurity of a man on a crutch?

"All I want is some cherries and whipped cream," he says to me with a cool directness as he pinches my cheek. "I want to spread the whipped cream all over your beautiful body and put a cherry on your dick, and then I want to lick it until I've licked it all up."

We're standing in front of the homeless geezers who doze on the chess tables by the southwest entrance to the park. I feel as if I've suddenly been thrust into the land of too much specificity, and an impasse where a specific response is required, something like "Oooh, baby, that sounds really hot," or "Oooh Carlos, that's what I want to do to you. I want to put cherries on your hungry titties and up your ass, and eat it all up until there's nothing left of you."

I feel like some sort of reply is expected, but I find I have nothing to say. And at the same time I think, cherries and whipped cream could be such great fun. I wish Carlos had surprised me with it, wish it hadn't become a fantasy that I feel I must fulfill, and I notice myself quickly losing interest. It's the sort of talk, I've been told, people crave on the sex lines, but I'm one of those literal-minded men who've never dialed the number, who has always preferred the mystery of sex with strangers in the dark, and such talk deflates me instead.

"I'll call you during the week," I say to Carlos, and that statement seems to frighten him. It clearly isn't the desired response. If this was a test I have flunked it, but Carlos doesn't quit easily.

"I love to do it with the curtains open wide," he whispers as he gives me a sloppy wet kiss on the cheek, "and I like to do it on the terrace in the middle of the day."

I watch him as he hobbles across Avenue A and wedges himself into the back seat of a cab. This is how he broke his leg, I think to myself: fucking on the terrace. This is how he got infected. He's just another slut, a total fucking sleaze—like me. I hear myself think these thoughts and am horrified at this judgment, this German loathing. And suddenly I can't wait to see him again.

We meet at my apartment the following Thursday, because Carlos has roommates, although it has occurred to me that I could have offered to come to him, since he will be dependent on crutches for another two weeks.

"I went shopping this afternoon," he announces on the phone in a breathless sort of way as we confirm the time, and it's clear his shopping was related to his plans for sex. "I will wear it tonight. I hope you will like it."

Oh shit, I think to myself and immediately want to cancel this rendezvous. He hobbles into my apartment a bit short of breath. I don't see that he's wearing anything new, and I'm somewhat relieved and also doubly curious now. As I tend to do when my interest in the other man is already waning, I rush to sex immediately. Carlos leans his crutches against my kitchen sink, and then we press our bodies into each other. He suddenly feels massive, his body, his face, his kisses, they are hoisted on me with a deep and burning desire, messy and yearning, and I love kissing him, love receiving these loose, roaming lips, until he begins to lick my cheeks, my temples, my eyelids, and my nose, and I know that I don't like being licked like this just yet, as if the green-eyed kitty were licking me clean.

I suspect it already as I hold him, but right afterward comes the moment of truth, the sweet and terrible moment that in some way or other it all boils down to, the moment that, I'm sure, is the only reason why my friend Angel hasn't had sex in years. The moment of disclosure, the moment the clothes come off. I'm one of those men who likes his guys a little big, and I'm not talking about what's inside his pants (there I care more about shape and form than I do about size).

But the moment Carlos peels off his clothes, it all looks just a bit too loose and a tad too wobbly, as if right in front if my eyes Carlos is coming undone. The moment when I know that I don't wish to have sex with this man, and yet here we both stand, naked in my kitchen. And then I look down to his dick, and I know immediately that this is the new purchase he's talked about. His genitals are tucked into a thin red glittering lamé thong that is partially hidden under the rolls of his stomach. I'm horrified. This is clearly intended as a turn on, but it has entirely the opposite effect. I feel like I'm suddenly standing in front of an out-of-shape show girl who's squeezed herself into a slip a size too small.

I throw Carlos onto my bed and immediately begin to yank this atrocity down his thighs, and it's not a task that is accomplished with any measure of grace. Carlos is already starting to moan, the pre-moaning I call it, the kind of moaning that has no relation to anything I'm doing. The live pre-recorded soundtrack. I toss the shimmering thing into a corner, and then I climb on top of him and kiss him at once, because I can't listen to the moaning anymore.

Skill always carries the encounter a certain distance, and even as I know that I'm not interested, as I simply propel myself through the motions and nibble on tits that lack a certain firmness I like, lick an ass that lacks a certain upward lift, I appreciate his skill in the bedroom. I don't even mind the moaning now. It becomes a comforting sort of background, like the numbing groans in a pornographic video, and for a few fleeting moments it transports me into the illusion of excitement. The red slip, I see that now, is in a touching sort of way the accurate costume for how Carlos maneuvers in bed. After he flips me down and climbs on top of me, he performs with the effortless skill of a seasoned dancer. Moves with agility, covers the floor with exquisite timing and grace, kicks his heels with remarkable precision, knows to make occasional eye contact with his audience to make sure it's still entertained. The shades to my bedroom are not drawn, they never are; there are no neighbors to look in, but Carlos doesn't know that, and this very fact may just enhance his sense of being on display. We end when I fuck him, his head down in my pillow, his wobbly round butt busting high into the air, and I suddenly feel like it is entirely too much work, and I can't wait to get it over with, as if I were scaling the rain forest and had to climb all the way to the top, when all I want to do is lounge by a waterfall and slurp a piña colada.

I draw the shades after we're done, as if it might make the bitter after-taste go away. I look at the two cherry-red bruises I left on his delicate chin, and then I notice the hickeys he left on both sides of my neck, and I'm amazed at how we can bruise each other in the act of fake passion.

"That was wonderful," Carlos whispers in that same breathless voice he had earlier on the phone and slips his thong back over his thighs.

"I'll call you later," I say to him, kiss him with a big sloppy kiss, as if I had to make up for the lack of commitment in my words. The moment he wedges himself out the door, one crutch first, then the other, I feel an immeasurable sense of relief.

I close the door and turn the lock, an automatic gesture here in the East Village of Manhattan, but today it also feels like a most deliberate act to keep him from walking back in. And yet, within minutes, I catch the afterglow, the second wave. I lie down on my bed, and instantly my body tingles again, with a soft and deliberate quaking, an inner tremor that rips through every pore of my skin. I close my eyes, and at once I'm enveloped by his weight again, this sense of his pale white flesh enveloping mine, his tongue traveling across the peaks and valleys of my body, tending to my soil, giving it moisture and pressure and reasons to grow. I brim and gloat with a sense of aliveness, with the power he has to keep me alive, minutes after he's left my room, and I notice the sadness that slips in as well, because I know I will not see him again.

I get his answering machine when I call and feel that sense of relief, the same sense I had as he walked out the door of my apartment. The message I leave is brief.

"I'm sorry I didn't get you live," I say and think to myself as I speak—what a liar you are, you had him live on Thursday, and the last thing you want right now is Carlos live. "I enjoyed being with you, but I don't think we're sexually compatible, so at this point I don't wish to see you again. Be well and take care of yourself."

All the things we don't say to get out of a situation, the things we withhold. I'm rather pleased I got off so easy and vow to not answer ads for a while, or maybe just not ads from white Puerto Ricans. Then I receive a letter from him in the mail. I open the envelope, unsure at first who it is who's writing me; after all, I know the secrets of his body, but I don't know his last name, and then I feel the tears well up inside of me. Maybe it's his hand writing, so elegant and clean and affectionately sweeping, with graceful swoops that circle full of passion, and maybe it's the fact that he wrote the letter at all, and I know that as I read his words, I still will not see him again.

Dear Achim, it says...
I received your message on Sunday, and it left me feeling
sad and confused. I believe you are a very beautiful per-

son, inside and out, and I had looked forward to spending more time with you. I don't understand when you say that we are not sexually compatible. I am so open and willing to explore. When you say that, I don't know what you mean. There are things I like, but it doesn't mean that you have to like them, or that I have to do them with you. I just wanted to love your body and you to love mine, and to make you happy. All I really wanted was some cherries and whipped cream. Please know this. This letter is not intended to change your mind, but you need to know that your phone call hurt me, and if you find yourself thinking of me, you know where I can be found...

EXIT 40

Fred Bernstein

I was 17 when my roommate told me I was gay.

I had never used the word, never really grasped the concept. Until that fall, my mind had been imprisoned in a strange, sexless autopia known as Long Island. All I knew was that I was in love with the gentle boy-man with whom I shared a 100-square-foot dorm room. I needed to be with him every waking minute, and then some. (When he slept, I stood nearby, watching, as if each breath was sacred.)

When I told him, three months into freshman year, that I loved him, Andrew (a relative sophisticate, having been sent off to prep school at age eleven) had the aplomb—not to mention the compassion—to respond: "I'm flattered. But falling in love with a straight man isn't going to do you any good. You need to meet someone who's gay, like you." To him, it was that simple.

(This wasn't a million years ago, although it feels that way. It was the 1970s, the last time a boy could grow up knowing he was "different," knowing he fell in love with other boys, and still not know the name for what he was, or would soon be.)

In that time and place, passion of any kind was suspect. My parents never touched. Nor, so far as I could tell, did any other couple in West Birchwood, a collection of immaculate, split-level houses off the Long Island Expressway, Exit 40. The two children per family (precisely one for each available bedroom) were conceived, ostensibly, without physical contact.

This was a place where each husband and wife merged into a unit engaged in a socioeconomic pursuit involving houses, cars, bar mitzvahs, summer camps, and, ultimately, college. Each couple interacted with the world through the medium of a joint checking account; it never occurred to me that it mattered how they felt about each other. In my naiveté, I imagined divorce—and there were occasional divorces—to be precipitated by disputes over the kinds of things I knew mattered to couples on Long Island: where to hold the next affair, whether to build a pool, whether to go to Miami or Nassau on the next vacation.

Were my parents in love with each other? Attracted to each other? It wouldn't have occurred to me to ask.

As to what would make me desirable, I had heard the same thing all my life: A boy needed an education. Education meant money, and money was key to a successful marriage. Become a doctor or a lawyer or, in my in my super-achieving world, doctor-and-lawyer. I'm sure girls on Long Island grew up knowing they had to look good. Not boys. "Nice eyes" or "great smile" was the most anyone ever said about our faces. And there was no discussion of male bodies. Muscles—this in the era of Charles Atlas, not Calvin Klein—had to do with strength, not appearance. And, anyway, Jews didn't think about such things.

So after several painful months, during which I reconciled myself to Andrew's lack of interest, I took his advice and placed an ad in the *Village Voice* (then an exuberant counterculture rag). I have no idea what my ad said—probably "College student, 17, likes architecture, journalism, travel, looking for same." And I have no idea how many responses I got (although if it did include my age, I'm sure more than a couple), or what any of the aspirant/correspondents told me. All I remember is that there was one letter I liked, from a Columbia student (and fellow Long Islander) named Stuart, and that I called him, and that we agreed to meet, and that I took a train to New York for dinner at an Italian restaurant on McDougal Alley. It was the first date I had ever been on. We talked about school, about movies, and about how lucky each of us was to meet another gay, Long Island, Jewish college student! By dessert, I pictured us moving in together.

But he had other ideas. "I had a good time," he told me at Penn Station. "But you're just not my type. The attraction isn't there."

The words stunned me; it was a thousand times worse than Andrew's rejection. That one I had understood, even expected. But this? What was this person saying?

I didn't look right? But I looked fine. No one had ever said I didn't. My hair was washed, my teeth were white, my shirt was ironed.

That was, in retrospect, the night I said good-bye to Exit 40. On Long Island, I knew my worth. (A valedictorian, no less!) On gay island, I didn't have a clue.

My date with Stuart was the beginning of a metamorphosis, in which I came to understand (and to deplore) the degree to which, at least between two men, looks matter. Decades in which my search for love would repeatedly founder on issues of attraction—so often, in fact, that questions of compatibility, on quotidian matters, seem quaint to the man I've become at 40. Decades in which the tyranny of the gym would overwhelm the gay community, and me.

Ever since that ad, I've lived life in a mirror.

PUBLIC NEWS

Erasmo Guerra

I bought the stationery at a department store in the mall. I could have gone to a better place, a card store for instance, but it was raining that afternoon, and the mall was on the way home from work. When I got home, I shut myself in my room, took out the newspaper, and read the ad again. The paper, a tiny Houston weekly called *Public News,* covered the alternative music and art scene, but its personal ads were legendary. Everyone read them, and read them all—since the ads weren't subdivided. They all ran together in one indiscriminate collection of short monologues from men and women seeking the opposite sex, the same sex, or just plain sex. Frequently, my desires got caught up with some-one else's, making me wonder if perhaps my dull wish for din-ner and a movie somehow masked the need to get my toes sucked and ass spanked by a swinging mixed-race couple.

Even the big-haired secretaries at the oil company where I worked enjoyed reading the ads, because ads like these appeared nowhere else, not in the *Houston Chronicle,* not the *Post,* not even the gay bulletin, *This Week In Texas,* also known as the *TWIT.* Another weekly was published then too, but unlike *PNews,* which focused on the bohemian downtown culture of the Mon-trose district, the other paper was more a listing of goings-on for the conservative suburban middle-class who worked in the city but lived in the outlying districts of Katy, Sugarland, or The Woodlands. The personals in this other paper were nothing more than a bland parade of desperate whinings, and so similar to one another in wants and needs that I sometimes wondered if they were not all written by the same staff writer.

I grabbed an issue of *PNews* every week but never considered submitting a response until I found two ads. The first was written by a nineteen year-old: straight-acting, inexperienced, tired of the bar and club scene. That was who I thought I was, too, at twenty-one. The other ad sounded more sedate, and I remember that I liked the images, the scenes painted with its few words: lazy weekend mornings with coffee and both the *Chronicle* and the *Post,* walks through Memorial Park and drives to Galveston; movies at the Post Oak Theater. What grabbed me however, what started me off with a few words in response, was the closing line, which asked, *"What are you going to do?"*

The interrogative hook reminded me of a song Madonna sang in which she breathily posed the same question, a daring demand more than anything. I was really into Madonna at one time, having been a closet-case from the distant South Texas Border, where if you didn't shoot your first *javelina,* or white-wing, by age ten, you were branded a *maricón.*

Down there along the Rio Grande, I never shot anything more than a wad of fantasies into my own slick palms. Once I moved to Houston, however, I began going out to the bars and clubs in Montrose. I was living, dancing to music I had only dreamed to, meeting different men, but still I wanted to meet someone special, enjoy the company of a serious man for more than one night. Why I thought answering a personal ad guaranteed I'd have a longer—longer meaning a somewhat better and more successful—relationship than with anyone I could have met in a bar, I didn't know. I was naive enough to believe it, however, and I wrote in my neatest hand.

The first letter I got back was three pages long and was something of a collage of photocopied images of Margaret Thatcher, wild turkeys, and phrases cut out of magazines. He addressed me by my initials since I hadn't given him my full name, but immediately he began guessing at it.

Eric? Ernie? Elwood?

He was writing the letter late at night because he'd just gotten home from work. He tended bar at a local posh hotel. He was tired and asked for my patience.

He wrote that the whole experience of writing a personal ad had been odd at best and disappointing at worst. He received five written responses and six phone messages. Mine was the only one he decided to answer. His name was Blaine. *Blaine,* I thought, reading it over. *Blaine? What kind of name is Blaine?* I went on reading. He said he never realized how important grammar, vocabulary, and punctuation were to him. Most of the responses were illiterate. I would be surprised, he wrote, at the people out there who couldn't form a cohesive sentence.

I must have mentioned Depeche Mode in my letter, because he said he liked them too. I thought I had written him about Madonna.

He went on to describe himself, though he noted that the physical was not so important to him. It sort of was, but it wasn't paramount. It wasn't in the top two. The statistics: 5' 8", 150 pounds, auburn hair, hazel eyes, straight white teeth with a slight gap in the middle even after six years of braces. He had a birthmark on his left arm. The picture he sent along, a black and white cut from a contact sheet, was about two or three years old. He was twenty-three.

A final page summed up "various facts" in no particular order. He hated the term *straight-acting.* There was no such thing as straight or gay behavior patterns—"end of topic." He loved a good kisser. Very important. He wanted to live in Western Europe: London or the French countryside. Maybe Seattle if the other two didn't work out. Money, per se—his words, not mine—was not important, but success and freedom were. He thought long-term gay relationships were possible, but was not sure people were meant to be together *forever.*

Edward? Elias? Efrim? He took another stab at figuring my name.

I liked that he would never get it.

Summer school was starting in a couple days, and he had an eight a.m. class from Monday to Thursday. So sleeping in, he regretted to inform me, would be relegated to Friday, Saturday, and Sunday.

It was my turn to drop him a note, now that I knew a little more about him. He actually wrote that and then signed off. Under the operatic flourish of his name was an address that I quickly found on a city map. The street stemmed off Memorial Drive, a grand boulevard of fabulous homes tucked in among a densely wooded area of oaks and pines. Below the address was his phone number. I didn't call right away because I didn't want to seem desperate. Then again, I had answered an ad, an act that most people considered desperate enough and a mark of social failure.

What shattered me completely, though, was when I called the next day and the voice at the other end was not Blaine. It was Michael, his roommate. I said I'd call back, not leaving a number, searching the letter to see if he'd mentioned the roommate. He hadn't, of course, and I figured he hadn't written about the roommate because the roommate was perhaps more than a roommate. On the phone, with his twang, the roommate sounded like a tall, good-looking blond. I was sure of it and of all the other thoughts choking my hopes like a muddy bayou. As fresh as I was to the whole gay scene, I knew two gay men living together shared more than toothpaste. Then again, I was living with a gay man too. He was older, and I wasn't attracted to him in the slightest. I met him through the *Post*. He'd listed the extra room in his apartment but asked me never to mention this to his friends, because to him it seemed about the worst way to meet anyone. I didn't tell him about Blaine. I wondered if I had told Blaine about him.

I called Blaine again later the same night, but he still wasn't home. I left my initials and number, feeling a bit guilty that I hadn't included it with my first letter. I hadn't even sent a photo. In retrospect, I wanted to risk as little as possible because for all I knew, Blaine could have been a formerly incarcerated pervert. Still, I felt like an idiot for playing it so safe, so scared. A few minutes later, the phone rang and it was Blaine.

He was at the hotel that night and wouldn't be off for a while. I gave him my full name, and he said it easily, though he rolled one too many letters where people usually refuse to even flip one. The call was quick and to the point. I suggested we meet at Biba's One's a Meal on Post Oak, because it was between his place and mine. I didn't tell him that I hadn't really thought of a place to go and had only thought of the diner right then on the phone because it was the one place a friend and I frequented.

The nineteen year-old never wrote back. I kept wondering what exactly it was about my response that turned him off. The stationery? It was a pastel blue with rows of crested waves, and at the top and bottom were hydroplanes, their propellers spinning. Not exactly macho. I should have thought about it more, written on spiral-bound notebook paper, pulled it out and sent it without bothering to clean up any of the messy threads. I could have masturbated on it too. Some nights I wondered if I'd put the right letter into the right envelope. Had I written to the nineteen year-old about Madonna? I checked the mailbox every afternoon, hoping I hadn't, and came away rejected every time.

When I walked into Biba's the evening Blaine and I were to meet, a few tables were already settled with men. There were no women in the diner other than the waitress, which was odd because this was not the House of Pies—also known as the House of Guys, because it attracted an almost exclusive gay crowd. This was Biba's, a regular diner, and I didn't know how I was going to identify Blaine from everyone else. I felt rattled and confused and paralyzed. Two men, sitting together in the corner, kept eyeing me as I stood by the entrance eyeing them and the other tables. For a moment, my sickened imagination took over and led me to think I'd been set-up:

There they were, Blaine and his roommate. I was now more than sure they were fucking behind my back. I saw that they were enjoying my torture and stuffing food into their mouths to keep from breaking into a riot of laughter. I scuttled off to the bathroom like a roach escaping the drop of a foot. Once there, I splashed my face with water, smelled my armpits, and went over what Blaine had mentioned in the letter. The statistics: five foot eight, one-fifty, auburn hair, straight white teeth with a gap. And the birthmark. He had one on his arm. I forgot which one, but if he wore a long-sleeve shirt, as I had, I wouldn't be able to see it. I took a breath, flushed the toilet just to let anyone within earshot think I was doing something normal, and stepped back out into the dining area.

The men all turned to me with slack, bored expressions, making me feel more than alone. I was ready to walk completely out of the diner and jump back into my car and head home, but the waitress blocked my path to the door and asked what I was going to have. I mumbled my order. The usual blue cheese burger with a side of fries. She shouted the order to the cook and then asked me if I was going to sit down. I did. I fell into a dark banquette and stared at the front glass door awash in the last brittle rays of sunset. I tried not to look at anyone.

He walked in at some point after I stopped watching the door and was anxiously devouring a Boston Cream pie I'd asked the waitress to bring as I waited for the burger. (And when he tells this story himself, Blaine always mentions the pie and how rude it was of me to have started eating.) He came in, and without a hesitation of any sort, stepped up to my table and said hello. He didn't even bother to look at anyone else in the diner. For many reasons, I was put off by it. I was offended by his confidence in thinking, in knowing really, that I was the guy who'd answered his ad. Was I that easy to spot? And did he think he could just now come up to me and say hello after the humiliation I'd suffered waiting for him, waiting which anyone else would not have endured for as long as I had?

I checked the greasy clock on the wall and then checked my watch. He was only five minutes late. I must have arrived at the diner too early without knowing it. I still felt wounded though, nearly rejected, and I was tempted to ask, do I know you? Instead, I finished the pie, smiled slightly, not the least bit interested in him. Besides, he wasn't what I expected anyway. His hair was auburn, as he mentioned in the letter, but for some unexplained reason I had imagined auburn coming closer to the blond I was used to seeing on all the guys at the clubs who weren't Black or Latino or Asian. In fact, the color of his hair was close to the shade of the burnt-orange paper he'd used to write his letter. And while he would never make the cover of the *TWIT,* he did have interesting chiseled features, and rich browns and muted greens puddled in his eyes.

He apologized for his lateness and asked if I'd finished dinner already. I said no and asked the waitress to keep my burger warm until Blaine ordered and both dinners could be brought out together. We talked for a moment, the other guys leaving the diner, the waitress wiping down the tables. Our disparate voices ricocheted against the bright checkerboard tiles and knocked into one another like bodies bumping on a dance floor. Our voices didn't quite find their rhythm, didn't hum together like the neon lights framing the windows. I was uneasy and then figured it wasn't anything he was saying but how he said it. There was a definite pattern to his speech that aggravated me. It was too exact and enunciated, the words drawn out in an exaggerated diction. He seemed to be on a large stage, making pronouncements to the far-flung seats so that they could clearly get what he was saying. Later, he told me about his extensive theater training in high school and at the University of Houston. Still, I was slightly bothered by the unnecessary drama.

After dinner, we caught a cabaret show at the nearby Tower Theater and then went dancing at a downtown club. Through it all, I wasn't especially nervous. Meeting Blaine that day had me thinking differently about him, about me, about being with other guys in general. I knew I would see him again, so I didn't have a desperate need to be with him completely, to go all the way the first night. It wasn't a ploy to attract him or to engender some kind of mystery to snare him with. I already felt that he liked me as much as I liked him. The proof? At the end of the night, sitting in his parked car, he asked for a kiss. I said—and I can't believe this now—that I would give him only one and then I had to go home.

Why he didn't just kick me out of the car and land my ass on the pavement outside, I didn't know. Even I wanted to kick myself because I knew this was not how a night was supposed to end. Any night I went to the bars I usually left with someone, anyone. The one-night stands were there to take like matchbooks, but this new me now wanted to give them up for something better. I wanted the comfort of a sustained fire rather than the scorch of a quick-to-die flare.

The single kiss that first night led to another dinner later that week. He prepared an Italian feast of mixed-green salad, tortellini, bread, and wine. He invited me to spend the night, which I did on the condition that I be allowed to sleep on the living-room couch. Again, he agreed, and I lay against the rough cushions, unable to sleep. I tiptoed to his room during the night and complained, through the crack he left his door open, that I couldn't sleep with him so close. A few months later we moved, with his roommate, to a two-story house.

I made a call to my parents and told them about Blaine, though I didn't say how I met him, because they would not have understood. *The Town Crier* back home only reported the weekly specials of the local supermarkets and the honors won by the enlisted men overseas. In the ensuing parental silence I repeated myself, but then I heard it, the slow swell of a heart-arresting *grito*, the kind that punctuates the start of a *ranchera* where a man sings a lament to the woman leaving him, or a love-sick woman to the man who beats her. A dial tone chimed in then and kept its steady one-note until an electronic horn blared in like an on-coming pick-up truck. A recording asked me to hang up and try my call again. I didn't. I merely hung up and fell into Blaine's waiting arms. I felt lucky to have him.

A few months crept by without a word passing between me and my parents. Eventually, their refusal to see me for who I was gave way to an invitation to spend the weekend. Blaine came too. We spent our days on the old couch, watching television with my dad, who only brought out his hunting rifles once, and listened to my mom tell Blaine how I liked my *enchiladas*. As if Blaine didn't know already. I never told them how I met him. I don't think they ever asked.

We were together two years and have been friends for the past five. My parents still ask about him. They liked him. Or they may have been permanently damaged, forever asking about Blaine because he happened to be the guy I was with when I admitted that I was indeed a *maricón* as they had always feared. I've had a few short-lived loves since, but my parents never seem to remember their names. No, my parents, whether they know it or not, hold onto the idea of Blaine and me together. They safeguard it like newspaper clippings announcing some grand *quinceañera* or wedding that never took place but still could.

Even Blaine and I half-jokingly agreed, when there was no chance for one more bittersweet reprise, to call one another in about ten years. Perhaps we'd be better suited for one another then. Not a year has passed, however, where we haven't been in close contact. In fact, we even now count ourselves as neighbors, living ten streets away from each other in Hell's Kitchen, New York City. We call each other on the phone, ask about how the other is coping, who we're dating, what we might be doing next.

Blaine is returning to Texas. He is returning for many reasons, but the one stuck to my heart—straight-pinned like a butterfly whose wings have gone the color of old newsprint—is his disappointment in never finding a man in this city willing to risk enough to have a genuine relationship. Even his three-day flings end badly.

I myself have refused to develop any long-term relationships. But I lie. And I lie because it is embarrassing to admit to every last one of those failed attempts at love. I want to believe, as Blaine wrote in his first letter, that long-term relationships are possible. I also want to believe that two people can stay together forever. I'm sure Blaine wants to believe this too. I hear it in his voice as he and I blame our troubles on the city, which doesn't seem to be the place for a sustained commitment of any kind. Of course, someone else could point out the pledge we've made to one another, quite unspoken, but real and everlasting. We are blind to it at the moment. In ten years we might have better clarity. For now, I eye the stacks of some weekly papers and think, and then think again. If I pick them up at all, it's only to read the horoscopes.

LESSONS

Jameson Currier

One particularly lonely and forlorn day this ad caught my eye:

Butt Play 101
Let me teach you how to enjoy your ass
and asshole. I will show you how
to experience ultimate pleasure
from the space between your legs.

I had never answered a *sexual* ad before. Of course, I had spent years reading them and mulling them over, but I only circled and called the romantic, dream date ones. As for sex, I'd always found enough action at the bars or the clubs or on the street or from the dating ads that I hadn't ever needed to turn to the "Sex Only" personals as an outlet. My goal has always been to find a worthwhile long-term relationship (or at least someone who would stick around after the third date), not someone who wanted to stick their sticky fingers up my butt in order to get their rocks off. Nonetheless, I circled the ad, part nostalgic after the recent break-up with a boyfriend and part curious about whether I should really consider a new method to snare a new one.

But the truth of it was, the real reason I circled the ad was because I had become a virgin (again). I had just emerged from a period when a lot of things had been going wrong, or, rather, a lot of people had been disappearing from me without saying good-bye, and those who weren't disappearing were afraid that they would be disappearing themselves, too, and so, instead of waiting to see I if was going to vanish as well, I had sequestered myself. I had drawn those willowy pink chenille curtains of mine closed, locked those over-painted louvered window gates up tighter than a chastity belt and decided to hide in the dark away from it all until it was safe to go back out in the sunlight again.

It never really got safe again, you know. Things never really got better, but I learned how to adjust to them; I learned to peek through the slats and wear sunglasses and hats and whatever other protective gear I could get my body into when I went outside. But then one day I found myself no longer fretting about my self-imposed exile and back out in the sun again—in the Sheep Meadow in Central Park carelessly sunbathing with my shirt off without even putting sun block on my skin, no less—and falling in love with a married man who was trying to fall out of love with his wife.

It was a complicated relationship for us both right from the start. Even though those gates of mine had been closed so long that even the locks were rusty, I was nonetheless definitely standing outside my closet door. He, alas, was hidden within his. But none of this hampered any of what happened between us in bed, of course. In fact, that's where the relationship, well, blossomed and grew, to mix a few metaphors. Soon enough we began experimenting and, well, his greatest desire was for me to teach him how to become a bottom, or, in more technical terms, how to become "the passive partner who receives the penetration of a male's penis." And I became more than a willing coach for him; he possessed a beautiful round and firm ass that could have belonged on a man ten years his junior. I spent hours getting that sphincter muscle of his to relax, lubing up a small butt plug until he was comfortable holding it inside his ass, then progressing to inserting a slender dildo, then gradually moving up to a larger one, then a wider one, until one day we reached the point when he was ready to take my cock up his ass. I remember thinking at the time, that if someone had bequeathed me that sort of time and attention then I would have no desire to find another boyfriend. I'd want to get married.

I should have realized during all these lessons that Trilbys don't stick around to marry their Svengalis. Once my boyfriend had mastered my cock, he soon began requesting to play the new role of top to my bottom. The only problem was, he wasn't interested in giving me the time and attention I had given him, nor was he interested in giving up being a bottom, either. Like I said, it was a complicated relationship—I was out and he was in and he wanted to be in and out with other guys. I never had the chance to switch from top to bottom with him, because we were too quickly switching between other partners and fighting too much about our positions. But he wasn't the only guy I had dated who, well, wanted to flip me over, if you catch my drift.

I should probably admit now that to many men I seem like the ideal bottom—boyish-looking and short, I don't even weigh in at 150 pounds. Which is why, I think, I get such a delicious personal pleasure out of turning the tables and demanding that I be a top with all of those, well, you know, hunky macho guys who want me to roll over and play bottom for them. But the truth is, even though I looked boyish and my boyfriend wasn't really my boyfriend anymore, I wasn't really boyish any longer. I suppose this is a round about way of saying that I wasn't getting any younger. And, as community folklore has it, of course, after so much time goes by, those closed gates soon look like a boarded-up wall; if you want to open the window, you have to start over again and knock out a hole if you want to see the sun. And so here I was a virgin again after all these years of isolation and waiting for the right guy to knock my window open.

The real truth is: I was a single and unattached aging gay man yearning for love. What I wanted was to find a better man than the kind of man I was usually meeting, and one of the methods I thought that might help me in my personal quest was if I were to, well, uh, make myself more versatile in the bedroom department. Knock my own gate down before someone else hit a brick wall, if you know what I mean.

And so, not long after that insight, I began perusing the personals in order to meet my dream man, a habit I had gravitated to for years and years and years whenever I felt the dating pool was getting shallow. I picked up newspapers and magazines at the bars, the community center, the bookstore, the newsstand—wherever I could find one that carried men-for-men personals. At home I would sit at my desk with a red felt-tip pen poised in my hand, ready to circle the most desirable ones. No matter how many personals I circled and notated in the "Romance Only" or "Let's Date" sections, I always seemed to ponder more and more over the "Raunch and Kink" or "Sex Only" sections, fascinated by the obsessive nature of so many gay men and at the same time frustrated that so many guys were looking for such specific requirements in order to obtain pleasure, and knowing, really, that my nature would most likely preclude any visits to the kinkier sides of gay life. The only thing I had ever desired out of a perfect sexual encounter was to give as much pleasure to my partner as I wanted him to provide to me. And that didn't necessarily include smelly jock straps or foot worship, though it also didn't preclude them either.

Which leads me, of course, back to the matter at hand. The ad for the butt professor. A few days after I saw the ad, while I was leaving voice mail messages for all of my potential dream dates, I decided, what the hell, let's respond to the butt player as well.

None of my Perfect Husbands responded, but the butt player did. Our short, introductory conversation on the phone went something like this.

"So you're into butt play?" he asked.

"Not really," I replied.

"You ever had anything up your ass before?" he asked.

"Not in a while."

"I've helped a lot of beginners," he said.

"I'm not exactly a beginner," I stated, "just starting over."

"Boyfriend?" he asked.

"Not any more."

"I can see you Sunday at nine," he said. His voice was cheerless and perfunctory, making it sound as if I had called for a doctor's appointment for a shot of penicillin. But it was exactly this sexless, clinical exchange that made me so easily accept his offer.

"Okay," I answered. We talked a few minutes more. He told me his address and that his name was Joey. He said he was in his early fifties and had salt-and-pepper hair. As I hung up the phone, I reminded myself that this was a learning experience—he was going to teach me to be a bottom, or, well, teach me to be a better bottom. Henry Higgins wasn't exactly the perfect man for Eliza Doolittle when they met, either, you know.

❖ ❖ ❖

I arrived at Joey's apartment nervous and tipsy and more than fifteen minutes late, which (even on gay median time) is more than a rude way to begin an association. I had indulged in a glass of wine at the bar on the corner of Joey's street, a trendy little smoke-filled, artsy-fartsy place with skinny women in black dresses and guys in dark T-shirts and gold hoop earrings. As I gulped down the last third of my drink, I reminded myself once again that this wasn't a date. This guy didn't advertise in the "Looking for Love" section, and I wasn't expecting Joey to be my Mr. Goodbar. He was only Mr. Chips, after all, and I could leave him as soon as he taught me, uh, well, how to enjoy the pleasure of a man's penetration.

"Want something to drink?" he asked me when he ushered me inside his apartment. My distress must have clearly shown on my face at that moment. Joey was more like sixty than fifty, and his salt and pepper hair was a unshaven beard. Otherwise, he was bald as a cue ball and had a puffy face that looked like a sandbag that had been punched and not regained its shape back. He was slightly shorter than I was but more than three hundred pounds overweight, a fact he hadn't mentioned to me on the phone. He was dressed in the kind of light, blowzy outfit that when worn by street people make you immediately cross to the other side of the street. If he had not lived in one of those high-tech, luxury, contemporary apartments that always seemed to end up photographed in *Metropolitan Home* or the Thursday section of the *Times,* I would have turned around and left, because this potential deamboat more closely resembled my worst nightmare.

I should probably add that the Sunday night I arrived at Joey's apartment, it was a warm, misty late spring evening that seemed to possess more humidity and mugginess than actual heat or raindrops. I stood in his doorway with a moist umbrella and my split ends growing into an afro. I felt so, well, old and troll-like myself at that moment that I was conscious I was standing on a clean beige carpet, worried that I had brought with me all the urban dirt and soot and grime I had carefully tried to avoid out on the street. Joey's apartment was clearly more showplace than a home. The smell of a bouquet of flowers that rested inside a crystal vase on a table near where I stood wafted up to my nose as I shook myself out of my damp jacket. The vestibule where I stood frozen like a stray dog that had been rescued opened up into a living room that was entirely decorated in beige—a sofa and matching wing chairs were upholstered in a neutral, beige fabric; prints of blank beige-colored squares framed by beige wood were hung on a beige-painted wall; a shiny beige lamp rested on a shiny beige end table.

"Any wine?" I asked Joey as he led me to the sofa. I took a cautious seat, resting my derriere lightly on the edge of a cushion as if I were going to leap out of the room at any instant, because I was embarrassed at shedding particles of dust into the immaculate surroundings. Beside me, a beige coffee table jutted out close to my knees, empty except for several *Playbills* arranged in the shape of a fan.

"Red or white?" he asked.

"Whatever's open," I answered.

During our entire greeting and exchange, Joey was beaming as if a Christmas gift had just walked through the door. I sat waiting for him to return, feeling like I had played this game a million times and was too old and tired to try it again tonight with an ancient geezer.

"I loved this show," I said, trying to deflect my discomfort when Joey returned with a glass of wine that looked more beige than white. I reached over and plucked a *Playbill* out of the arrangement, the fan quickly disintegrating into an unorganized mess. As I tried to straighten it all up, the thought occurred to me as I made an even larger mess that murderers don't like show tunes—do they? But wasn't Joey too old to be a murderer? Isn't it usually the wealthy sixty-year-old man whose throat is slashed the next morning? Joey seemed unperturbed by the mess I had made on his coffee table. In fact, he seemed to be a bit too amused by my nervous stumbling about, as if I were a six-month old child who had tottered into the room on his own two legs for the first time, and whom he was about to applaud at any minute. When I looked up, I noticed Joey was smiling, or, rather, I noticed that Joey's mouth had widened to reveal a set of conspicuously fake beige teeth.

"The dancing was terrific," he said, "but the music was abysmal." He waved his hand in the air on his last word, as if shooing away a fly, but then he started talking again about a theatrical wig maker he knew who worked backstage and, as the gossip started flying out of his mouth, his hand took to waving back and forth as if it were a flag flapping in the wind on Independence Day.

I didn't really mind all the talk about the theater, however. I was grateful for the distraction from the matter at hand. We sat and kibitzed about a lighting designer stepping out of his boundaries to become a director and a composer known for his S/M tendencies. In fact, we talked so long about the theater that I completely forgot the reason why I was there in the first place. Joey was becoming a friend, not a potential teacher, and his fuzzy potato head no longer looked as if it belonged to a derelict. I could see the honesty in his face even if I couldn't imagine him successfully pleasuring my ass. But then Joey abruptly ended the conversation by leaning over and saying, "Well, shall we get started?" Suddenly his wrist was no longer limp but firmly placed against my shoulder and reaching around to remove my empty glass from the coffee table.

"Uh, sure," I answered, not really certain I wanted to go through with it.

"You can leave you clothes on the chair," he said to me as a doctor might say before leaving a patient alone in a room. In fact, Joey did leave me alone in the room when he left with the empty glasses in his hand, but he had returned by the time I had managed to stand up from the couch and fumbled with the buttons on my shirt. Joey walked to set of louvered doors which I had thought was a closet, but after he had opened them revealed a full-size bed built into a small nook that must have once been a laundry room. Along the bottom of the bed were a row of drawers built into the frame and Joey began pulling out an assortment of materials from the middle drawer: a pair of latex gloves, a box of condoms, a giant industrial-sized bottle of lubricant, four or five different sized dildos, none of which I felt certain that I could accommodate, a box of baby wipes and a plastic mat, which he unfolded and placed on top of the beige bedspread. I was deliberately wasting my time with my clothes, folding them and refolding them as he moved swiftly about his little alcove. Finally, he turned and looked at me standing sheepishly in my underwear and T-shirt.

"I sterilize all the dildos in the dishwasher," he said, as if that were my most crucial concern about sticking a giant object up my ass.

"The dishwasher?" I responded, flabbergasted by a mental image of a row of dildos sitting straight up in a car wash. The

next thing I knew I was standing behind him staring at the para-
phernalia on the bed, all articles that had been withdrawn from
the drawer in order to entertain my ass. Things had never seemed
this complicated when I had played the same game with my ex-
boyfriend. But that was the difference, wasn't it? It *was* a game
with my boyfriend. This was a lesson.

"And I always use condoms on the dildos," he said. Next, he
patted the plastic mat on the bed. "Take your shorts off and sit
up here," he added. Joey seemed to realize as he said it that there
was no place for me to sit on the bed because of all his equipment, and he started rearranging things to make a space for me,
or, worse, make a place for us. I realized the moment that I
dropped my briefs that I should have thought twice before agreeing to all of this. Was I that desperate to learn how to enjoy my
ass? Shouldn't I have really concentrated on finding a boyfriend
first? I looked down at my cock and noticed it was smaller and
more frightened than I had seen it look in years.

"Have you had many responses to your ad?" I asked, when I
was seated on the edge of the bed, shifting myself onto the mat.
Somehow Joey was already completely undressed and I was
amazed that his body looked no different from when he had been
wearing his billowy outfit. His body was as lumpy and wavy as
beige fabric that had been sat on all day. The only difference
between his body and his clothing was a chain around his neck
that dangled a gold Hebrew symbol, now visible against the
sparse, gray fluff of his chest. And then there was his erection,
too, of course: a small, slender dick that popped straight out at
me like a breadstick misplaced in an Easter basket.

"Nope," he said, "you're my first. I just took the ad last week."

Great, I thought. I'm a virgin again. And a guinea pig. And
stupid.

❈ ❈ ❈

But it was then that the lesson began. Or the life unfolded. Isn't
that what teaching is all about? The passing of knowledge of wis-
dom gained not so much on one subject but on the cumulative
experiences of many?

"When I first met my lover I was strictly a top," Joey said. I was
on my back with my legs bent and my kneecaps parallel to the

ceiling. "I wasn't interested in somebody sticking something inside me, because all I wanted to do was to stick something myself, you know. Then, after we were together for about four years, we started changing roles. He didn't always want to be the bottom, so I experimented with it some and decided I liked it so we changed roles. He was the top and I was the bottom. That lasted for a few more years, and then he decided he wanted to be the bottom again. That's when we started getting all this stuff," he said, waving his hand at his assortment of dildos.

"I think that's more than I can handle," I said, twisting my body to look at the smallest dildo, which in my estimation was about twelve inches long and eight inches around.

"You think so? We'll see."

Joey had positioned himself at the end of the bed, a plump round period to my wavy exclamation point. He lifted one of my legs and rested it against his shoulder. The next thing I knew, his wet gloved finger was in my rectum, and I could feel him twiddling with my prostate gland. I leaned up to watch his hand inside me, expecting him to say at any point, "Scalpel," or "Sutures," but instead he said, "You're very tight."

I nodded, wishing that there were some music playing or somebody kissing me or a video being shown or, better yet, that I had another glass of beige wine in my hand. Instead, all I heard was Joey beginning to breathe harder, like someone who has asthma. I lay back down against the mat, hearing it crinkle as my skin pressed against it. I closed my eyes and tried to imagine myself a thousand miles away, but, instead, only heard the *slumpf, slumpf, slumpf* of Joey pumping more lubricant out of the bottle and into his hand and then into my ass.

"It's the small ones that are the hardest, you know," he said.

I leaned my head up again and looked at him in surprise. "It's the truth. It's all about stretching. The walls don't stretch that much with the tiny ones. The big ones just force you to relax in order to accommodate them. Give me a big, fat dick any day. It's so much easier to manage and it's a lot more fun." He started laughing, a high-sounding hiccup that started in the back of his throat and ended with the quivering of his shoulders and saggy chest.

It was such an odd moment from someone I had heretofore regarded as a clinical, professional worker. "It's all about relaxing, you know," he said, still chuckling. "Once you learn how to relax those muscles down there, you can take a football. I had a friend who used to work in the emergency room, and he used to tell me about all sorts of guys coming in with cucumbers or tennis balls or light bulbs stuck up their asses."

The thought of a light bulb up my ass was definitely unappealing, and I pumped a swipe of lube from the bottle and wrapped the oily palm of my hand around my cock, trying to force myself to become harder. Above me, I heard Joey gasp.

"What's wrong?" I asked.

"Ahh, why did you do that?" he asked.

"Do what?" I asked, shocked.

"I wanted to suck your dick. Now I can't take it in my mouth. And you have such a beautiful dick."

"Ohhh," I said, really sorry he hadn't acted quicker. "Thank you," I added, feeling like a moronic pupil who had disappointed his teacher.

Next, he took a slender dildo I hadn't noticed before, the kind I had once used on my ex-boyfriend, lubed it up and inserted into my ass. It went in easily, though I could feel the walls of my ass caving into the dildo instead of stretching them further. "You've been practicing," he said.

"Not really. Those Kagle exercises don't work for me."

"Oh, sure they do," he said. "You're just uptight. What are you so nervous about?"

Life, I thought. I'm nervous because I'm still alive after all these years. The only thing that worked out for me was that I didn't die when everyone else did.

"Open your eyes," he said and lightly slapped my chest.

I could feel the residue of lube where his hand had grazed my skin.

"I'm not going to hurt you," he said. "I won't do anything you don't want me to do. You can trust me. In a few lessons, you'll be able to take King Dong over there."

"King Dong?"

"The super deluxe double-headed one," he said and nodded at the giant dildo with a cock head on each end. "My boyfriend and I used to play with that one a lot. There was a time when we were both bottoms. Come to think of it, there was a time when everyone in the city was a bottom. It was difficult to find a top some nights."

I gave him a smile and leaned back and started pumping my cock again. I felt myself growing thicker and he took the slender dildo out of my ass and lubed up a wider and longer one. Before I knew it, it was inside my ass, and I was rock hard, pumping my cock and arching my back away from the mat. Suddenly I felt a decade younger, and a memory washed over me of a man I had dated on Fire Island. Joey bent my legs and rubbed my thighs just as the man had. And then he held the dildo far up inside me, cupped my balls and rubbed them with his slippery hands. Then he reached one arm up and twisted my left nipple.

"The first time I was fucked, my boyfriend was so impatient he made me bleed," Joey said. "I turned him into a great lover, though. Then he left me. Then he came back. Said he couldn't find anyone better in bed. Oh, he could find others to have sex with, don't get me wrong. But none of them had my touch. It worked for both of us though. He made me feel so beautiful."

Joey was breathing hard through his mouth by now, and he moaned and moved one hand to my cock and stroked it as he returned to lightly pushing the dildo in and out of my ass. "That okay?" he asked.

I nodded back at him.

"I miss him," Joey said. "He died about three years ago."

He stopped pushing the dildo in and out of me and pulled himself up out of his hunched over position. "That doesn't bother you, does it? Everything we're doing is safe."

I nodded back at him again that it was all right to continue. I was aware that we hadn't kissed one another, aware that not a single drop of body fluid had been exchanged between us. No tears. No sweat. As I looked at Joey's face as he worked over my ass and cock, alternating one hand between stroking his cock and my own, I realized he had survived, as I had, but his road might have been more difficult than my own. I sensed that the puffiness that bloated his face was not entirely the result of the ravages of aging but from the use of medication or the overuse of alcohol.

But I also realized he was enjoying his task, the first time it had occurred to me that he must have taken the ad out because he enjoyed sticking something up a guy's butt, enjoyed giving a guy pleasure this way, that perhaps maybe this was his fantasy, his fetish, the scene he wanted to play. Older teacher instructing the younger pupil. The thought of it made me smile, and the delight surged through me like a jolt of electricity. I felt my body finally become sensitive to his touch. My first shot came like a wave of release, replaced almost immediately by a flood of tension and pressure and then a second shot into Joey's waiting palm.

Before he had a chance to remove the dildo from my ass or wipe my cum from his hand, I reached my hand up and clutched his cock and gave him a few quick pumps with my slick, hollowed fist. He came instantly, his cum spilling over my wrist and onto the mat with a drip, drip, drip. He laughed as he caught his breath.

"Thank you," he said.

Thank you, I repeated in my mind, embarrassed that he had thanked me for letting him fuck me with a dildo and then quickly jerk him off. As I dried myself off with the baby wipes and paper towels, it occurred to me then that teaching was such a selfless act. In that way it bore such a striking resemblance to being in love—doing something for someone else without the expectation or need of anything being returned. You don't expect someone to thank you. Lovers can be the best teachers. And teachers can be the best lovers, too. But I was aware that my encounter with Joey had not been without a certain level of self-absorption and self-need. His. And mine. Joey had knocked a window out in my wall for me. And I think I had helped him withdraw some quirkiness from his drawer.

When I was dressed and standing at the doorway in my still damp jacket, Joey held his hand out for me to shake. Instead of taking it, I leaned over and kissed him on his fuzzy cheek. He smiled and held the door open for me. As I stepped outside, I realized that I had revealed so little of myself other than the intimacy of my body. I hadn't even told him about my ex-boyfriend. But it was already too late. I felt myself headed back into my shuttered, private little world. But before he closed the door behind me, I turned back and said, "Thank you. It was fun."

And then I was back out on the street again, slapping my tennis shoes against the puddles of water like a teenager, eager to be a teacher again.

WHAT I WANTED, WHAT I NEEDED

Nels P. Highberg

Boy seeks Daddy
in looks but not attitude. GWM, 25, 5'11", 180,
br/gr, seeks GWM, 35-50. Looking for strong arms,
nice smile, kind eyes, and soft stomach.
Need a man to enhance my life, not be it.

"**W**hy did you answer my ad?" I reached in the basket between us for another roll, knowing his answer.

"I don't know. Why did you go out with me?" He looked up at me and smiled.

"I don't know. You seemed like a nice guy." I picked up my fork and knife and began cutting my prime rib.

"Yeah, but you weren't looking for a nice guy." We both started laughing.

Gary and I met on November 2, 1994, and tonight was the third anniversary of that meeting. As always, we went to Cooker, the restaurant where he took me that first night. Cooker called what they served American Cuisine, *cuisine* being used to justify charging more for steak and potatoes than if they'd called it *food.* We liked to make fun of the waiters and waitresses for smiling too much and sounding way too happy to be serving us. And we always rolled our eyes at the managers who visited our table a couple of times each visit, asking, "So, how's everything? Good?" unless something was actually wrong with the meal.

It was an old joke between us that Gary didn't fit the ad I had placed in the *Columbus Guardian,* the weekly newspaper that had personal ads for straight people as well as gays and lesbians.

He had the smile, eyes, and arms. And he had the soft stomach, or, as he liked to say, "Well, I was fat, which is what you wanted." Still, he was three years younger than the minimum age I had set, he abhorred the "Daddy" label in every way, and he was looking for a husband, a long-term committed relationship.

Quite frankly, I just wanted sex. It had been a year since I moved to Columbus, Ohio, to begin graduate school. As an undergraduate at the University of Houston, finding sex was never a problem. With the city's abundance of adult bookstores and bathhouses, I could usually find quick, satisfying, anonymous sex in just a couple of hours. In Columbus, the bookstores didn't have back rooms and the bathhouse closed a few months after my arrival. What had worked in the past wasn't working anymore.

My friends knew I wanted to broaden my social activities beyond campus. One of them, John, suggested a personal ad. He'd tried it a few times and encouraged me to do it. "It's free to place one," he kept reminding me. "You'll meet lots of guys. Come on, do it." So I did.

The newspaper ad came with voice mail, so guys could call up and leave messages for me. The first night I checked, a Friday, five guys had responded. One sounded like he was reading from a script:

"Hello, I am a bisexual white male, 45, who likes football and auto racing."

He told me I could reach him by sending a letter to a post office box across town; I chose not to write the address down.

Two other guys sounded okay enough, but one guy, *man,* he sounded like what I needed: direct, clear about what he wanted, and not into games. All he said in a baritone voice was, "Hi, I'm Dave and I'm your man, so give me a call."

I started to get hard before I could finish writing his number on the notebook at my desk, and I called him back first. He answered, said hi, and told me, "Well, let's get together, what about lunch Sunday?" I didn't have a car, so we decided to meet in the parking lot outside my apartment building at 11:30. The conversation ended within three minutes.

He was in his late forties and looked like Dennis Franz from *NYPD Blue,* only with smoother skin and a bushier mustache. Somehow, after we ordered sandwiches at some deli near campus, he was able to slide how much he enjoyed sex into the conversation, asking, "So, what are you into?" Within the hour, he had his back against the door to my bedroom, pants around his ankles, and dick down my throat. This was what I was into.

Gary was the fifth guy who called that first night. He sounded nervous, saying "uh" and "um" a few times, but that seemed normal and didn't bother me as much as the guys who sounded like they had been recording messages for quite a long time. When I called him the next day, he hesitated the first few minutes of our conversation, and I did, too. I don't remember what we discussed. It was probably about Ohio State, since he had earned his B.A. in economics there, and I was a graduate student in OSU's Department of Women's Studies. Or about Texas, since I had lived there for so long, and he had spent the '80s worshipping Dallas and had always wanted to visit the state.

I do remember one specific thing he said. He described his hairline as "receding." Months later, when I started spending every weekend at his place, I would bug him about this, the way we always play with each other about lots of things. "You know" I'd start out, "the proper word, dear, would have been 'receded' since your hairline has been at the back of your head for years. I mean, it's stopped 'receding' by now."

Still, even if I don't recall many details from the first night we spoke on the phone, two hours passed before we arranged to meet the following Wednesday for dinner. It felt good to talk to someone for so long. The first dinner we shared at Cooker wasn't much different. I described working in women's studies and teaching a course on women writers. Gary tried to establish a connection.

"Oh, yeah," he replied, "I know a little about those ideas. I see Camille Paglia on CNN all the time."

I wasn't a Paglia fan, and I let him know that pretty quickly. Months later, he told me, "Geez, I was just trying to have a conversation, and you ripped my head off."

He thought he really blew it after, as he put it, I "ranted for a few minutes." Actually, I barely recalled the conversation. I just remember that we talked. And I hoped we'd have sex later.

Sitting across from him as we ordered, I wondered how much hair he had on his chest. He wore a dark blue, crew neck sweater over a white, button down shirt, so I couldn't determine anything in the restaurant. But I felt comfortable talking with him and watching him laugh and look at me nervously. I knew things would progress naturally.

One way I like to play with Gary, whenever we talk about that first date, is to say, "Yeah, we had a really nice dinner, and then you drove us back to your place and took advantage of me. You just rushed me right upstairs and said, 'Well, here's the bedroom' and smiled at me."

This really bugs him. He always yells back in shock, "I did not! We walked to the parking lot, and when I asked what we should do next, you asked if we could go back to my place. I remember. You said, 'Well, if your place is presentable, let's go over there.' I just hoped we'd talk and maybe I'd get to kiss you. I was just giving you a tour."

When he agreed to go back to his place, I assumed we would have sex, and I really believed that he thought the same thing. I didn't know it then, but our attitudes about sex, or maybe I should say our expectations, differed. He can remember every man he's ever slept with; I get confused when I think past the first month of college. Still, he didn't put up a fight when I stood in the doorway to his bedroom and leaned over to kiss him, and he didn't mind when I pulled him towards the bed.

It took me a while to realize that we kissed more than anything else. He didn't try to push me onto my knees or lift my ass in the air, and I liked lying there, stretched out across his blue bedspread. He was certainly different from the men in my past.

I really noticed and appreciated the difference a couple of months later.

On a Saturday morning towards the end of January, the phone woke me from a long sleep. One of my best friends from Texas, Richard, called from the hospital. After a few minutes, he told me that he had AIDS. I asked about his doctors and his medications, and he told me about his parents and brothers, how their support surprised him. After hanging up the phone, I sat in shock. Richard wasn't the first of my friends to face an AIDS or HIV diagnosis, but previous experience didn't make it easier.

By then, Gary and I had been dating steadily. He called a few minutes after I spoke with Richard, and I told him what I had just learned. Before long, Gary knocked on my door. We gathered my dirty laundry and a few things I had to read for classes, and he spent the day washing my clothes and cooking dinner. I lay on the couch and flipped through the TV channels for hours. It started to sleet and snow, and he told me to stay the night. He took care of me, giving me time to deal with what was happening.

I wasn't used to being taken care of, not like this. I thought I wanted freedom, my own space, the ability to go wherever and suck whomever I wanted. But I liked how I felt with Gary. I felt calmer, distracted from the usual stresses. I liked feeling that he was looking out for me.

Three years after the night we met, we sat in the same restaurant, across from the table where we sat in 1994. Gary smiled and said, "I really got to you. You may not have wanted it then, but it happened."

"Whatever." I pointed my fork at him. "You're always so damned insufferably pleased with yourself. I'm still the best thing that ever happened to you."

Gary stared directly into my eyes. "Ditto."

I spent a lot of time the night I wrote the ad obsessing over each and every word. In the end, the language didn't really matter. Well, maybe it did, since something made him respond, and something made me call him back even when he didn't fit the image I had set up in my head.

I met a woman in graduate school who thought about placing her own personal ad, but she was worried that she wouldn't find what she was looking for. I told her that that might be just what she needed.

DAD

Patrick Arthur Dakin

I know I'm not the best writer in the world, but it's important to me to tell this story. Many strange things have happened to me in my life, but this was the strangest.

I grew up fast. My childhood flew by and, before I knew it, I was turning into a man. As soon as I hit seventeen, I was ready to leave home to pursue a better life—not really financially but sexually. I was ready to get my own apartment and ready to meet a guy.

I had been attracted to men all through high school, but I never gave in to what I felt. I was too nervous about my dad's reaction and my mother's. My parents had recently suffered a bad divorce, and my mother had left "to find God." My father got full custody of me when I was fifteen, and I knew my mother would use my being gay to prove what a bad father I had. My father had his problems. He sometimes drank too much, but he was a generally honest and outgoing man. We never talked much. We just lived together and sort of enjoyed our own separate lives.

On my seventeenth birthday, I moved out on my own and decided it was time to do something I had never dared do before. I was finally going to answer a personal ad. I sat in my living room with the local paper trying to find a voice personals phone number. I found the one for Vermont and quickly grabbed the telephone. I remember my trembling hands trying to push the right numbers. I put the receiver to my ear and listened to the instructions. After about five minutes of pointless instructions, I pressed the number three. Five seconds later the ads started.

It was the very first ad. It sounded so strange. I will never forget listening to the voice, knowing I recognized it and trying to figure out who it was. I listened to the description:

"Hi my name is Dale. I am a forty-four year old manager living in the town of Springfield. I am six feet three inches tall and weigh 200 pounds. I have black hair with a mustache and have blue eyes. I would like to meet another guy for good times outside and in. I also want someone honest. Thank you and I hope to hear from that special someone."

My mind was racing as I listened. It took about ten seconds before I realized who it was. It was my father. The description was exactly him—even the name was his. It was too strange. After his message beeped, I blurted out, "Hi, Dad" and quickly hung up the phone. So many feelings ran through my head. My body and my brain felt numb. It was too much to know and such a weird way to find out. I had to go talk to him. I jumped up and ran to my car.

The ride was very fast, probably too fast. I was determined to see him and talk this through with him. After about fifteen minutes of driving, I arrived at his house. I saw him upstairs through the bay window sitting at the table drinking coffee. I took a deep breath and walked up the porch to the front door. My heart was pounding and my head ached with the nervous tension of knowing what was about to happen.

I saw my father turn in the kitchen to greet me.

"Hello, Patrick. What's wrong? You look stressed out. Let me guess–bad day at work." He was speaking quickly. It was just small talk. I could tell he had had lots of coffee.

"No, Dad. I have something I really need to talk to you about." I walked over and sat down.

"Is it good or is it bad?" he asked.

"It's something very awkward, and I don't know how to say it."

"Don't worry. It's not like I can ground you," he replied sarcastically.

"Okay, I'll just say it. I know. I know that you're gay. Why haven't you told me? Is that why Mom left?"

My hands fidgeted with my watch while I waited for him to take in what I had just said to him. My eyes met his, and I could see all the pain he had felt. His eyes glassed over, and his voice began to quiver slightly. It was odd seeing him like this, because my father always seemed so strong. Seeing him this upset was very rare. He took a very deep breath and looked at me.

"I always have been, Patrick. Your mother and I married very young. She was pregnant with your brother. We had to get married. I loved your mother very much. When I told her, she just wanted to pray and cry to God for forgiveness. She was angry that I didn't feel that it was bad thing. She left after I told her." His words trembled while he said this. He was very nervous.

"So tell me, how did you find out?" he asked.

"Well, I have something to tell you, too, Dad. I'm gay. I found your personal ad in the paper." I was in shock that I actually told him. I felt like a huge weight had been lifted off my chest. He looked at me dumbfounded. He seemed quite surprised by the news.

"Well," he finally said, "this is quite the news. Are you okay with it?"

"Yes, Dad, I'm fine. I am actually quite fine about it. It was bad in school for a while, but I never said anything. Besides I don't go there anymore, so I feel a lot better now."

"Your mother is going to blame me, you know."

"I'll tell her the truth. That's the right thing to do"

"Patrick, don't worry. I love you the way you are, but I want you to be careful."

"I will, Dad. Oh, also, Dad—nice personal ad."

"You liked it?"

"Fit you to a tee."

We talked for hours after that. We laughed, and we cried. My father and I got to know each other really well that night, and it really helped us become friends.

Things have been strange since that day. My mother and my whole family knows now. They handled it okay, and they keep telling me how much they love me and my father. My dad and I joke about how ironic it is. He often teases me about making the talk show rounds.

To this day I have never used the personal ads again. I can meet guys at other places. And besides I am afraid of who I might find next time I try my luck at the personals.

ARCHAEOLOGICS

Achim Nowak

My friends all warned me it would happen, and sure enough, they were right—all of those who have never answered an ad, never placed one, because they simply don't know how to lie well enough. They're terrified, more than I am, of that first glance, that moment when someone we have never met finally gets to look at us and makes his decision. When everything that was said on the phone—the connection that seemed so readily established, the sweet feelings we felt—when it all is erased.

I walk into Manatus, a diner in the West Village, right on time, and look for the face that I know from the photo I received, or, to be more precise, I look for the body that goes with the face. My ad specified that I wished to date a man who desired a long-term relationship, but the one I wanted to meet right away was Roger. Roger, who sent me the sleazy snapshot. Jeans pulled down from the waist, zipper half open, a bare frame solid and broad, tits hard and bursting on a chest that looks massive and full, a shoulder that flings wide over a waist that is narrow, and pecs that puff like a pair of vanilla soufflés. His face is beautiful, a somewhat banal all-American mid-Western kind of beauty, with lines that are beginning to harden; they give him that maturing Marlboro Man look.

The photo has been taken in a wood-paneled basement, somewhere in New Jersey, I imagine, even though Roger lives in the West Village, but it has a basement, a rugged, regular guy, intensely lustful, locked-up-in-the boonies look. It's all enhanced by the fact that the photo is blurry. The blurriness is subtle; if anything, it heightens the allure, the allure of this working class hunk, this blurry dreamy vision in whose imaginary arms I have already drowned three nights in a row now, releasing myself into sleep.

I survey the room. He's not here yet, and, well, I think to myself, he's allowed to be a few minutes late, although we're in his neighborhood, and I came west from *East* Seventh Street, the other side of the divide. But I notice a man sitting by himself at the table by the wall, nearest to the window, the furthest table away from the entrance, and he looks at me with a question mark on his face, and as he looks in my direction he seems at the same time to shrink further into the wall, as if he wished to crash right through it and go shopping in the jewelry store that's on the other side. I, too, feel suddenly like a big question mark. But the *photo,* I think to myself, the *photo.* Maybe this guy's having a blind date with someone else, and maybe they haven't exchanged photos, maybe that's why he's confused.

"Roger?" I ask as I step up to his table, and he replies by simply nodding his head and mumbling "uhuh," as if it were just too painful to answer in the affirmative and acknowledge that he is who he is.

I sit down and suddenly feel that all the wires in my circuits are crossed, and a heat is rushing up my arms, and it's not an erotic heat. It's the heat of having stepped into someone else's scenario, the heat of having walked into the story they all told me about. I don't wish to be rude and just blatantly stare at him and say, "Look what the hell happened to you, you look nothing like that picture. Or was it your picture, was that tasty, hunky mouth-watering body really your own? Was it ever?"

I peek at Roger, at the hair that's still blond, but clearly not a blond that nature has graced him with, look at this face that's etched with hard, deep lines. They're rugged all right, but there's a rugged that's sexy and a rugged that's worn out. This skin is sallow and drained. These eyes are a charcoal aquamarine and speak of years of sadness. If he's the one from the photo—and I'm beginning to believe he is—his body has shrunk, all of him seems to have diminished. There was a stature in that photo that is nowhere to be found.

My ad was in the *Body Positive* magazine, and I immediately have this other thought, the sort that's inevitable in the Positive dating scene. Maybe Roger just got out of the hospital, maybe that explains it, and he's on his way back. But I've dated those boys. I know what those bodies look like, the dying skin and the shrunken bones that are trying to bulk up. No, that's not what happened to Roger, I think to myself. This is just someone who's getting old a bit too fast. Taking a Dorian Gray kind of turn. Desired for years, and then it finally shows. The sort of fate which, I fear, will come to me overnight.

"How's your health?" I ask Roger just to be sure, though I don't know why I think he'll give me a straight answer, not after that photo he sent.

"Fine," he says. "Fine. Never been sick." The answer that makes him instantly more desirable, because none of us like to hear the alternative, and I believe him. These are the beauties of Positive dating; it's the sort of question I don't ask on a regular date, where status is a matter we meticulously avoid.

Roger and I babble about this and that, and nothing falls from his lips that especially strikes my fancy. I realize that I'm a little worn out. Roger's the eighth date I've been on since I placed the ad, none particularly successful, but none attained with such ruthless deception. I think of the photo again, the beauty of that man, and my mind flashes back to a man I had sex with in the Continental Baths, fifteen years ago in Washington, D.C.

His body was delectable, the body of a bodybuilder before bodybuilders became too hard. It was a massive bodybuilder frame on a medium-sized man, and though he was big, there was a sweet, soft roundness to that flesh. I liked the fact that he was older than me, maybe fifteen or twenty years older, but fifteen years older when you're twenty-three is much different from fifteen years older when you're thirty-eight. I stepped into his cubicle in the baths, and before we ever touched, he pulled out a photo of himself. "Used to be a Colt model," he said, and I looked at the photo, a nude man standing like a Greek statue on top of a rock, behind him nothing but a blazing sky.

The model was beautiful, as they all are in those old black and whites, a glistening torso posing for the gods, but I was suddenly confused. The man in the cubicle no longer looked like this man. I couldn't find the resemblance, and if it was there at all, it was faint. We went through the motions of making love. He was adept at what he did, and when we were done he gave me his phone number. "Please call me," he said. "Please. Come out for dinner." The photo was still laying on top of his clothes, and maybe it was because he lived so far away, out beyond the Beltway, but I just couldn't bring myself to go.

Roger is talking to me while we pay at the cash register, but all I notice again is just how small he looks, and it isn't the smallness of his body, it's the shame he carries, the shame of false advertising, because he must know that he's a letdown to everyone he meets.

"Want to see my apartment?" he asks furtively as we trip out of Manatus onto the Bleecker Street sidewalk, teeming with homies from New Jersey and the Bronx who're letting loose in the Village—and they all look more entrancing than Roger.

"Sure," I say, and I too find myself flushing with shame now, the shame of going home with this wasted human being, this tattered shell. If he were at least vivacious. If he were interesting, if he had a grand spirit, but there's nothing, absolutely nothing there. We hurry down Christopher Street, and I can't wait until we turn onto Washington, because I don't want to run into anyone I know, don't want to explain that I'm on my way to have sex with Roger, and there is no other way I can explain him away, because my friends will know at once there's nothing else I could possibly do with Roger, and I wish I had met him in the evening, when all men look prettier, not on a Saturday afternoon at two, when the sunshine on Christopher knows no mercy.

He lives close by, two blocks north of the strip. Just as he pulls out his key chain—and I notice the key chain (it's a massive, masculine silver loop with way too many keys on it, the sort of key chain that engenders hope)—just as he gets ready to move it toward the lock in the front door of his building, it drops and falls through a grate that covers the ground on both sides of the entrance way. Drops and disappears from view.

"Phewww," he says out loud, spewing the sound without saying anything else. It's the strongest display of emotion I've seen in Roger since we met. I'm spewing myself now, spewing silently inside my brain—we were so close, so close—because I don't know how much longer I can feign interest. Roger is looking less and less like a Marlboro Man.

"It's Saturday," he elaborates now. "Shit, the super's not here today." I stand in this silent moment, feeling helpless, stand next to Roger who looks more and more like a daddy, though he's probably less than ten years my senior. But I don't want a daddy that's helpless. If I'm going to play with daddy, I want a daddy who's in charge, not a daddy who gets lost with his little boy on the way home.

"My friend Betsy has a set of keys," Roger says. "She lives around the corner."

This is the moment, the perfect time to bolt, but I also realize—this is what happens when you go on eight dates in two weeks and still haven't gotten laid.

Betsy lives on the other side of Christopher, right next door to the bookstore at the corner of Hudson, where I've made love to other daddies in whose company I would never wish to see the light of day. Betsy buzzes us in, and we climb up to her apartment, which spans the entire third floor. Betsy's a hippie, and her apartment is a hippie apartment, very floral and velvety and much too ornate. I like it. Betsy's friendly, a bit chatty, and clearly a hell of a lot more interesting than Roger, but then I'm not here to sleep with Betsy. And she's a relic, I realize, a relic from the Sixties, standing there in her long Moroccan caftan, the even gray hair flowing down to her breasts, the Balinese bird earrings, the silver turquoise rings on every finger, and I, of course, am about to walk out of here to have sex with a relic of my own.

"I'm so happy to meet you," Betsy says and extends her arm in a surprisingly formal welcome. And suddenly I get suspicious. Is this a welcome because it was all set up—Roger dropping the keys, us stopping by to see Betsy? Is this what Roger always does—bring over the boys? Or is it the welcome of stunned bemusement that Roger would have anyone at all?

Ten minutes later I step into Roger's apartment. It confirms every hunch and every fear I had. It's situated in the back of his building. A studio, nicely fixed up, in the sort of sad way in which New Yorkers try to make a studio a home. A built-in wall unit occupies two sides of the room. Custom made and over-designed, this unit covers every inch of these two walls and contains everything that makes up Roger's life. I rather like the design, modern and sleek. The only thing I don't care for is the gray of the wood, it matches the sad grayness of Roger's skin. And it's a *studio,* a *tiny* studio, a space that's half the size of my small studio in the East Village. My god, I think to myself, nobody should be Roger's age and live in a studio that's the size of a walk-in closet in most suburban homes. Nobody should live in a studio the size of mine, but then I have ten more years of hope. One of my little delusions.

Roger settles on the diminutive sofa sectional that's part of the wall unit, and immediately lights a cigarette. You don't date smokers, I tell myself. You don't *do* it with smokers. The smell of smoke and the smell of liquor on a man's breath always send me running. Remind me, every time, why jerking off is so much more reliable (it offers predictable pleasures and none of the down parts). I stare at Roger and find myself getting livid, because this is what always happens, this moment right here, when a smoker waits until he has lured you into his world.

I want to kiss him now, kiss him not because I really want to kiss him but because I just want to get it over with, but it's hard to kiss a man with a cigarette, and it's hard to kiss a man you don't want to kiss. It does occur to me that we could just forgo the kissing, but kissing is part of what I love best, though I don't think it's Roger I want to kiss. I stroke his knee, gently, softly; he understands. Out, out goes his cigarette, and he grabs me and sticks his tongue into my mouth. I don't know when it happens, the moment his tongue is inside, or the moment his arms grab my shoulders as he moves in, but an unimagined power erupts from inside Roger.

I feel it in his mouth, which burns, a hot deep furnace, a tongue that's charging like a weapon into my mouth, a gun burning with smoke, and I suck it in, this smell of cigarette smoke, this manly smoke. He's my Marlboro Man after all. I feel his hands clutching my shoulders, strong, so strong, and all of a sudden it's just his mouth burning, burning so wonderfully hot, so wide open, so willing to press into me, fearless and wild, and a tongue so desperately wet, and I feel the smoke of joy in this mouth, the smoke of peace, the smoke of fresh life. And that is what we are now, mouth to mouth, and I don't know who is resuscitating whom, because it's simply been much too long.

When his mouth goes down and takes my dick, I feel it again, the heat, as if my dick were baking now, fresh into the furnace, rising, rising, running for the flames. It feels so unbelievably good and necessary. Roger is starting to yelp, but I press him down harder, press my fingers into the gray roots of his hair and press them deep into my groin. When he comes up for air I unzip his fly, and at first, he wants to stop, doesn't want me to take him in. I'm annoyed now. I like a daddy who wants to please his boy, and he has been pleasing me, pleasing me better than I might have hoped, but now I want to show my gratitude. Doesn't he realize how fortunate he is—usually I'm much too selfish to want to blow the other.

I yank out his dick, and I realize at once why he didn't want it out. He has one of the tiniest dicks I've ever seen on a man, and it's hard, clearly hard. It will not be rising any farther, and I imagine him flushing with shame again. He must have anticipated this moment when I first walked into Manatus, the horror of this recognition that must have been a constant in his life. I take his dick into my mouth, it enters so completely and perfectly, and there is even room to spare. That's what I so love about small dicks, they fit. I've never liked the big ones, the ones that rise as big as mine, because then you have to work, and I don't want sex to be work, no, I want sex that's easy, a dick that accommodates, like a pacifier that can still all the yearning and all the terror and pain. I draw it in, his dick, deeper and deeper. My mouth is firmly nestled in the jungles of his pubic hair. It will go no deeper, but I try, as if with this act of sucking, this hot, burning sucking, I had embarked on an archaeological dig. As if this afternoon I might suck away all his shame.

We come by lying back and jerking off together, and though we both haven't been with a man in a long time, we shoot dribbles, and I realize that this is what Roger and I do daily, alone.

When I say good-bye, I tell him I'll call, though I'm not sure I will. It's also possible I might, but already I feel it take over as I look around—the grayness of the walls in Roger's apartment, the grayness of his skin that looks dim now in the shadowed light, the gray blond of his hair, the grayness of his heart.

I call my friend Arturo instead, first thing when I get home, and tell him of my meeting with Roger. I stop my tale at the moment we stepped out of Manatus.

"Oh Roger," Arturo says, "Yeah, he answered my ad last month. I met him at Manatus. Did he send you a picture?"

"Yeah," I reply, and I'm suddenly *incensed* that Arturo never mentioned Roger to me. Never told me that he had placed an ad in the first place. I wonder what lies Arturo invented about himself, as I lean down and stare at Roger's photo, which lies next to my bed, and look out to the empty roof deck behind my window.

"Damn", Arturo says and giggles. "He sure was a tired old queen."

And I don't know what else he doesn't tell.

REBEL

Tom Reilly

It was in the late Sixties when I first met Rebel. I had answered a personal ad and met Tom. Todd had also answered Tom's personal ad, and I eventually got to meet him; and, when I did, Rebel was with him. Tom moved into my fifty-dollar-a-month loft in Chelsea. We continued seeing Rebel and Todd, but Rebel took a real liking to me. Todd and Rebel did not stay together for very long, but I did do a large painting of the two of them sitting together holding hands. This was part of an exhibition I had in 1973 of mostly naked gay and lesbian couples. I also did several paintings of Rebel naked with a huge teddy bear. In any case, Rebel had his own key to my place and would come and go unannounced, a kind of half-presence. I would hear the motorcycle engine revving up 26th Street and, moments later, Rebel would appear in my doorway, dressed in his army fatigues, ready to ride off into the night and the dark leather bars of the city.

Tom and Rebel were both poets. Our ménage à trois lasted several years. Tom was a story I am not going to try to tell now. Rebel loved me with the devotion and loyalty of a golden retriever. He was six-foot-two, blond, muscular, with a pale baby face, blue eyes full of pain. He also had a very large uncircumcised dick. He was about 28 years old and a recently discharged Vietnam vet. He never talked about what happened over there, but something happened that had left him empty and withdrawn. His only love (besides me) was his motorcycle, an old Triumph. And *Triumph* was to be the title of his first poetry collection.

We did share poetry. We both loved Cavafy and Auden. We would sit for hours in front of my fireplace, burning packing crates we had dragged in from the street, drinking dark rum. In spirit, we were in a café in Cavafy's Alexandria. We would go to readings at St. Mark's Poetry Project. We had both read John Rechy and, of course, Ginsberg. (Tom had studied with Allen's father in Paterson, New Jersey, and Allen would sometimes come by late at night for talk, and sex—with all three of us.) This was a time when there was no recognized gay literature, no gay studies departments. It was shortly after Stonewall. There was much excitement about the Gay Liberation Front and, shortly after-wards, the Gay Activists' Alliance. It was a time when many gay men were coming out of isolation and having a wild time doing it. It was in reference to this spirit that Rebel was calling his man-uscript *Triumph.*

Tom and I went our separate ways.

Rebel and I led a hand-to-mouth existence. Usually we ended up working the same day jobs together, but then we would dance all night on cobblestoned Wooster Street in front of the Gay Activists' Alliance Firehouse, get our drugs on St. Mark's Place, and go to leather bars together. I couldn't afford even a leather jacket, but one night I picked up a sanitation worker, with his truck, and talked him out of his uniform. So I'd go to the bars in uniform, ready to "pick up the garbage." Usually this meant leav-ing Rebel sitting alone at the bar when I went off with someone. Many times I simply stood him up. But I knew he'd always for-give me, without receiving an explanation or apology.

Rebel saw himself as my slave. And sometimes we'd act out his S/M fantasies. My arrogance and selfishness were real turn-ons for him, but, unfortunately, I was so self-centered that even his pain bored me. We tried everything he could think of, and still, self-absorbed as I was, I found him emotionally empty and boring.

Rebel started finding satisfaction in other places. He would show me the marks from whips and belts, red welts that criss-crossed his entire body. I understood his need, but I was repelled, maybe even frightened. I didn't want to explore my own dark side any further than I already had. I was consciously trying to change—to become more vulnerable, to become more loving. And Rebel was not the person I could do this with.

I knew Rebel and I had run our course. I had a party—maybe 150 people—and, early in the evening, I found a very drunk Rebel telling a group of my Ivy League undergraduate students all about the joys of scat, urging them each to get portable toilet seats. I grabbed him by the collar, dragged him to the hallway, punched him in the face, and told him I would never see him again.

Years went by. Occasionally I would hear rumors that Rebel was performing at private S/M clubs, getting electric shocks, being bled until he passed out. I heard he was living with a transvestite.

More years went by, and one day there he was. I was walking on Madison Avenue, and there was Rebel, in a dark suit and tie, with a briefcase. We said hello, and he apologized for his costume. He had a job. Until then I'd never seen him in anything but army fatigues, leather, or nothing at all.

Still more years later, someone saw his name on the AIDS Quilt. And now I feel the loss of a brother I was unable to love. He found freedom in bondage and joy in pain. But this was not where I wanted my own life to go. A few of his poems were published, but no one remembers where; and, to my knowledge, none of it now exists.

But, in my hand, I have a drawing I did for his first book cover, *Triumph.*

DHEA, TESTOSTERONE, MINOXIDIL, FRUITION, AND EYE ZONE

David Sanders

I met Mike, the man of my dreams, the man that I thought I had been waiting for all of my life, on a cold February night in New York City.

About four weeks prior to that night, I had been out on the town with Dimitris, my Greek ex-lover, who had been vacationing in New York City over the holidays. At what used to be our favorite Chinese restaurant, Dimitris gave me a "good talking to." The gist of his harangue was this: "Get out there, David, and start trying to meet someone. You're not getting any younger!"

I was only thirty-five at the time, but I went home and opened my medicine cabinet. DHEA capsules. Testosterone patches. Minoxidil bottles. Fruition and Eye Zone. Dimitris was right. Time was running out, and although I was definitely trying to preserve myself, the question I suddenly had to ask myself was, for whom? Because I really wasn't trying to meet anyone. So I determined that night that I would jump start my search for a lover by writing my first personal ad.

I had answered ads before. Dimitris was a case in point, but I had never written one myself. I think somewhere in those neural nooks and crannies of mine I believed that the writing and placement of an ad moved you into another club, the club of love losers and pathetic geeks who could not succeed in meeting someone in the traditional places: on the subway, in an elevator, at a bar.

Of course, once I made up my mind to do it, I wasn't hesitant in the least. And I wrote a pretty damn good ad. I received more than thirty responses, which I winnowed down to a series of blind dates. The last one, the ninth one, was with Mike.

I remember everything about that night. I was twelve minutes late. Intentionally late. I went out and bought a picture frame at the corner store so that I would be—because I didn't want to appear eager, even though I was. I had liked Mike on the phone. His voice was incredibly sexy. Deep and lush and nuanced. But then, he's a singer, a baritone.

We had agreed to meet at the smoky little piano bar in Chelsea where Mike occasionally belts out a Broadway tune. I walked in confidently, but, having only spoken to him briefly on the phone a few times, of course I was wondering what he would look like. To be honest, as I peered beyond the long mahogany bar into the darkly-lit table portion of the room, I wasn't expecting very much. For two reasons. My eight previous blind dates had been such disappointments. And I had already scanned the faces of every man seated at the bar and saw no one that I wanted to meet. So at this point I knew that if there wasn't someone I was attracted to at the tables, I was screwed again into having to spend a polite hour chatting with a man for whom I felt absolutely no attraction.

Most of us in the personal ads scene say that we're looking for friends too, but I've come to realize in this last go-round that it's just a line we use for others and for ourselves. The truth is that I wasn't looking for a friend the night I met Mike. I was looking for the man of my romantic and sexual dreams. I was looking for a mate. I was looking for the intimate conversation that can be sustained over long periods of time when you're in bed with the right person. Because it's all the same thing really, when it's right, isn't it? Talking and trusting and fucking and feeling. Isn't it all the same?

When I finally found Mike seated at a back corner table, I could feel my heart begin to race. He was exactly what I had hoped for. Shorter than me, more compact, dark wavy hair, deep, intense brown eyes, and a strong jaw. Mike was dressed like a preppy college boy. He smiled at me. I smiled at him. Excitedly, simultaneously, as in a Robert Altman film, we said each other's names. Obviously we were both happy at what we saw.

We sat down together, and Mike began chatting. I was more quiet, withdrawn. The more I'm attracted to a man, the less I am able to speak. Yet with Mike, I forced myself from my own muteness. I knew immediately that I did not want to contribute in any way to ruining what I felt was possible. I tried to be as witty and charming as he seemed naturally to be. I thought it was working. Within minutes, he touched my arm, near the elbow. This was important. His laughter and smiles amidst the story that he was telling me were not necessarily specific to me, but his intentional touch, the placing of his hand on my forearm and elbow, was the first jolt of Mike that I felt.

It was not the last. There was too much human electricity in the air. We went to dinner. Spanish. Over paella we told each other the basic stories of our lives. As we were finishing up our sangria, Mike let me know that he did not want the night to end.

"What would you like to do now?" he asked me.

"Why don't we walk to my apartment for coffee," I answered, knowing full well that I had no coffee. "It's only a few blocks away."

He smiled, happily agreeing.

I had known from the first moment that I saw him that I had to kiss him that night. Enjoying talking to him had made my ache for him twice as strong. I was impatient, antsy, horny. The door to my apartment had barely touched the jamb when I pushed myself into his body and crushed my lips onto his. Awkwardly, amidst our frantic kissing, we landed on the couch, and there we kissed for hours. I had never kissed so fiercely and deeply as I kissed Mike that night and every night when we were first together. I was overwhelmed by my passion for his mouth and his tongue and his smell and the taste of his throat and the texture of his skin and lips and the smell of his neck and ears and hair. I had never felt such heightened desire and loss of separateness as I did in those hours of kissing Mike. Our kissing was like a drowning within desire. Indeed, there were times when each of us felt almost asphyxiated by the coupling of our lips and tongues. There were moments when we just stopped and looked at each other and breathed freely, amazed at the intensity of our feelings, until we would begin again.

That first night, we were still dressed, but Mike mounted me on my couch. We were still kissing and he spread his legs across my hips and thighs. That night he gave me an image to hold, a preview of the eventual night when we would actually make love. I knew at that moment that, if he was the man who he seemed to be, I was going to love him. There was nothing to stop me from loving him. We had already tasted each other, and we had been transformed by it. I knew that physically we could reach the highest levels of passion, and I knew that we had much more in common than I'd had with previous lovers.

After Mike left that night, I found myself wondering if my years of searching had ended, if I had finally found that sweet prince that I had been longing for, waiting for, to shower love and affection on. The person that I would be able to talk to and laugh with and help and love for the rest of my life. The person who would share my deepest passions and loves. I wanted to sing with Mike. To paint him. To write music and poetry with him. To travel around the world with him. To learn more about faith and philosophy and God from him. To kiss him forever. For the first time in a long time, I felt like a truly lucky person.

And he didn't push me for sex. I never sleep with a man right away, and I remember Mike saying to me, "I like the pace that we're following." But there was a point, five weeks in, when I couldn't wait any longer. We had been kissing, again for hours, and I began to undress him. First it was just our shirts. But the sensation of our flesh exposed and touching, the heat and softness of our skin, was too much for me. And the incredible sensation of his nipples. He can be driven wild by the right lick and bite of his nipples. Before I could stop myself, I was removing his pants and shorts to lick him, to taste him. I was already in love with Mike, and now I had him inside my mouth.

He was a perfect fit. Not too big for my mouth. I loved the smell of his groin, but I couldn't linger there for long, because Mike moved. It was clear that he wanted to taste me too. I shifted around and then mounted his face. He took me in with a frenzy. It was intensely erotic. I thought about letting Mike inside of me that night. I wanted to sit on top of him and ride him. I wanted him to utter dirty commands at me. The imperative is the language of fucking. I wanted him to use it. I wanted us to come together that night. I wanted us to be one.

But we didn't make love that night. Maybe I was still holding back because of Jim. Jim. Three letters. A short name for a short man. Jim, the ex-lover. Jim, the current lover. Can you hate someone you've never met? Maybe not, but you sure can envy them.

What night was it that Mike told me about Jim? You'd think that I could remember that. I remember so many details about our relationship, but that one detail is fuzzy. But Mike did tell me.

There was disclosure. I don't think it would have qualified as full disclosure under SEC regulations, but I have to say that Mike did inform me of his relationship with Jim. In fact, he told me that he still loved Jim when he left him in Austin six weeks before he had moved back to New York and answered my ad. But he also told me that he had left a lover who had committed selfish, insensitive, and manipulative acts. A lover that he no longer wanted to be with.

Jim had moved to Texas without Mike's consent, assuming that Mike would acquiesce and follow him. And as if that insult weren't enough, once Jim had Mike down in Texas, he decided that he was going to adopt a child. When Mike insisted that he wasn't ready for such a commitment, that he wasn't ready to be a father, Jim went ahead anyway and started the adoption process. When Mike told Jim that he might leave, Jim scoffed, not believing it. But then Mike did it. He packed up and moved back to his apartment in New York and left Jim in Austin. Nine weeks later we were lovers.

And for a while I was right. We were lovers—dream lovers. The first two months were nothing short of glorious. I had never experienced a better beginning with a lover. Mike would say to me every time that we were together: "I'm so happy that I met you." I believed him and felt the same way. He quickly introduced me to all of his friends. Mike's friends are important to him, and they became important to me. Within the first month, I was in his circle. We felt like a couple. We talked every day and saw each other at least twice a week. Once during the week and on Friday or Saturday evening for a sleep-over. Some weeks we'd see each other five or six times. Our schedules were hectic, but we found time for each other.

At first he wouldn't even let me stay over at his place. Too many memories of Jim. Jim and he had lived there for a few months at some point in their on-and-off-again relationship. Eventually, we did start spending time there. I think it was in his Mission-style bed that we made love for the first time.

I was really nervous. It had been a while since I'd been with someone. And it had been a long wait for someone like Mike. You think you'd know how to act or what to do and say when you meet the person you've been waiting for such a long time. But waiting isn't practice or preparation, it's just waiting. And longing. And all that longing can turn into a lot of nerves. And sex and nervousness don't necessarily create phallic cement.

When it happened, I remember how embarrassed I was. I gave up and laid my head next to his and apologized. I know that in my mind I had just lost him for being so inept.

"I'm sorry," I said, "but I'm nervous. It's been a while. I'm sorry I failed."

Mike looked at me in the dark. Already I wasn't afraid to return his look, to stare deeply into his eyes.

"What do you mean 'failed?'" he said sweetly. "You didn't fail. It's fine."

He was wonderful and loving at a man's most embarrassing moment. I remember thinking how much I admired him. Who needs Viagra when you've got a man who's so kind and sensitive? I was incredibly turned on. Kindness and integrity, love, is such a fucking turn-on. I started kissing and sucking him everywhere. Our excitement built up again. This time everything worked. We both came hard. Then we slept our first night at his apartment. The next morning we awoke with renewed passion, and Mike specifically seduced me and excited me and guided me into himself. I was so excited at his wanting me so much. It felt like it was love not just sex.

There were so many other wonderful times. One night he was coming over for dinner at my house, and he said that he wanted a fire. He got one. We had a picnic of takeout pizza and wine on a woolen blanket in front of a cozy little fire in my living room. We kissed each other and sucked each other, and I think we made love again on that blanket. We must have, because my kneecaps were raw to the touch for the next four days from rubbing against the wool of that blanket.

But the things I loved most about Mike had nothing to do with sex. They were the small, quiet things that can unexpectedly steal your heart. Like at dinner parties with our friends. At some point in the evening, after dinner, when I was sitting on the sofa, Mike would usually move closer to me or sit down at my feet while putting his hands on me somehow. Neither of us are the clinging, hovering type. But he would always come near to me—to connect physically. And I would respond. Casually, of course, because we were in a room full of people. So I would just touch his neck or caress the back of his head or shoulder with my warm hand. But inside I was moved. It was a beautiful thing to see him do this, to see him want to be close to me and touch me, and in front of others.

And there was something else that he did that really moved me, something that no one ever witnessed. In bed, before or after love making, he would climb on top of me. He'd lay his entire body on top of my entire body, and I would just hold him in my arms. These moments, the two of us laid out like that, were perfect, encapsulated moments to me. I never wanted them to end. In fact, I loved it so much when he did this to me that I began to wonder whether it was something specific to me or not. I needed to know if he did it with everyone or just with me. I suppose I was really asking if he had done it with Jim. So one morning I did ask. I asked him why he did it and if it was something that he had done with other lovers. He said that he hadn't done it with anyone else and that he did it because he cared about me. I was so moved.

But these beautiful, encapsulated moments did not last. Somewhere in his inner life, in a place I had no access to, Mike was still thinking about Jim. I could sense that there were things he was holding back, that he was maintaining some kind of safety barrier. And I tried to break through, repeatedly. I tried to make Mike open up about his feelings. I believed then, and still do now, that if he could have talked to me about his feelings for Jim, then we might have been able to form a stronger emotional bond, and maybe things would have ended differently. Of course, I was so much in love that I wanted to believe that everything would still work out.

It didn't though. It didn't work out. By the fourth month, it was clear that Jim was in the picture again. He had moved back to New York for the summer, and he had his adorable little girl with him. Mike began to see Jim at certain parties and functions, and they began to talk again. The little girl, Annie, precocious and beautiful, became an object of Mike's affection. By the fifth month, Mike and I were on a two-week hiatus so that he could think clearly about what he should do.

Unfortunately I had the same two interminable weeks to think about what I should do. I was a total wreck. I felt self-destructive. I ate a lot of ice cream. I drank a lot of beer. I wondered if it were possible to O.D. on DHEA. I sprayed Minoxidil on my neck and ears. I wanted to hurt myself because in my heart I think that I already knew that I had lost Mike. Because what's a safer bet, the past or the future? How do you compete with a five-year history and a beautiful little orphan girl? What could I offer Mike beyond my love? Beyond the acts of kindness and love that I had already shown him?

It's hard to believe that it's been eight months since Mike and I broke up, five since Mike and Jim moved in together with their little girl. Rumor has it that Mike has another beautiful apartment, most of it bankrolled by Jim. They entertain on a regular basis. They live in New York now, not Texas. A matter of compromise, I suppose.

But I try not to pay attention to what's happening in their lives. Because I have to move on with my life. All I really know are two things. I know that I loved Mike. And I know that he held onto me until the final moment when he knew that he could have Jim back again.

I still have questions, of course: Like, did Mike love me, as he said he did in our last phone conversation a few days after we broke up, or was he just using me? I wish someday that I could know for certain. I wish that he could help me to continue to admire him and respect him the way that I once did. I want to. I wish that he could share with me what he truly felt for me and what he feels for me now.

There's an old proverb from the Middle East: "There is no truth, only versions." I can't say that I like the idea that we can never know the truth about anything. But in matters of the heart it does seem to be that way.

The last time that Mike saw me, he held me and kissed me and told me how much he cared about me. Two days later he called me from Jim's Fire Island rental and told me that he had decided to go back to his former lover. On the phone he said, "This whole thing has been about me."

What was he acknowledging there? Was he really confessing to me then what he had known all along? That he had selfishly used me for the previous five months?

I don't know what else to say in this little story about my love affair with Mike. Except that meeting, loving, and losing Mike has been the most bittersweet episode in my life. I have shed some tears, believe me. Holding onto a romantic dream all these years is hard enough, but finding it and losing it, having to dismantle that dream, is pretty devastating.

But I'm putting my life back together. Ironically, for quite some time I'd thought about joining a therapy group. Thanks to Mike, I finally have. Every Wednesday evening for two hours I find myself squirming in a very uncomfortable vinyl chair. But the talk there has been quite comfortable and comforting, too.

Actually, I met my therapist by answering a personal ad a few months after Mike, still looking for love. When the man on the other end of the line told me that he was a therapist, I launched right into the story of my ordeal with Mike. I told him that I was more interested in finding a therapist than in finding a new boyfriend. Before I knew it, I was joining his gay men's group.

Of course the end of this story is the same as the beginning: I'm trying not to love somebody that I love. Which is a horrible thing that we all have to do from time to time. But at least I've grown a little wiser from the experience. And I haven't given up believing in love or in the personals. I met Dimitris, my greatest love, through the personals. I met Mike, my greatest lover, through the personals. And if anyone asks me, this is my advice: Answer or write those ads. Maybe you'll find the man of your dreams. Maybe you'll find a therapist. Or maybe you'll discover what I did—that self-preservation is a little more complicated than just DHEA, testosterone, Minoxidil, Fruition and Eye Zone.

MISSING PAUL

Marc J. Heft

When I signed onto the Internet, back in 1994—way before it was the mass medium it is today, when it was still controlled largely by propeller heads and a few of us cool people that had slipped under the radar—I had only one purpose in mind: I was going to find me a man on this thing!

And I did. I met all sorts of boys. I met boys who were funny, boys who were weird, boys who were smart, and boys who were dumb as a bag of dirt. Each encounter was carefully orchestrated to insure that they could be easily prolonged if we were enjoying ourselves, or easily ended if I found my eyes rolling to the back of head as I slipped into a coma trying to force continued interest in the screen.

Paul and I first talked on-line in the *nycm4m* (New York City Men for Men) chat room, a place I found myself spending more time than I cared to admit. In our first chat, we talked about all the things that boys talk about on-line: what movies we had seen, where we worked and lived—your basic run-of-the-airwaves cyberchat. Of course, I looked up Paul's on-line profile in order to gather as much information as possible to keep the conversation going.

I did ask him my standard ice-breaker: "You are not an ax-wielding psycho killer are you?—not that you would tell me anyway" (meaning it as a joke of course, but not entirely). I followed it up with a little smiley face :-) just to let him know that I was kidding and to show him how incredibly clever I could be.

Just when I was beginning to feel fairly comfortable chatting away in relative anonymity, Paul popped the first big question in the pre-date cyber-ritual.

"So Marc, do you have a gif?"

Oh, no, I thought, *the dreaded gif exchange!*

Now this is a very critical moment in the cyber process. This either catapults you to the next level or stops you dead in your tracks. *What do I say?* I thought. *If I say yes, then I have to send it; if I say no, then he won't know what I look like and may lose interest. What if he is way better looking than me and I feel inferior; what if I am way better looking than him and he stalks me on line for the rest of my cyber life?*

"Yes, Paul, I do have a gif. Do you?"

"Yes," he answered. "Wanna swap?"

"Sure," I said with another one of those smiley faces to give some levity to the situation and to communicate that I know this is all in good fun. Hehehehe... No ego damage possible here. Ha! (We both know, of course, that we will be scrutinizing these photos for the slightest imperfection. We'll be on those images like a jeweler looking for flaws in a five-karat ice-blue diamond.)

I checked my mailbox and found his e-mail: It was given the acceptably unobnoxious title "Mypic." A lot of boys go for damage control at this point by using file names for their gifs like badpic.gif, cuterinperson.gif or ilookbetternow.gif.

I began the download. First the black box appeared on my computer screen, and I knew that within seconds my anticipation would be over and I would get to see him for the first time. Will he be beautiful? Will he be sexy? Will he be hideous, fat, thin, short, tall, blond, dark? *Hurry!*—I can't wait anymore. Then the unthinkable happened: I lost my modem connection, and my program shut down. (This, as all Internet users know, is an all-too-common occurrence.)

Nooooooooo!!! A blood-curdling scream pierced the silence of my apartment. It seemed to be coming out of my mouth. Naturally, I panicked. *Oh, no! What do I do? He will think I saw his picture and was so horrified that I ran screaming into the night. I will have damaged the boy forever. Quick! sign back on!*

The first try was busy. I double-panicked, then tried again. Success! I heard that glorious modem sound and knew that within seconds my connection would be re-established. I found him again and offered a phrase that I had had occasion to utter many times before (and have had since):

"Sorry, got bumped." I followed it with another smiley face hoping he was not upset.

His response popped up on my screen:

"No prob. Did you get my pic?"

"Yes," I replied. "I'll download it now. Did you get mine?"

"Yes."

Oh, no, I thought. *That's not good. He didn't comment. He is trying to spare my feelings. He thinks I'm hideous. I am never leaving the house again.*

Then a second line—equally as short but much more fulfilling: "Cute." Followed by a little smiley face of his own. My heart resumed beating.

I downloaded his picture and thought the same thing. *Cute,* I said to myself and then to him. It was not a very good quality picture but good enough for me to want to proceed. We survived the hair-raising picture exchange and are both still here and interested, a miracle.

"So," I asked him as casually as possible. "Do you want to talk on the phone?"

Now this is also a critical hurdle, because you are asking the person to get off the computer, where it is entirely possible that he is simultaneously having six conversations identical to—or even better than—the one he's having with you. You are asking him to dismiss all the other contestants—*Thank you for playing. We have some lovely parting gifts for you. Jay, tell them what they've won!*—and choose you as the winner, at least for now.

"Sure," Paul answered. "Give me a few minutes."

Now, I always try at this point to get them to give me their phone number, instead of the other way around. This ensures that if, after the phone conversation, I decide they don't get to participate in the swim suit competition, we won't ever have to speak again. Remember, I have done this before. I am a professional. Unfortunately, while I was thinking how smart I was about to be, Paul beat me to it.

"Give me your number and I will call you," he said.

Not wanting to sound paranoid or like I have anything to hide, I gave him my number.

The phone rang a mere five minutes later. A good sign, indeed.

"Hello," I said, wanting to sound mysterious, sexy, funny, intelligent, warm and well-adjusted in just a single word—not an easy task, mind you.

"Hi, Marc. It's Paul."

I thought to myself, *No kidding? I was expecting it to be Brad Pitt at 2:30 in the morning, calling to invite me over for a pajama party!!*

I said something dorky like, "I know. I recognize your voice from the computer," which I followed by even dorkier nervous laughter. We talked for a few minutes. *Hey, this doesn't suck,* I found myself thinking, which is always a surprise.

It turned out Paul lives in the East Village and is a writer. At the very moment he revealed this information to me, I began planning our lives together.

"So," I blurted out, taking control of the situation, "wanna meet?"

"It's almost three in the morning."

"Not *now.*" (I am trying not to appear shocked that he would think I might actually leave my house at this hour to meet a complete and total stranger—something I would never do, no matter how tempting it might be.)

We agreed to meet the next afternoon for coffee.

Now, Paul may have beaten me to the phone number thing, but I was certainly not going to make the same mistake twice. I quickly suggested a location that was my standard meeting place for all Internet encounters: It's close to my house, and they don't serve anything that takes more than five minutes to eat. At least I don't have to travel to be disappointed, and I don't have to suffer through a multiple-course dinner.

I told him to sit in the outdoor bench to the right of the entrance and that I would meet him at *exactly* five o'clock.

I managed to get his phone number *Just In Case Something Comes Up.*

* * *

At 4 o'clock the next afternoon I had to run home and drop off the Bed, Bath & Beyond bags before my date. It would be way too stereotypical to bring them. I mean, I might as well have had a Judy Garland album in one hand and a bouquet of calla lilies in the other! By the time I got back to my apartment, I realized I had a scant twenty minutes to make myself gorgeous—not enough time. I decided to just go for non-repulsive.

Of course, my head was giving me the usual instructions: *Don't talk too much. Let him say something once in a while. Look interested and intelligent, warm and caring, funny and.... Yeah, yeah, yeah. Shut up. I know the drill.*

As I crossed Christopher Street, I glanced over to the coffee bar. There on the bench was Paul, right on time. I looked over and thought, *He doesn't look exactly like his picture,* but then again they never do. He wasn't bad, though. I didn't have that nauseous feeling when I saw him, and my Flee Now instinct was nowhere to be found.

"Hi Paul," I said in my cheery, emotionally available voice.

"Hi," he replied in a slightly flat, lifeless tone.

"How are you?"

"Good," he responded, somewhat uncomfortably. "How are you?"

"Fine, thanks. Great day, isn't it? Beautiful weather."

Oh, no, I remember thinking, *fifteen seconds into the date and we're already talking about the weather. This is not a good sign. Not to worry,* I reassured myself, *I am the professional. I will take control.*

And so I did. I started talking a mile a minute. At one point I almost passed out from lack of oxygen—*Breathe, Marc. Breathe!* I decided I needed to give him a chance to speak.

After a few minutes of painful silence, it was obvious that this strategy was not going to work. I started to ask him direct questions in the hopes of stimulating some semblance of a conversation.

Apparently seeing through my strategy, Paul responded to each question with a one-word answer.

Now, I have seen this many times before. It is known MIPP, or Meeting-in-Person Paralysis, and it happens to approximately one in five boys on Internet dates according to my extensive data. It can pass, and you move forward—or it doesn't, and you remember why you picked this coffee bar in the first place.

After about five minutes with Paul, I noticed that this was not just MIPP, but that he evidently has a serious personality disorder or perhaps he hadn't quite got his Lithium/Prozac combination down right. As I said, it has happened before, but I decided to give him a bit more time, since he had such potential on-line and on the phone. I stood up to go inside and asked Paul if he would like something.

"No," he responded. "I'm fine, thanks."

What I wanted to say was: "I can see that, you inconsiderate freak. You obviously did not feel it was necessary to wait for me to order coffee."

I decided, however, that this might have sounded rude and, besides, he could still stab me from behind.

Once inside, I ordered a cup of tea, nothing to eat, being fairly certain that I would need to pull the rip cord any minute and bail. Food would just hinder my getaway. Finally, the nose-ringed, attitude-ridden, tip-expecting serving shrew handed me my tea, but it was way too hot. It needed some cooling down time. Hhmmmm this could be a problem. I asked the charming young lady to give me an ice cube. You would have thought I'd asked her to paint my apartment from the annoyed look she gave me. I scanned the room while waiting for the morsel of ice that would help quicken my escape.

I looked around the crowd and wondered how these people had met and if any of them were here doing the same two-step of death as Prozac Patty and me. I took my tea with ice, not to be mistaken for ice tea, and re-joined Paul on our bench.

We had a few more minutes of excruciatingly dull conversation while I tried to finish my tea without burning the skin off my tongue. There was another thing that I had noticed after a few more minutes of sitting and talking with Paul: He is one of those people who avoids direct eye contact at all costs. This is a most annoying character trait as far as I am concerned. I was really getting the signal loud and clear: This child was s-t-r-a-n-g-e.

We were at Defcon Four, and I needed to get out of this situation, immediately, if not sooner. This boy was giving me the heebies. This is the kind of person who keeps a shoe box full of beheaded Barbie dolls under his bed and refers to them as "his girls."

Too bad, he was kinda normal and funny on the phone. I made my move. I stood up, said it was nice meeting him but that I needed to be on my way. I informed him that I had dinner plans. I shook his soggy, moist, fish-like hand and was gone before he knew what hit him.

I was indeed a professional at this. But my timing, like my intuition, was off a bit. The date lasted 25 minutes, five minutes longer than usual when they are that much fun. I blamed it on the temperature of the tea.

All in all I had managed to depart relatively emotionally unharmed. I was not rude or unpleasant, which I would never be (unless absolutely necessary), but I did not lead Paul to believe that we would *ever* see each other again. I proceeded to meet my friend for dinner, a friend I met on-line and regaled him with my tale of the latest Internet debacle.

❖   ❖   ❖

When I got home, I found three messages on my answering machine. The first was from my mother, asking how my weekend was and asking me to call her when I had a moment in my busy schedule, which half made me smile and half made me want to delete the message immediately. The second was from a friend asking if I wanted to see a movie the following evening. (*Absolutely.*)

The third message, much to my dismay, was from Paul. It went something like this:

"Hi Marc, this is Paul. I waited for you at the coffee bar this afternoon, but you never showed up. Oh, well, maybe something happened. Call me if you want to reschedule. Bye."

I stared blankly at the answering machine until it hit me like a ton of bricks, like one of those flashback sequences in a movie when all the pieces suddenly fit together. Paul never actually said my name the entire time we were sitting there together, he'd avoided making eye contact with me, and he was nothing like the guy I had spoken to the night before on the phone. There was, of course, a very good reason for these things: The horror of this encounter was that the guy on the bench that afternoon was not Paul. I dialed his number.

"Hi, Paul. It's Marc"

"Oh. Hi, Marc," he replied in a tone that was perfectly acceptable from someone who thought he had been blown off by a stranger. I then started to tell him what happened. At one point he interrupted me and said, "Did you ask the girl behind the counter for ice for your tea?"

"Yes, yes that was me," I answered, with complete relief realizing now that he would know I was telling the truth and had not callously failed to show up for our date.

"Well, who the hell was that guy you were talking to?"

"I have absolutely no idea," I replied.

"Then why were you talking to him?"

"Because he was sitting on our bench, and I mistook him for you."

I asked Paul why, if he had recognized me from my photo, he didn't say hello or ask if it was me.

He said that he thought it was me, but he wasn't sure. When he saw that I was with someone else, he assumed it wasn't me. He said that he could not sit at our pre-arranged bench because when he arrived the fake Paul was already sitting in it, so he sat inside instead.

The absurd hilarity of the situation hit me, and I started to laugh. I laughed really, really hard—until tears were streaming down my face. All of a sudden it dawned on me that there was only silence on the other end of the phone.

"Paul," I asked, "are you still there?"

"Yup."

"Don't you think that this is absolutely hilarious?"

"No, not really."

"You don't?" I said in disbelief.

"No."

Well that one simple statement probably saved me weeks of dating before I found out that he was not the boy for me. If something like that just didn't hit him right smack in the funny bone, then I am pretty certain that there was no future for us.

I apologized to him for the mix-up, and he said that it was okay. I wished him well, and he did the same. We said our good-nights, both knowing that our meeting was just not meant to be.

I walked upstairs and looked into the den at my computer. We glared at each other for a moment. I smiled and thought, *What if he is on there tonight and I miss him?*

I sat down, signed on, and waited, impatiently. Finally came that oh-so familiar, automated voice: "Welcome. You've got mail."

I'll read it later, I thought to myself. *I've got a chat room to get to.*

BERLIN CONNECTION

Owen Levy

He answered my personal ad in the contact column of one of the city magazines. I thought this might be one way to meet some new faces when I was living in Berlin right after reunification of Germany. Of the ten or so answers I received, his seemed the most promising. I telephoned, and he suggested we meet the following Saturday by the statue of Kaiser Friedrich across from the entrance to the Charlottenburg Palace. We'd already exchanged snapshots, so the biggest hurdle was out of the way. Now it was time to see if we could get something going.

It had been raining on and off all day, but he was right on time. I knew because I had arrived five minutes earlier.

Gut impressions were good, and we started strolling the castle grounds. The intermittent rain was romantic, but a small problem, since neither of us had brought along rain gear. We got out of one heavy downpour by forking over five marks to visit an exhibition of porcelains in one of the miniature châteaux that dotted the landscaped park.

The verbal rapport came easily enough, though my German was hardly fluent, and he seemed reluctant to use his English. The fine eighteenth- and nineteenth-century porcelain figurines, serving pieces, and elaborately detailed tea sets from the castle's permanent collection provided an opulent backdrop for our first meeting, I thought.

We shared impressions of the porcelains, all the while circling like stalking beasts, unsure of one another's nature, guards up but not defensively. I was drawn to his large prominent mouth, the soft thick lips jutting over straight white teeth. On the stairs between galleries, I tried to swipe a kiss, but he artfully finessed the attempt. An awkward moment followed—but obviously not one he was going to hold against me.

The rain let up enough for us to walk through the sculpture garden overlooking the boat basin. I liked the way his trim athletic body filled out his jeans and decided I definitely wanted to see what was under them. His intentions were not so plain. It started raining again, and we headed for the front gate. Something hot to drink and a cozy place to sit were in order. Since we had both come by car, I suggested he follow me over to one of my favorite neighborhood bakery cafés.

The smaller tables were all occupied, so we sat opposite a serene elderly woman who was smoking alone at one end of a family-sized table. The waitress took our order, and we settled back in the deeply cushioned, vintage easy chairs that were the café's second big draw. As he made polite chatter, I was thinking about the explicit letter he'd written answering my ad, which I worded with numerous double-entendres. Somehow all of the directness took on a muted tone as he discussed the potential for relationships and how important it was to build up to something. I readily agreed, mouthing *"Langsam anfangen"* ("Slow beginning"), remembering an earlier bittersweet affair that had come and gone much too fast.

After our snack we walked along the nearby promenade that runs along the Spree river. We didn't talk much, but it didn't seem we had to. When it started raining again, he suggested we take in a movie. We checked a schedule, and in deference to my language skills, he suggested seeing something in English with German subtitles. We drove in my car to the neighborhood of the cinema and grabbed a crunchy meal in a nearby vegetarian restaurant before the movie. It was beginning to feel like a real date, the kind of date that might actually go somewhere.

The film was okay. It was the director's latest, but it just didn't live up to his first film, we both agreed—but the company remained satisfying. Driving him back to pick up his car, we played touchy-hands on the gear shift stick and shared a hurried good-night kiss before he jumped out. I waved and drove off but soon noticed he was right behind me, though he lived in another direction. It looked like he was driving to one of the bars he said he'd been going to a lot lately. Next time I looked, he was gone. I drove home.

When I got back to the apartment, I was charged up with pleasant thoughts of my new prospective intended. I liked the idea that we hadn't jumped right into bed. Maybe there was something here worth nurturing. We'd agreed to get together on Tuesday, but we hadn't made it clear who would call whom. When I hadn't heard from him by the end of the day, I rang.

He sounded apprehensive, talking in a low monotone. It gradually came out that he was on the tail end of a relationship with some poor fellow who had tried to commit suicide and whom he was helping to get therapy. He wasn't able to meet me that evening because Andreas was due back soon from the doctor, and he was afraid Andreas might attempt to harm himself further or, not finding him home, trash the apartment. (When I mentioned to my friend Victor that I'd lost a date because an ex-lover was threatening to commit suicide, he laughed and said it sounded like a lie to him.)

He suggested we get together Saturday night and he would call me. I was a little skeptical since I knew he'd be working that day and would also have to the next. The phone didn't ring within the designated time frame Saturday afternoon. I felt very centered that day and decided not to make any effort to call him when he got home. Being stood up twice in one week was enough.

When I didn't hear from him by Monday, I decided to call and demand my picture back. I'd been reluctant to send it in the first place, but now, the way things were, I just wanted to get it back and put the whole interlude behind me.

I woke him from an afternoon nap. He seemed even more down than before as he explained that arrangements had been made for his ex-friend to move to a treatment facility and that he was waiting for him to come home so he could pack and give back the keys. He thought he should be able to get to my place by nine o'clock, if I wanted to see him. I bought into it without further recriminations.

The appointed hour came... and went. When I'd given up on him completely, the door buzzer sounded. He stood tentatively in the threshold until I stepped aside. He asked if it was all right to come in. I led him into the living room, closed the door and waited for him to do the talking.

He was confused, he said. So many bad things were happening in his life right now. Beside the ex-lover, there was his apartment, which he hated, job uncertainty (with performance reviews about to come up), his parents wanting to know about his life in Berlin, and his brother, who was having his own problems with a shaky marriage. Besides which, he'd been so determined to find a relationship that he had put a personal ad in a national magazine with his home phone number in it and was now getting calls day and night. This was all by way of explaining why he was three hours late and had stood me up twice.

His clothes smelled of cigarette smoke, and since he didn't smoke, it was a telltale sign he'd made a stop before coming to see me. When I commented on the smell, he said he'd stopped by a café and had two teas—black and peppermint—on his way. I casually mentioned that it was customary to let people know when you're going to be appreciably late for an appointment.

We talked some more, dissecting what we were looking for in a relationship, and how, on the one hand, he wanted one really badly, but on the other, was unable to change his behavior. He said he acted badly and he knew he did, and it was up to me to decide whether he should go or not. Very dramatic.

We started kissing a bit. Then a bit more, but I could feel him holding back. "My body wants to," he said, "but my head can't tonight."

I urged him just to go with the moment. I was getting excited and wanted to consummate this damn thing. But finally he was able to pull himself away even though his nipples were rigid, and he had to adjust his trousers when he got up.

As I was showing him to the door, he said it was up to me to keep in touch and that, by the way, his phone was being disconnected on Friday. (Victor's Golden Rule of relationships is "Never date anybody who doesn't have a telephone!")

Late one night, a few days later, the phone rang. It was him. He said he was calling from a pay phone on Savignyplatz, which was a few blocks from my apartment. I invited him to come over, and without hesitation, he agreed.

Savignyplatz is about five minutes by car but it took him about forty. Either he had trouble finding a parking spot, or he was really calling from his place, which was a good half-hour drive away.

I lit some candles, turned off the lights, and stuck a couple of condoms in the edge of the mattress. When he arrived, I led him right into the bedroom. He sat down on the edge of the bed, said he was feeling a little tired and had to get up early to go for an AIDS test. He asked if he could stay the night. I said sure.

Like a couple of Boy Scouts, we both stripped down to our underwear and crawled into bed. We kissed and fondled each other a little, but I didn't push it, and soon we both rolled over to go to sleep. In the wee hours, I started caressing him, and he responded—though he remained passive, which meant I had to do all the work.

I'd been waiting a long time for this tryst, and it was obvious he was willing to let me have my way with him. I was really excited, perhaps too much so. As I mounted him and penetrated, I came prematurely before the first really deep thrust. I kept feeding it to him anyway and pulled him to a climax. We fell back off to sleep.

He was up by seven, dressed and out the door in ten minutes. I decided this was a nice beginning: Once a week he'd call, come over and be gone in the morning.

I didn't hear from him for two weeks, and I knew his birthday was coming up. I sent him a postcard with a picture of the château where we'd seen the porcelain exhibition on our first meeting in the rain.

No response.

On his birthday, I toyed with the idea of driving out to his place, but it was already late, and I was too unclear about the exact route to take a chance at night. In between, there had been other new acquaintances to occupy me, so I tried not to lose any more sleep over him, though I had to admit I was still attracted.

A few days later I was driving Victor out to a shopping center to redeem a gift certificate and realized that if I took an alternate route back I could see where my classified affair lived. I rang his buzzer but there was no answer, so I scribbled a note and stuffed it into the mailbox.

Days passed and still not a peep.

Victor and I were reading apartment share notices on the bulletin board of a gay café when Victor thought he recognized the handwriting and phrasing style on one. (I had let Victor read all the responses to my ad.) I checked the contact book at the bar, and it turned out it was from exactly whom we suspected. He had submitted it a week before his birthday. There was a phone number. I wrote it down thinking it might be new but later it turned out to be the same line that had been disconnected.

I knew that sooner or later we would run into each other. The Berlin scene just wasn't that large. Unlike Paris or London, things at the time were pretty much localized in one neighborhood. I recalled him talking about this café he liked to go to, and one rainy Sunday when I had a couple of hours to kill, I drove by and checked it out. It was crowded and smoky, and since I'd heard the food wasn't very good, it was easy to turn around and leave after seeing he wasn't there.

I was walking in the direction of another strip of gay hangouts when I passed a porno book and video store I'd frequently seen advertised but had never visited. I decided it was as good a time as any to pop in and see what was up.

The layout was instantly recognizable. Display cases filled with dildos and other toys, books, magazines and shelves of videos to buy or rent, all of it just a front for a thriving back-room porno theater. I was debating whether to blow twelve marks on a quick excursion into the back when who should come through the front door?

He looked really surprised to see me, and for some reason, it didn't surprise me at all. He acted as if we'd seen each other recently, and wasn't this a happy coincidence? I let him get away with that as we cautiously shared pleasantries. I asked if he got the postcard.

"Yes," he said and kissed me thank you.

And my note?

Yeah, he'd gotten that too and was planning to call me. As he spoke, he turned toward the cashier and doled out the price of admission. I'd have thought he'd have the decency—or deceit—to at least wait until we wound up our conversation.

Obviously there was no further point to all this, so I told him pointblank: "Send my photo back when you get a chance."

He seemed stunned by the request but immediately said he'd bring it by one day this week. I said I had to work on Monday and Tuesday, so he said he'd call on Wednesday.

He gave me another kiss, and this time I noted that his breath had the dead smell of a mouth that had recently been sucking more than one cock. He nodded good-bye as he disappeared behind the door leading to the screening booths. I headed back out into the rain.

A few days later my picture came in the mail. No note and no return address.

LIE

Eric Latzky

Lie, he said.

Absolutely, his boyfriend concurred. It was a sultry September afternoon as we sat in lounge chairs on a weathered wood deck by the pool in the gated compound of a rented modernist wood-and-glass house, engulfed by rustling trees and blueberry bushes dense with greenery from a summer's growth. On the earthly boardwalk boulevard just beyond this heavenly space, a slow, steady stream of overgrown boys, ripe as the day, with hairless, waxed torsos and perfect tan lines, continued their strutting, high-season parade with the transgressive showmanship of white shoes worn after Labor Day. In breezeless intervals when the trees were quiet, we could hear waves breaking further in the distance.

Lie?

Definitely, he said.

I put down my cool, sweating glass of iced tea, took off my sun glasses, picked up a pencil and a notebook that had been waiting impatiently on a table next to my chair, and leaned back into a long, loud breath.

Sell yourself, his boyfriend suggested in an attempt to redirect the discourse, aware of my ambivalence.

I lifted the pencil, scribbled a few statistics and announced the results:

5'7", 170#, shaved head,
slightly husky but attractive, writer.

The response was swift.

I said *lie,* he said with an unmistakable tone of disdain.

Smooth the edges... Embellish, his boyfriend came back with a smile.

Our house was next to the last on the main walk, just before the edge of the beach forest. Meat Rack-view, the real estate agent had said, floating this trial balloon as a racy marketing ploy. To some this was a selling point, and members of the house had staged a political moment at a pre-season meeting in support of allocating household funds to purchase a pair of night-vision binoculars in lieu of a VCR. The thought of a summer in proximity to a real-life version of the pornographic ideal was *very* exciting to some in our crowd.

I raised the pencil again and drew a big X-mark through the former entry while throwing my friend a chilly glance that melted into a softer stare as I turned to his boyfriend.

5'7 1/2", 165#, shaved head, writer,
work in the arts, attractive guy getting in shape.

Again, I read it aloud.

He opened his mouth to speak, then turned his head away from me without saying anything, which his boyfriend took as a quick cue.

Good. More!

The night-vision binoculars never materialized, but keen observation and literary descriptions of the wealth of male perfection became a sport of the summer. Stories unfolded of distant appreciations of Adonis incarnates, actual meetings with well-toned and sometimes well-employed young men, and even a rare report of a handsome intellect. Occasionally, an account came of all these aspects in a single package, recounted over a rapt full-house dinner on an idyllic August Saturday eve followed by sardonic pool-side star-gazing in which any number of the members dared introspectively dream of love with such a complete creature.

Good-looking guy, 5'8", 162#, perfectly shaped
shaved head, gym 3x week, published writer,
successful arts professional, downtown soul
living uptown, looking for a peer of the realm.

I was beginning to believe these personal improvements. I liked this new vision of me, superior and free of flaws, buoyed and bolstered, hugely homosexual.

I drew a breath to speak, but before a single word came forth, I picked up the pencil again and began to cross out, then write more, furiously.

PAST PERFECT

Jessie McHallon Hall

Apollo Seeks Zeus
*Tall, blond, uninhibited, 28. I have a body of Epic
proportions and genuinely prefer older men,
any race, any size for soulful service.
I'm a nonsmoker, D/D free. UB2.*

"**I**t's too good to be true," Marvin said, dribbling skim milk from his oatmeal down his scraggly would-be goatee.

"Well, I know it's not the usual," I agreed over our ritual Saturday brunch at the Fiddler Café. "But what have I got to lose?"

"Your dignity. Your self-respect. Your virginity."

"Lost, lost, and lost," I said trying to get an egg yolk onto my buttered bagel without breaking it.

"Your illusions..."

"Left 'em in the maternity ward."

"Your life?"

"Oh, Marvin, you're so *dramatic.*"

"Does he say if his name is Dahmer?"

The first two times I called I got his answering machine.
"Hi, I'm not here. Leave a message."
I hung up.

"His *voice* sounds nice," I told Marvin eight seconds later.
"What do you mean *nice?*"

"Well, he doesn't sound like a thug. He doesn't sound like a fruitcake. And he doesn't sound like he's from New York. He just sounds... I don't know. *Nice."*

"I'm from New York," Marv reminded me.

"Marv," I reminded him, "you went to Bronx High School of Science. You went to Yale."

"Spoken like a true Choatie," he sneered and hung up on me.

The fifth time I left a message.

"Hi," I said. And hung up.

I waited an hour.

"Hello?" he said.

"Oh," I answered.

"Hello?"

"Sorry. I didn't think I'd get a live person."

"I know what you mean," he said with a slight baritone laugh deep in his throat. "I'm Alex. What can I do for you?"

"I saw your ad in *Frontiers,"* I managed to get out. "You sound great."

"What is it you're looking for?" he asked, a question that always floors me, for some reason.

I mean, what am I going to say?

Oh, I'm looking for a hot young stud of impossible beauty who will give me total pleasure and offer no resistance no matter what I ask. The stud in question will be sensitive and bright and have a great sense of humor and won't kill me after I come. He will be respectful of his elders, but not want a daddy, and it won't bother him that I'm way past the gay expiration date and big enough around the equator to fit adolescent twins in my jeans.

What I said was:

"Well, I'd like to meet someone who looks like you say you look and who doesn't object to middle-aged men and who likes affection with his sex."

"Sounds like you found him," he said and asked when he could come over.

"Tonight?" Marvin practically gagged into the phone.

"I like a man who goes after what he wants," I said, trying to sound blasé.

"No, you don't," Marv corrected. "You think Hamlet was impetuous!"

"Marv, all I said was I thought there were excellent reasons for not just killing his uncle..."

"What time?" Marv demanded. "I'm going to sit in my car in the street. If there is any trouble, you scream out the window. I'll bring the cell phone. I'll preset the speed dial for 911."

"Don't be ridiculous!" I said. "I'll be fine. And, besides, if he's as hot as he says he is, I won't want to know you're out there with your finger on the trigger. Or on anything else!"

At 10:02 p.m., there was a knock on the door.

He was late, but I forgave him, since I couldn't remember whether or not I'd set the clock two minutes ahead on purpose to trick myself.

I opened the little metal grate in the door to check him out. My eye was even with the canyon between his alpine pecs. I slammed the grate closed and opened the door.

"Hi," he said as simple as Simon.

"Hi," I said, thinking it was the wrong thing.

"I'm Alex," he said, extending his hand. I took it. It was the size of a small dog and as hard and muscular as a big one.

Alex was tall. Six foot five would be my guess. He was blond—naturally, unobnoxiously and neatly groomed blond (his eyes were greenish blue). And he was built. Colt Studios built. A brick shithouse in jeans, a red muscle shirt (and how *well* that shirt deserved its name stretched across his chest and shoulders), and flip flops, like he just stepped off the beach. He had a face somewhere between a movie star and a choirboy in one of those states in the middle of the country that starts with M. He was carrying a little gym bag that looked like the kind of thing a cat burglar would carry his tools in.

I showed Alex in. I showed him the living room. The kitchen. The study. The bedroom.

"It's a really nice place," he said, looking over this and that. "Do you mind if I take a shower?"

"No, not at all," I said, thinking things were getting off to a weird start.

"I just got off a boat," he said, "and I'm kinda salty."

I gave him a clean white towel. He smiled as he closed the door behind him.

I paced up and down the hall, thinking how much I liked salt.

I nearly jumped out of my skin when the phone rang.

"Is it okay?"
Marvin.
"He is fucking *gorgeous!*" I whispered into the phone. "Where are you?"
"I'm out front."
"Go home!" I ordered.
"Where is *he*?" Marvin persisted.
"He's in the shower."
"You're already finished?"
"No, we're not already fi— I thought you said you were outside. How the fuck could we be finished? He just walked in the door."
"Well, what's he doing in the shower?"
"He's taking a shower, that's all," I said as the sound of the water went off. "And he's finished. Go home."
"I am staying right here."
I hung up on him.
Not for the first time. Or the last.

I went into the study and looked at what I could see of my reflection in the window you could see the Hollywood sign from. It was a flawless L.A. night. I heard the bathroom door open and went back into the living room. He wasn't in it. He wasn't in the kitchen.
Alex was in the bedroom. He was on the bed. He had wrapped the towel around his waist, but he'd folded it in half first, so it looked like one of those tiny sarongs the bar boys wear in Hawaii, only it was white, so it looked like all those boys in bathhouses back in the '70s. He had his hands up behind his head in perfect "do me" position.
Okay, I thought. Crude, but acceptable. I approached.
Alex had perfect tan skin without the trace of a hair or a blemish anywhere I could see. But he wasn't shaved. There just weren't any follicles. I felt like a yeti. I could not keep my eyes of his torso, his *tiny* little waist, those cobble-stone abs, nipples like chocolate kisses. His thighs were enormous, and every muscle was defined. They seemed to be held onto his body by a network of veins that wriggled like indigo reptiles under his skin when he moved.

As I got near him, he sat up.

"Aren't you wearing too much clothing?" he asked.

"Possibly," I said, standing in front of him.

"Here," he offered, and pulled my sweatshirt up over my head. He was Tarzan. I was Jane Curtain. Or Oliver Hardy.

"Very nice," he said when it was off and shifted a bit so he could kiss the gray, hairy hollow between my tits. "I love hair."

He rubbed his hands over my chest. He plucked at my nipples with his fingers (callused–from weight lifting, no doubt). He put his hands on my hips and kept kissing my chest, my belly.

Then he made a single quick gesture with both hands, slipping them between me and the elastic waist band of my shorts, and without hesitation, peeled them off me. They dropped to the floor. My rock-hard dick was aimed in the direction of his mouth.

He laughed.

"Too small?" I asked.

"Too soon," he said. His laughter echoed in his chest cavity and resonated with the springs in the mattress. "Let's start with a little massage," he said and stood up. "Face down, head up by the pillows."

Now there's one thing I have learned in my life. When clear directions to a desired destination are offered... follow the directions.

The phone rang.

"Oh," he said. "You want to get it?"

"No," I said, "but if I don't something paramilitary might happen."

"Huh?"

"Never mind," I said and picked up the phone.

"Hello?"

"It's me."

"Go home."

"Is he there?"

"Yes."

"Is he naked?"

"Yes."

"Is he big?"

"I'll call you tomorrow."

I hung up.

"Do you mind if I use powder," he asked.

"Powder?"

"Talcum powder, instead of oil."

I didn't mind.

He reached into his gym bag, grabbed some classic Johnson & Johnson and sprinkled cold talc on my back, butt, thighs.

Then he started rubbing my back as soft as he could. At first, there was barely any contact at all, just the hard crusty ridges of those calluses. I was thinking of rose thorns, the skin of sharks, and every little nerve ending my skin ever thought of having was standing at attention like an army of microscopic erect dicks. Gradually he got more and more into it, massaging deeper and deeper. I do not remember telling him to stop at any point. The smell of the talc was heaven. As he was massaging my ass, I started dribbling out my dick, which was stuck underneath me. I wondered if I was having some kind of flashback to the nascent libido of my infancy, it felt so good. I made a mental note that my mother must have done at least one thing right, after all.

Then he reached underneath me and pulled my dick backward until it was breathing between my thighs as he worked on them.

When he straddled one leg, I realized with a not-unpleasant shock that he wasn't wearing his little white towel any more. His seemingly heavy balls were rubbing on my leg, and his dick was obviously hard.

I rolled over onto my back. He straddled my hips and held my hands down on the bed with his. He was leaning over me... *looming* over me, I should say. It was like sailing past Gibraltar. His blond hair was hanging down over his face like the forelock of a billy goat. He could have killed me any time he wanted, and I might have let him. He moved his face down to mine. I could feel his breath on my face as he moved his face toward mine. Then he veered off to the left and went to work on my neck.

I made a noise that was part purr, part gasp at the unbelievable sensation of it. I could not help think that he had my jugular vein between his teeth for a time, but just when I was starting to get nervous, he started working the other side of my neck with his tongue. Like the good host I always try to be, I was thrashing around on the bed, pushing up with my hips at his butt, the sweat-slick crack of which was making the perfect temporary home for my dick. That's when the looked me straight in the eye.

"Can I kiss you?" he asked.

"Of course," I said, and he did. And I kissed him.

"My turn," he said after a wonderful while and flopped onto his back.

There was no doubt about his beauty. There was something of a boy about him, most notably his seeming lack of shame, but he was, as they say, all man. He was stretched out there, his beautiful big dick as hard as they get and pretty much as big as I'd ever seen up close. (It reminded me of the "pickle," the first musical instrument I ever played, in first grade, which was really just a kazoo in a kosher dill-sized plastic casing.) His balls were tucked high around the base of it in downy, light brown hair.

It was too much. I went to work on him with my mouth and fiddled his nipples with my fingertips. I love sucking dick, and I was having the time of my life. His nipples were obviously of the highly sensitive variety, and he was rolling under my tongue and fingers.

I moved off his dick and onto his balls. He spread his legs, and I dove down between them. I put my tongue on his asshole, and I thought he was going to come. I spit on my thumb and started playing with his asshole while massaging the whole area with my other hand. That's when he pulled his thighs back with his hands, and I realized what Alex had in mind.

A butch bottom, I thought with glee—God's perfect creation and as rare as justice.

I dove at his asshole with my lips and tongue, finding the only body hair on him. He was practically bouncing the bed off the floor and groaning like mad. I went at the pulsing sphincter with my thumb again, with more pressure this time.

"Oh, yes," he hissed, *"please."*

The magic word.

I reached across him to the bedside table and opened the drawer. I grabbed a new dick-shaped bottle of lube, pulled the top up with my teeth, and gobbed some into my hand.

There was no point beating around the bush. I went in with two fingers.

He pulled his vascular thighs so far apart I thought the tendons in his groin would snap.

I grabbed for a condom, but he took it out of my hand. He opened the pack with his teeth and rolled it down my dick. It had been a long time since I had actually been able to toss a fuck in a rubber, but I wasn't worried about losing this erection.

Then he did something I've only seen in circuses. He some-how wiggled his massive shoulders through his thighs so that his shoulders were holding his thighs down and apart, offering unob-structed access to his hairless asshole.

I went in with three fingers until I located the flat disk of his prostate. He was oozing all over his taut stomach. His little out-ie of a belly button looked like an acorn melting through ice in a spring wood.

Then I slipped into him, easy as a hand into a glove and just as warm. He was digging his hands into my chest and I was rak-ing my nails across his glutes. He was practically having a seizure, and he was beating the pillows out of the way with his head, his hair falling into his eyes.

Now, there is nothing I like more than shooting a load into a man's asshole. There is no feeling like on earth that comes close. Shooting into a condom, even if it is burrowed into the buggery burrow of a beautiful bodybuilder, doesn't touch it for a pure experience. I was, however, getting perilously close to shooting.

My knees were aching, and I was pumping, his dick in both my hands. I could see his ample balls shrink up into his body before he let loose, the first wad spurting out of him like a comet and splashing on the glass of the picture over the bed behind him. The second and third hit him in the face. The next few hit him in the neck, then the chest, then the stomach, puddling around his navel.

I pulled out of him, making him shudder with a sharp moan. I ripped off the rubber, flung it aside with a snap, grabbed my dick, leaned back, and gave myself a couple of fast, short jerks before I burst. I hit the wall, the pillows, his face, his chest.

Not giving a shit who heard what, I let out as massive a sex roar as I have ever bellowed, and Alex joined me, practically howling out his approval.

When my body finally gave up its last spasm, I collapsed onto him. He wrapped his arms around me and kissed my head all over.

After what seemed like hours, we managed to get ourselves into the shower. He was remarkably tender. I never did actually get soft until well after we were drying off. He wrapped me in the big bath towel, and I dried his sculpted back with the oversized bath sheet.

I watched him get dressed, smiling all the time. Because he wasn't wearing much in the way of clothes, it didn't take long for him to finish. His hair was plastered into a respectable arrangement. His skin was glowing with the day's sun and the night's... sin? *Phooey!*

"Thank you," I said as he was leaving.

"Thank *you*," he said. "Will you call me?"

"You have any doubt?"

"You wouldn't be the first who didn't," he said.

I didn't believe him. I still don't believe that anyone could resist a second helping of him. Or a sixtieth.

I called the next day. Machine.

The next day. Machine.

"Well, he's not going to answer, that's all," Marvin said the following Saturday, finally giving in to believing the evening had taken place just as I described it.

"He was the one who was worried that *I* wasn't going to call *him."*

"He probably does see other people," Marvin suggested.

"Maybe he's out of town," I countered.

"Maybe he's dead," Marvin offered, always willing to trump my bid.

"Now who's being a drama queen? Maybe he's busy."

"Maybe he's some kind of weird perverse straight man running around giving gay men exactly the kind of sex they want and then refusing ever to see them again, like some horrible heterosexual form of torture."

"I think that's it," I said.

"Yes, that's definitely it," he decided, letting a drool of grapefruit juice slip out the right side of his mouth.

The next time I called Alex, the phone had been disconnected. His ad disappeared from *Frontiers.*

About two years later, I was wandering along the tourist shops and cafés that line the harbor of Paphos in Cyprus. It was warm November, long after the tourists had, for the most part, departed. It should have been the rainy season, but the rain had taken a vacation elsewhere.

Suddenly, something caught my eye from the postcard rack of a refreshment stand. I pulled it out. There he was, Alex, sitting on a rock in the ocean surf I instantly identified as Zuma Beach. His blond hair carefully coifed, his massive upper body cantilevered over his impossibly thin waist; his prodigious thighs and beautiful butt were as naked as he was that night in my bedroom in L.A.

GREETINGS FROM CYPRUS, the card said.

There were no other clues.

I've got that picture postcard of Alex on the rocks hanging over my desk now. It's next to that drawing by Leonardo da Vinci of the perfectly proportioned man with his arms stretched out to a circle, the navel at the epicenter but the genitals at the focal point.

Clearly, Alex would have failed the da Vinci perfection test.

He didn't fail mine.

PISS ELEGANT

Barry Lowe

It's no fun walking around the snooty eastern suburbs of Sydney in a leather harness, leather jeans, and biker boots at the best of times. It's even less fun when it's the coldest night of the year, when you're lost and the only people to approach for directions are a gaggle of highly lavender-coifed matrons with sun-bleached skin the toughness of your accessories walking their poodles, which growl at you as if the leather you're wearing is one of their long lost relatives.

And it's least fun when you know you're running twenty minutes late for a hot date with a very strict master who must, by this time, be extremely pissed off.

Dungeon Master
Eastern suburbs, strict master seeks slaves
with eager and insatiable mouths for froth fest
and forced feeding. No stamina? Then don't reply.

The personal ad was as brief as it was belligerent. Almost defiant in its cockiness, it had caught my eye in one of our local bar rags, and I'd responded promptly and subserviently, stressing my unlimited capacity for humiliation and, in turn, received a handwritten reply scrawled on the back of a flyer for local supermarket specials giving me explicit instructions on where, when, and how low to grovel.

But here I was—eagerly anticipating the prospect of a warm (recycled) beer—unable to find the address. I suspected I had been deliberately misled in order to make my punishment more pleasurable for him and all the more painful for me. Eventually, however, I did manage to come across the block of apartments, the well-disguised entrance of which was as inviting as a hemorrhoidal sphincter muscle, and, being the good slave I am, I pressed the bell and adopted a submissive position on the spiky door mat emblazoned with the words HAVE A NICE LIFE and waited for the inevitable.

I heard the locks being turned and the door opening.

"I've been very bad, Master. I'm late, and I deserve to be punished, sir," I whimpered, not daring to look up.

"Jesus Christ, can't any of you guys get it right?" he said. Then he shouted up the stair well. "Todd, there's another one of your slaves down here. Can't you give them the correct fuckin' address instead of doing this to me every time?"

"What's this bastard like, Scott?" a voice boomed from above. "Most of 'em have been dogs."

"I'd give this one a seven," was all Scott called.

"Okay fucker!" Master Todd yelled from the landing. "Crawl up here on your hands and knees, and I wanna see that tongue work overtime clearing up the crud off those steps."

This command to someone who wouldn't so much as lift a finger at home to dust a shelf or polish a doorknob?

For this stranger, though, I was willing to perform my dog act slowly up the tiled stairs—they were comparatively clean although the taste of Pledge does leave a nasty aftertaste. I heard Scott, grumbling his displeasure, close the front door to his flat.

After the stairs, my lint-coated tongue did its damnedest to polish Todd's knee-length leather boots, and even though I thought they would have passed parade muster at any barracks, he was well displeased. That resulted in the first of my punishments—a few well directed swats across my bare, and by this time freezing, back.

Bearing up under the blows, I scrambled my way into his flat and across the parquet floors. Parquet? I thought that went out in the '70s? Maybe it was retro-parquet. Ah well, you can't be too preoccupied with the exegesis of flooring inlay when, I suspected, the parquet was not so much a commitment to interior design as a hint that the lounge-room rather than the bathroom was to be our playpen.

Todd was a pig—not as in pig in shit, as in slob: cascading

beer gut and fetid beer breath. As masters go, however, he had a good line in verbal abuse and corporal, make that *corpulent,* punishment. But when he told me he wanted the "fuckin' parquet floor to gleam like the side of a Qantas Jumbo Jet," I reared on my knees, looked him right in the eye, and informed him: "I'm a slave, mate, not a fuckin' cleaner."

For my troubles I got a severe lick of his crop and quickly ducked back on all fours, my tongue resolutely flicking in and out like a pop-eyed gecko. To help keep my throat well-lubricated for the task ahead, Todd had unzipped and I felt a warm splash on my back and head as he released the built-up beer he'd been guzzling while awaiting my arrival. I slurped as best I could as the wet stain spread across the tiles like a seasonal flood.

I had been doing my best imitation of a sponge for about fifteen minutes when there was a loud thump, and I heard Scott's angry voice from the apartment below: "Are you fuckin' pissing again, Todd? 'Cause it's dripping down my light fittings and short-circuited the TV. Will you cut it out!"

Ungraciously, Todd screamed back before fetching a glass from the kitchen and, flopping his flaccid knob, began to dribble what little piss he had retained into it. "Here," he said and belched. "I like to see fine things desecrated. It turns me on."

Just then Todd's flatmate arrived home and shrieked, "That's our best fucking crystal!" and "Urgh!"—as he grabbed the glass and tipped its contents down the sink. The gurgling drain more or less paralleled the sounds my stomach was attempting to suppress.

"What you want for dinner?" Todd's flatmate asked when he'd scrubbed the glass to such pristine cleanliness it would have done an obsessive-compulsive proud. A grunt from Todd somehow translated into a preference for lentil curry and peas. And a desire to watch *Sixty Minutes,* because they'd advertised this really rather gripping debate on the parlous state of the economy.

Now, I'm as interested as the next slave in how the sales tax will affect the price of my next sling, or whether the import duty on Crisco will force me to a cheaper brand—but not when I'm being dragged through puddles of stale piss with a tongue coated with last week's mold while being swatted on the back with a crop and a ten-inch butt plug protruding from my well-beaten ass yelling, "Yes, sir! No, sir! Three bags full, sir!"

Todd's flatmate complained that he couldn't hear the TV for all our grunting and verbal sparring and turned the volume up. This led downstairs Scott to pound his ceiling with a vigor that suggested this was not an uncommon occurrence. He was obviously releasing a lot of pent-up frustration.

"Chow's ready," Todd's flatmate said, and suddenly the two of them sat down to the lentil curry and salad. My meal was under the table: Todd's red and very swollen dick. "I've been using the Accu-Jack," he'd confided earlier. Prodding it with my tongue was like rimming a sponge cake; all I really felt like doing was sticking a candle in it and singing *Happy Birthday.*

As I was working the swollen appendage in my mouth, Todd moved uncomfortably on the chair, and the long liquid *phhht* of a lethal fart assaulted my nostrils. Without so much as a "pardon me" he continued to shovel the curry into his mouth and again shifted in his seat.

I abhor bad manners, and enough is enough even for the best-behaved slave, and I was brimful of it. I stood up suddenly and my limp and very dissatisfied cock brushed the edge of the table.

"Hey, get your dick out of the lettuce," Todd's flatmate yelled.

Mustering my leather gear and a little pride, I marched out, slamming the door behind me. This commotion brought Scott to his door itching for another verbal onslaught, but he just gaped as I descended the stairs nude.

"I pissed in their salad," I said by way of explanation. And kept walking.

PERSONALS

Robert E. Penn

I haven't placed or answered a boy-meets-boy *newspaper* ad for years. This is true for one reason only: I found the process severely wanting. Lies, lies, and more lies—and anticipation, letter screening, setting up dates, small talk, no payoff, time wasted. The papers didn't work for me.

However, I am not out of the loop. There is AOL after all. If a profile isn't a want ad, I don't know what is. There are the stats, the name, the age, all possibly fictitious, of course. Most importantly, there are the statement of hobbies and personal quote. Those are genuinely revealing.

I first got on AOL in late 1996. I created a realistic profile, and I met one or two people who mostly wanted to talk about writing or orchid raising. I was sorely disappointed. When I returned in early 1997, I created a profile that stressed the *social* sides of me. I started collecting dates and encounters. My profile appears below. It's generally true, except the birth date. But any man who wants me on AOL can see my gif before meeting. No one has doubted me on age to date.

CougarBGM

Member Name: *Rob a.k.a. CougarBGM: Cougar is a graceful North American feline; BGM=Black, Gay, Man. Definitely male, not into fronting.*
Location: *Manhattan, east 20's. You can find me most mornings at the municipal gym on East 23rd.*
Birthdate: *Pisces*
Sex: *Male*

Marital Status: Single, 5'9", 155, 41c, 31w
Hobbies: Laughter, sharing intimate feelings, photography, music, literature, visual stimulation—painting, sculpture, film, theater, drawing—writing; light brown eyes, shaved head, full close-cropped beard, great smile.
Computers: ThinkPad and body language, good sex is a start but real connections count more.
Occupation: Let's meet face to face. If you won't or can't kiss, don't IM. No smokers, drinkers, or drug users, please. Allergic to cats.
Personal Quote: There's no time but the present. (For meeting, talking, networking or another path: kissing, hugging, and more.) Hot top sex and high relationship potential. LTR leads to an occasional flip.

One very cold night, I was horny and got in the chat called *blkm4blkm2*. A guy came all the way into Manhattan from New Jersey, because he was very horny, too. Unfortunately, once he arrived at my door, I realized he was not my type for sex, and sex is all we had chatted about—first on-line, then via telephone—before he crossed the river. We spent some time talking about literature and out black gay men and each other and then fell asleep.

I think it's pretty amazing that I could fall asleep with a stranger for whom I felt no attraction. It used to be that I was so set on having a good time according to my idea of a good time that I wouldn't sleep until my every wish had been fulfilled. With AOL, I feel like it's all a crap game and so there are few to no expectations. I never saw that guy again but I did turn him on to some literature by black gay men. Maybe he's cruising legit book stores now and will read this anthology.

The best response my profile got occurred when I visited the chat *m4mover40*. I thought that I would end up in a room filled with men my age so that I could avoid dealing with fear and other feelings related to dating a younger man—again. As it turned, out the room was for younger men who like men over 40. My room would probably be *mover404mover40* (mover forty for mover forty). Hah!

A young man and I chatted after each of us found the other's profile to be interesting. He was sweet and tender, and we decided to take a chance at meeting. He has a roommate, so I invited him over. The handsome 24-year-old showed up on my 48-year-old door step, and sparks flew. We dated and made it for several weeks. We listened intently to each other, and then he started to fall in love. I didn't mind the prospect of having a lover but had some reservations because of a few closet-like things he had said.

I bit the bullet and asked him if he had come out to his parents. In fact, his parents had learned of his sexual "period" from his former fiancée, who had told them so that all three—fiancée and parents—could try to get him cured before the marriage. He did a good thing for himself by moving far away from home.

But he is still on his road toward self-acceptance, and I think he should have the privilege of learning by experience rather than from a man twice his age who has already learned some of the lessons. Besides, I have a strong caretaker and paternal personality and would probably try to protect him day in and day out. The prospect of losing my discipline and not giving him the room to learn led me to end the relationship.

I am glad that we met through our ads. I have to say that AOL profiles allow each man to get a bit of information about another guy before making virtual contact. Chatting on-line is a good filter before exchanging images and talking on the phone. Meeting for coffee before going on a date or getting it on can slow the pace and allow for more getting to know one another. For some, all those steps might be frustrating.

The young man I met is fine. Great smile. We made love well together and often lay in each other's arms talking or watching a video. I can't complain. If it were possible for us to maintain a casual friendship, we might still see each other on a regular basis now. That wasn't what turned out for us.

I saw him a couple of weeks ago. I was as happy to see him as he was to see me. We caught up with one another and I am happy to know that he's doing well.

So am I.

THE EARTH MOVED

Roy Cameron

Fourth of July weekend in San Francisco, 1989. Some friends and I had come to the Living Sober Convention, and although I had come to The City many times on business, it was not one of my favorite places to be. I was living in Southern California, in Glendale, with my mother. I was recuperating from a heart attack I experienced in Denver. She wasn't charging any rent, but, to give each other some space, I had agreed to stay out of the house on the weekends. Normally, I went to Palm Springs. In fact, all my friends expected me to move there. I had become a personal trainer, so I could take my "business" with me anywhere. But something strange happened that weekend in San Francisco.

I don't know why—it was a good weekend, but it wasn't *great*—as I was driving home with my friends Dale and Denny, I got this unmistakable feeling in my gut that San Francisco was the place for me. I didn't understand it, but I had been clear-headed for enough years to follow such feelings, especially when they were so strong.

My mother thought I was crazy, and all my friends agreed with her. I sold everything I had, including my Dodge station wagon, and I moved to San Francisco October first, 1989, with my cat, Rooty Toot, and a single bed.

It wasn't long before I thought I needed a double.

I had always been an avid reader of *Drummer* magazine. I advertised regularly and had fairly decent luck in meeting guys. I rarely responded to ads taken by others. After all, I was a buff young top, a combination that was clearly a winner. But one day, I was reading the *Drummer* ads and found one from a bottom that for some reason stood out from the rest. I can't tell you why, most of the ads are pretty much the same, yet I was intrigued. After putting it off awhile, I answered the ad. I sent a short note, my phone number, and a picture showing off what I thought was important back then. That was probably around the 13th or 14th of October.

A few days later, On October 17th at 5:03 p.m., two very important things were going on in The City. First, of course, was the Earthquake, the biggest since the one in 1906 that destroyed San Francisco. Meanwhile, over on Shipley Street, my *Drummer* advertiser had just opened my letter. Oh yes, and there was some kind of baseball game going on.

My letter was being read by a young man named Paul, and just as he had decided he wanted to meet me, his office building began to collapse. Paul escaped unscathed, but my letter, picture, and phone number were irretrievably buried in the rubble.

About two weeks later, I was leaving my apartment on Market Street to go to a client named John, who lived just above 18th Street and Castro. As I opened my outside door, a remarkably fine-looking young man walked by. He glanced and smiled. I politely returned the smile and was sorry I was in a rush. I turned it over. After all, in San Francisco it is said, "If you miss meeting someone today, you will meet them again within the week." (Try it—it works.)

I walked up the to Market and Noe, and this same handsome gentleman was standing at the corner waiting for the light to change. I stood behind him admiring his body and noticed all his keys and flags were on the left side. I remember thinking to myself that I didn't have enough time to spend any of it convincing an obvious bottom he is not a top. I didn't realize at that time he was just very comfortable with his sexuality.

I stopped at the cash machine at Castro and Market, finished my transaction and looked up, and there he was again. I smiled and walked on. Somewhere down the street, I must have stopped to chat with a friend, because by the time I got down to Wild Wild West, here was this handsome bearded man again standing on the sidewalk and smiling at me. My client lived a few doors up and I went in for our session.

I was picked up at 7:30 that night by new friends Curtis and Albee and my old friend from Texas, Buz. We were going to a piercing and bondage demonstration at an apartment somewhere south of Market. While the demonstration was going on, piercing not being one of my favorite activities, I was quietly looking away, pretending to cruise the crowd. To my surprise, here was this same hot man again sitting in the other room staring at me. I thought how odd it was to have seen him basically five times in the short course of a few hours. Then we had a break.

He walked up to me and said, "I want to meet you. I'm Paul."

"My name is Roy," I said. "Nice to meet you." He went on.

"Did you by any chance send a letter and picture to a personal ad box in *Drummer?*" he asked.

"Yes," I answered, "but the guy never answered me."

"I'm the guy," Paul said. "I work at *Drummer.* I received your letter the day before, and I was just getting to opening my mail. I had opened your letter and saw your picture and was picking up the phone to call you, when the building started to shake. Of course we all dropped what we were doing and ran out to the street. I've been looking for you for two weeks."

Rather surprised, I exchanged numbers with him. I had no idea that my life had just turned a very important corner. The universe had just given me my life partner, my soul mate.

It took a couple of days to finally get together. We met for coffee at Sweet Inspirations a few days later and just talked. He loved the way I looked, the fact I had a cat, and that I was a trainer. He was a editor and a writer of S/M stories. He wanted to be a boxer and power lifter. He asked me what my idea of a true relationship was, and I replied, "I don't know you well enough to have that conversation with you yet."

He smiled, and I fell in love with him over a piece of carrot cake and coffee.

Every time I would open my door and see that perfect smile, those beautiful deep eyes, and trimmed beard, my heart would leap. I was terribly smitten and surprised he was too. He became my rock, my cheerleader, and—most important—he was my companion, my partner. The sex was pretty fabulous, too.

We had about a year and half together before his illness took over. I knew from the beginning he was positive, but we always played safe, and even in those years, I had friends who had been positive for a long time. I was so in love and planning to spend the rest of my life with him. I never thought he would get ill. But he did.

After the initial arguing with Kaiser over how sick he really was, Paul was finally admitted to the hospital. The bureaucracy had let his illness spread while they decided what to do with this "patient number." They were playing roulette with my soul mate, and I was furious. For some reason, right from the beginning, I knew he was going to die.

It was a difficult time. I went to the hospital every day. Paul wanted to keep his illness a secret, so I was fielding phone calls from confused friends. The country was at war with Iraq.

I started having nightmares. I woke up one night and thought I heard a drum being played like the ones at military funerals. I went to the window on Market Street and there, below, were thousands of skeletons, marching and beating drums. At the front was Paul. He turned as he passed to look at me. I screamed and woke up sweating.

He came home from the hospital, but was soon re-admitted. On November 22nd, I was asked to make the decision to take him off life support and take him home. I sat in the lobby and wondered why my Higher Power had put me in this position. I knew Paul was almost a vegetable by then; there was no way he was going to recover, and he had clearly stated he wanted to die at home with me and our cat, Miss Booters. He was taken off support, brought home by ambulance, and at nine in the morning of November 27th of 1991, he died.

There is a tree in his memory in Golden Gate Park in San Francisco. His ashes were scattered in the Indian Canyons area of the Aqua Caliente Indian reservation in Southern California. His picture still sits on my desk, and I have had only two dates since his passing. I had found the man I wanted to spend the rest of my life with in the personals ads of *Drummer,* and living without him has been hard. I remain grateful for the time we were given and the privilege of taking care of him during and after his illness.

If I had it to do over again, knowing everything I know now, I still would have sent that letter and the Polaroid picture that would change my life forever.

DOMINANT SEXUAL ANIMAL

Doug Harrison

I was relieved to find a parking spot near Starbucks, but not too close. I could leisurely scan the coffee-soused patrons seated outside without any commitment. Yes, there he was. No doubt. Lounging in the cheap white lawn chair like a big, lazy cat, his arms folded across his lap, his lanky legs stretched in front of him. Black leather cap. Silver tinted sunglasses. Black mustache. Handsome, aquiline face. White tank top that showed the muscular arms, shoulders, and chest to best advantage. Black leather bar vest. Tight, faded 501's. Conspicuous bulge in crotch. Black boots.

Damn! A hot Leather Daddy here in the heart of Silicon Valley. I'll lick your boots clean anytime, sir. For once I won't have to drive an hour to San Francisco to get fucked.

My thoughts went back to his ad:

Dominant Sexual Animal
Hot, hung topman, bodybuilder, tall, 44" chest, 31" waist, defined, moderately hairy, 40, seeks hot bottoms for light or heavy leathersex. Must be muscular, slim, firm butt. Safe, sane. Limits respected. Candid photo, detailed reply, gets same.

Well, I reasoned, I'm muscular and slim. The firm butt's in question, but that can be disguised until the moment of truth. And, so they say, I look ten or fifteen years younger than I really am. The hell with the photo; a letter should get things started.

My response was succinct:

> *I'm writing this letter not with the expectation that we'll play (although that could be a possibility), but with the hope that we can become acquainted. I live in Sunnyvale, and I'm eager to meet other men on the Peninsula who are into leather.*
>
> *I've been into the leather scene for about ten years and am an active top in the San Francisco scene. I'm also a very piggy bottom. I'm a hot, 6-ft. bodybuilder who is hung, slim, muscular with prominent veins and moderately hairy with a mustache. I really enjoy heavy leather-sex and also sensitive scenes.*
>
> *Let's talk!*

A few days later there was a message on my answering machine. It was delivered in a low, sexy voice and suggested we meet at Starbucks at four o'clock on Sunday afternoon.

I approached his table.

We sure as hell should be sitting together. Two Castro clones among geeks in ridiculous jogging suits, tennis skirts, and baggy shorts. He's really hot, but I've got him beat in the body building department.

I looked into his eyes.

"Hi, I'm Doug."

"I'm Eric," he said through a cautious smile and rose to his 6'2" height to gasp my hand. The handshake was firm, but not too hard. His forearms were covered with black hair, not too delicate, but not coarse. I liked the pattern the interlocking curls made. The color matched the color of his chest hair, which spread from the edge of his tank top to his clavicle.

I wonder what he looks like with his shirt off. Or, better yet, completely bare-ass. I'll bet he has tight, hairy buns.

"I always like to be early for my appointments. I ordered you an espresso."

Pompous ass. What makes you think I like espresso?

"Thanks," I said. We sat down.

"You give good face." I looked puzzled. "I mean, you have a nice smile."

"Thanks again. So do you."

"So you'd like to get together and play? What do you like? What are your boundaries?"

Despite his opening salvo of rapid-fire questions, I didn't pause before answering. I had been through this before.

"I'm a switch. I play at San Francisco parties and privately at my house and friends' homes. I specialize in flogging as a top. When I bottom, I really like heavy tit play, I get off on flogging, and I enjoy play piercing and electricity. I'm in an open relationship. My partner Mark and I are okay with each other playing around. However, we've agreed not to be fucked by anyone else. That's reserved as something special between us."

"Too bad. Are you sure? I really like to fuck. And I can tell I'd enjoy getting into your pants. Maybe you two will change your minds. I don't like my bottoms to have limits."

"Well, there are lots of other things we can do."

"Yeah, I suppose. We'll find out. What times are good for you?"

"I'm pretty flexible, aside from Saturday nights."

"Well, my lover Jordan doesn't like me to be out much, so I'm only available Saturday and Sunday afternoons."

"Sunday would be best for me," I replied. "Where?"

"At your place; Jordan doesn't want me bringing tricks home. But I would like to meet Mark sometime, if he looks anything like you. Maybe we could do a three-way, if he's into that sort of thing."

"He sure is! If things work out between you and me, we could try a four-way."

"Oh, no, that wouldn't fly. Jordan doesn't want to be around when I get it on with someone else. So, it'll have to be either a three-way or just the two of us. But first, I'd like to get to know you better, so let's meet for coffee again next week, after work."

"Okay. Tuesday at six at Whole Foods?"

"Sure."

We shook hands and I left.

Next Tuesday I arrived at 5:50. He was seated at a small table outside the market, a manila folder on the table in front of him.

Why is he always here ahead of me?

"Hi," I said. Again the smile and firm handshake.

"Care for a drink?"

At least he didn't order for me.

"No, thank you."

"It really annoys me when these tables aren't arranged neatly. You'd think these people would care more about how things look."

They look okay to me.

"Jordan thinks I'm too fussy when we go for walks and I complain about people's messy flower gardens. But, if they're going to plant flowers, it's no more effort to plant the seeds evenly. And they could at least keep them weeded."

"Well," I replied, "not every one has that much free time. At least they're trying."

"They should try harder. If I had that sloppy an attitude, I'd never write a decent computer program. As it is, it seems like I'm always fixing someone else's bugs.

"But enough about work. I brought a questionnaire for you to fill out. I want to know as much as possible about my bottoms. I'll keep it with the others in my filing system." He handed me four stapled sheets of paper containing neatly typed questions.

Damn, is this a civil service position?

I quickly skimmed the survey, resisting the urge to throw it in his face and leave.

NAME, AGE, HEIGHT, WEIGHT, OCCUPATION, HOBBIES, COLOR OF HAIR, COLOR OF EYES.

He sure must have a bad memory.

MUSTACHE OR BEARD? BODY HAIR? TATTOOS? PIERCINGS?

Does this really matter?

HOW LONG HAVE YOU BEEN IN THE SCENE? DO YOU ENJOY ORAL SEX? DO YOU ENJOY ANAL SEX?

Oh, good grief!

NUMBER THE FOLLOWING ACTIVITIES IN THE ORDER YOU MOST ENJOY THEM: FLOGGING, SPANKING, CANING, PADDLING, BONDAGE, BULL WHIPPING, TIT TORTURE, COCK AND BALL TORTURE, BUTTPLAY, FISTING, PISS SCENES, SCAT, ELECTRICITY, PLAY PIERCING, BRANDING, KNIFE PLAY, HUMILIATION, DISCIPLINE.

Get over it, Sister! Where's your sense of adventure?

DESCRIBE YOUR BEST SCENE. DESCRIBE YOUR WORST SCENE.

Oh, boy, essay questions!

ARE YOU ON ANY MEDICATION?

At last, a relevant question for my personnel file!

DO YOU SMOKE? DO YOU DRINK? DO YOU DO DRUGS?

None of your damn business!

DO YOU HAVE A LOVER? DOES HE KNOW YOU ARE DATING? IS HE COMFORTABLE WITH THIS?

You should talk!

Eric shoved a black pen into my hand and I began to write. I left some questions blank.

I finished the survey and slid it across the table. He scanned it.

"Describe your most memorable scene to me," he commanded.

"Well," I answered, "I've been around the track a few times, and had a lot of memorable scenes. Some because of their intensity, some because of their humor, some because of their transcendence, one or two because they were so different."

"Pick one."

"OK. I was at a play party—I go there once a month. I met this hot top and he started yanking on my nipples. Well, this went on for a long time. He pinched and pulled them, till I didn't know if I was groaning in pleasure or screaming in pain. He slapped my chest, and punched me in the stomach. He knew how to throw his punches, and I knew how to take them. I really like getting roughed up by a tough daddy!

"The rough play really got him hard. He forced me to my knees and shoved his dick down my throat. He grabbed the back of my head and fucked my face until I could hardly breathe. I was gagging and the tears were running down my cheeks. I could tell he was about to come.

"He stopped, raised me to my feet, and shackled me to a St. Andrew's cross.

"I knew what was coming. I'd seen his large collection of whips. He began with a soft flogger that kissed my back. I guess he changed to something with heavier tails, because the caresses became dull thuds. It was mesmerizing, and I stopped thinking about what he was using and started to float away.

"The thudding remained, but the blows became sharper and sharper. I wasn't conscious of the restraints, or my body, or, for that matter, my mind. I existed only in the now.

"I was writhing. I was screaming. I was crying. As anchored as I was, I was floating. Floating in a plethora of swirling colors, reds, greens, and blues. I was a fleck of dust swirling in a kaleidoscope.

"And then I felt something cool on my back. He must have been blowing his warm breath on me, but it felt refreshingly cold after the whip stings.

"And then I was sitting on the floor, leaning against him. He was holding me tightly as I sobbed.

"'Let it all out,' he said. 'Let the good come in. I'm here. You're beautiful. You're loved.'

"My sobbing gradually subsided, and I looked into his eyes. Rather, I should say, I looked into his soul. He gave me not a ride, not a scene, but a soul-searching experience which is what this S/M business is all about."

I slowly came out of my reverie and smiled at Eric.

"Okay. Let's get together next week."

"I thought you could only play on weekends."

"Jordan decided he wants me all to himself on weekends, so we'll have to fit our play time in during the week."

"When?"

"After work, but I have to be home before he gets there. So, that means between four and six PM. How about next Thursday."

"That sounds OK with me. But, tell me, how ferocious a top can you be, if he has you so pussy-whipped?"

His scowl was momentary. "He's working through some difficulties. I'll be at your place next Thursday."

I left.

The following week I rearranged an already overcrowded calendar so I could leave work early on Thursday.

Is juggling these important meetings worth it, so I can rush home to change into some provocative leather for a two-hour date? Oh well, I'll try anything once.

Next Wednesday I spent a long evening preparing my playroom for Eric's visit. I wanted everything neat and tidy for the control freak.

The fateful day arrived. At two o'clock I checked my answering machine.

"This is Eric. I'm really tired and have to reschedule. Give me a call."

I leaned back in my desk chair. Surges of fire twisted my belly like nonforgiving, angry hands wringing sludge from a saturated towel. I took a deep breath, my grimace slowly softened, and a smile emerged. I reached for the phone and dialed a San Francisco number.

"Hello?"

"Hi, it's Doug. Are you free tonight?"

"For you, handsome, I'm available. Besides, I have a few new toys I'd like to try on you. How's about I take the five o'clock train?"

"Great! I'll meet you at the station, and we can go to dinner. You'll stay the night?"

"Sure, Bob's out of town for a few days. He's happy when I have a good time instead of dawdling around the house. Damn, I'm getting hard just thinking about fucking you silly and falling asleep spooning you with your hands and legs shackled."

I was rubbing my crotch.

"Sounds great to me! I'll take you to the train station tomorrow morning. Looking forward to it!"

"*Ciao*, sexy."

I hung up the phone and turned to my computer. I erased Eric's entry from the phone log.

NONE OF THE ABOVE

J'son M. Lee

BM

23yo 5'10", straight, masculine and attractive,
seeking one-time only oral encounter with BM.
You must be 21-25yo, masculine, straight-acting,
clean, D/D free and very private.

I ran across the ad one Friday night while flipping through the "Matches" section of the Washington *CityPaper*. It caught my eye in the "None of the Above" column after I read through all the "Men Seeking Men" entries without finding anything new or interesting. For some reason, I kept returning to it. I knew that responding to it and eventually meeting this man could be dangerous. However, against my better judgment, I responded. His voice message radiated with a confidence that was a cross between self-assurance and cockiness. It was the cockiness that caused me to hang up without leaving a message; it was the same cockiness that compelled me to call again and leave a message.

Although it seemed like days, it was more a matter of several hours passing, and still there was no response from this mystery man. To be honest, I didn't really expect to hear from him.

Nonetheless, I found myself waiting by the phone until late Saturday afternoon. Frustrated and restless, I went upstairs to check my mail. When I returned, my caller ID box was blinking. Could he have called? I checked my messages.

"Hey, J'son, what's up? It's Rod. You left me a message and I am returning your call. I'm going to be out for several hours, so I'll call you really late tonight if that's possible. Peace."

I felt as if he had made his "courtesy call" and that was going to be it. Moments later, the phone rang. My heart raced. Could it be him? I collected myself and in a low voice I answered, "Hello?"

The voice on the other end asked, "May I speak to J'son?"

I responded, "This is he."

We connected instantly. Through our conversation, I discovered that Rod was a recent college graduate and aspired to become a screenwriter. However, there were a couple of things that he began to share that were beyond anything I had ever expected. Rod was engaged; his fiancée was six months pregnant; they shared an apartment. She was aware of his desire to have a sexual encounter with a man and was totally supportive of it. In fact, she helped him rewrite his ad twenty-six times until they were both satisfied.

Rod and I exchanged stories of our sexual escapades. He and his fiancée had done everything imaginable! However, he had often fantasized about being with another man. He didn't want to enter into marriage with this desire unfulfilled. He didn't want to have any regrets.

Rod had a busy day ahead of him and asked if he could call me when he returned home. He expressed that he really enjoyed our conversation and wanted to call and "vibe" more with me later. Although Rod was obviously intelligent, his speech had a certain roughness. At times, I would have to deduce what he meant by the way that he formulated his sentences, because many of his words were not a part of my everyday vocabulary. To be honest, the roughness of his speech was actually a turn-on. I was always considered a "goody-goody" and successfully communicating with him made me feel "down" (as Rod would say). Although there was only a six-year difference in our ages, his manner of speech made me realize I was getting old.

Sure enough, Rod did call back. Although it was only 11:30, he apologized for calling so late. I would have waited up all night if I had to. I was unusually intrigued by this man. Our conversation this time was even more enlightening. We shared concerns about health and cleanliness, particularly about AIDS. He couldn't see leaving this world knowing he had a girl and a child who depended on him.

We stayed on the phone until four a.m., talking about everything under the moon. I could tell that he was as intrigued by me

as I was by him. In fact, he suggested we meet in the next couple of days. Days? I couldn't wait days. I knew I wanted this man,
particularly after he described himself in more detail. I think he
was really uncomfortable describing himself to another man. He
always prefaced his descriptions with "my girl says" this or "my
girl says" that. He said she often complimented him on his full
lips, his "Chinese" eyes, his hairiness, his Will Smith ears, and
the size of his dick. He stressed that he was very blessed in this
area. He asked me if I believed that a man's dick was three inches smaller than his shoe size. He had a size twelve foot. I love a
man with big feet!

Rod and I agreed to meet on Sunday night after he got off
work to see if there was a physical attraction. This would be
judged by whether or not he thought his girlfriend would be
attracted to me and if he thought I was competition for him.
These plans were tentative, and he said he would call me Sunday
afternoon to confirm.

I got up on Sunday morning and went to church. I'm embarrassed to admit this, but the entire time I was there, I was totally distracted by thoughts of Rod. After church, I returned home.
By ten p.m. I hadn't heard from Rod. I wasn't worried because,
from our earlier conversation, I believed that Rod was a man of
his word. About a half an hour later, the phone rang. It was Rod,
asking for directions.

Within an hour, there was a knock at my door. I had grown incredibly uneasy. I was confident I would be attracted to him, but
would he be attracted to me? Was I masculine enough for him?
Why was I doubting myself? I couldn't appear insecure. Naturally
I spent too much time considering the possibility that he was a
serial killer!

I opened the door and there he was, everything he described
and more. He greeted me with a handshake and a simultaneous
"What's up, man?"

He wore shades on his head similar to the ones Dwayne
Wayne wore in "A Different World." He walked past me pimping,
as if asserting his youth and masculinity.

We sat on the sofa and shared glances and awkward
moments, but we soon were very comfortable and talked like
"boys." He asked if he was everything that I thought. I quickly

conceded that he was. He said that I definitely would be competition for him were I straight. I felt flattered. He interrupted our
conversation and asked if he could use the phone to call home.

"Hey, Sweetie," he said into the phone. "Just callin' to let you
know that I'm here... Yeah, I'm okay... I love you, too."

This was really strange, but I loved it. Although I initially ques-
tioned his fiancée's knowledge of his desire, this call alleviated
my doubts.

After he got off the phone, we resumed our conversation.
Although somewhat unsure, I was pretty confident that I would be
the man that Rod would choose. So, as a "fierce" gay man would,
I directed the conversation to the purpose of our meeting.
More specifically, I wanted to know what his expectations were.

He said he would entertain the thought of anything sexually
with the exception of kissing and intercourse. As I was not really keen on the thought of intercourse with a total stranger either,
this was perfect, but I'd definitely have to work on the kissing
part. Rod talked of several things he would be interested in doing
but was unsure if he could actually go through with them.

"My entire body is sensitive, especially my thighs," he said.

Unexpectedly, he commanded, "I want you to suck my dick."
The thought of this excited me. He also wanted me to taste his
ass, only he had to be on his stomach. He said, "If I'm on my
back with my legs up, I'll feel like a bitch."

Rod began to break down the dichotomy between hetero-
sexuality and homosexuality. He commented that he saw beyond
my sexuality and thought of me as one of his "boys." I don't think
he had ever connected with a gay male on this level. I think he
realized we were more alike than not.

Rod was becoming very comfortable with me.

"If I asked you to take your shirt off," he asked, "would you?"

I told him that I would, but that it would be awkward, because
he would be sitting beside me fully clothed. Upon his request, I
took it off anyway, followed by my shoes, my shorts, until I was
sitting on my sofa totally naked. I was reminded of Eartha Kitt in
the movie *Boomerang*—"I [didn't] have any panties on!"

"Damn man, you have a nice chest... Boyee if you were
straight—"

I blushed.

"Would you like for me to touch your chest?" he asked.

"Yes," I replied.

He caressed my chest with an awkward, mechanical stroke that reflected his inexperience.

"Where else would you like for me to touch you?" he asked.

"At this point, it wouldn't matter. It will all be good," I responded.

His hands moved down to my dick. He stroked it as if he had never stroked his own. I loved it. There was something incredibly erotic about his innocence.

"Do you want me to rub your ass?"

I did.

I stretched out on the sofa. As I lay on my stomach, Rod began to explore my backside. I could feel his fascination with every touch. As my moans intensified, so did his touches. I could feel his cool breath between my cheeks. It never occurred to me that Rod was checking me for cleanliness until I hear him say, "You are so clean. I really like that."

One of the first things I told Rod I wanted to do to him was give him a massage. I knew that he would need to be relaxed. I was really surprised when he said to me, "I want you to give me that massage now." I stood up and led him into my den of iniquity. He asked me to light a candle. I lit the strawberry-and-cream–scented candle, and the room filled with sweetness.

"I want you to undress me," Rod said. "I'll go down to my boxers."

He didn't have to tell me twice. I removed his shirt. His entire body was covered in a soft bed of hair. I caressed his chest as I stared into his eyes. Rod's eyes were diabolic. They were naturally squinted and pierced my entire body as if seeing through me. I was overpowered. I simply melted as I stared into his eyes.

I loosened his belt, and he assisted me in undoing his pants. I dropped to my knees to remove the pants from around his ankles. As I rose, I brushed my face against the very visible bulge in his boxers. I wanted it so badly I could taste it. As he lifted me to my feet, I stared into those eyes again. They weakened me, and my eyes dropped to his naturally lined lips. His lips reminded me of juicy peaches. I wanted so badly to kiss him, but I remembered his reservations. He saw kissing as something very intimate.

I asked Rod if I could touch his dick. He let me. It was long... thick... and hot. It had an unyielding left curve and pulsed as I stroked it through the thin cotton.

"Would you like to see it?" he asked.

"Yes," I breathed.

Rod walked over and turned on the lights. He removed his boxers. He was wearing a red thong—obviously too small for that beautiful dick. He showed me every inch of it and handled it with the confidence of a man who knew his "piece" was all that. It was obvious he was proud of it. This was probably the first time I saw his youthfulness. It was like he had a new toy.

He turned off the lights and stretched out on the bed. I massaged his shoulders. They were very tense. I worked my way down his back to one of the plumpest asses I had ever laid eyes on. As I massaged it, he rose and crashed like the waves of the ocean. I could tell that this was his spot. I moved to his thighs. He moaned with delight.

I asked Rod to turn over, and I massaged his chest. As I worked my way down, I tried switching from hands to lips. He stopped me.

"No, not tonight," he said.

"Please," I begged.

"No, it's nothing personal against you. I just haven't discussed this with my girl. I can tell her what we've done so far, but not this. Not yet."

I respected his wishes and continued to kiss his body. Rod began to tease me. He rubbed his dick against my face. He took it in his hands and rubbed it against my cheek, on my neck, against my other cheek and across my lips. He repeated this several times. Each time I stuck my tongue out in hopes of tasting it. It was warm and smooth against my lips. I begged, but it was no use. He said that my begging turned him on, that it was flattering how much I wanted him. Frustrated, I collapsed in his arms hoping they would give me some relief.

"When my girl masturbates for me, it really turns me on. Would you feel comfortable doing that for me?"

I needed to relieve myself, so I agreed. Rod caressed my body as I stroked my dick. I invited him to join me, but he just wanted to watch. I had never done this before. Rod began to talk to me.

"Come on, J'son. Let me know when you're gonna come."

I rose and crashed. It was so weird, and probably vain, but I was turning myself the fuck on. It turned me on even more to watch Rod enjoying me.

"Rod, Rod," I breathed.

"Yeah, yeah. Come on, boy. Are you gonna come?"

"Yeah, here it comes!"

As I exploded in ecstasy, Rod was visibly excited. He took my dick and rubbed it in my cum. My dick was so sensitive. My body jerked with pleasure. I couldn't take it. I tried to remove his hand, but he wouldn't let me. We both laughed. He laid his head on my chest and just held me.

When I drove Rod home, he told me he'd call me in fifteen minutes to make sure I'd gotten home okay. When Rod called, he gave me some very exciting news: He and his fiancée had talked, and they agreed that I would be the one. In fact, she asked him why he went as far as he did and not all the way. I guess good things do come to those who wait.

❖ ❖ ❖

I woke up Monday morning around eight a.m. Although Rod and I didn't get off the phone until about four, I wasn't tired. In fact, I felt rejuvenated. My thoughts of Rod gave my physical body the energy it needed to have a productive day at work.

When I returned home from work, there was a message on my answering machine.

"Hey, what's up?... Uh, J'son, this is Rod... hum... just callin'... I know you're probably not home... probably at work... but anyway, just hopin' that you were havin' good day that's all... pretty much all I wanted to say... just hope your day has went good... Hum... just enjoying the conversation we've been having... I thought you might like to hear from me. That's it... thought it would probably make your day. I'll talk to you soon. Peace."

Rod called again late Monday night. Since Wednesday was his day off, we agreed that it would be "the day." I had actually hoped that I could see him sooner, but I didn't want to suggest it. I didn't want to pressure him or make him uncomfortable. I wanted Rod to suggest and initiate anything that was to happen. He acted at a pace that was unnerving. He knew how badly I wanted him. It made me wonder if his uneasiness was a subconscious effort at maintaining a sense of control of the situation.

But he decided to come over right away. When he got there, he suggested that we take a shower together. He undressed before me and revealed his very sexy white net underwear. Rod loved provocative underwear, and I loved seeing him in it. After several heated moments, I took them off of him. We stood in front of each other in the bathroom totally naked. We held and caressed each other as the room filled with steam from the shower. He asked me to turn the lights out. This was so erotic to me. We got into the shower and I lathered his entire body. I paid special attention to those areas I was most interested in tasting. Rod embraced me as if nothing or no one else in the world mattered. His touches were much less mechanical than they were on Sunday, and I didn't sense any nervousness. Maybe it was because the lights were out.

We went from the shower to the bedroom. I turned on the CD player, and I got lost in Rod's arms while Rachelle Ferrell sang "Waiting" in the background.

I had to keep reminding myself that all of this was going to end on Wednesday; however, I was feeling things I thought were no longer possible. As Rod lay on top of me, he stared deeply into my eyes. I wanted to kiss him and he sensed it.

"You want me to kiss you, don't you?" he asked.

"Yes."

"How bad?" he taunted.

"Really bad."

"I guess I can try it once," Rod said.

Rod had the sexiest lips I had ever seen. When he kissed me, it reminded me of when I was a child and I would practice—kissing myself in the mirror. Rod was my reflection in the mirror, but I could feel that he really was not comfortable kissing me. As he tried over and over again, his kisses filled with a passion and sweetness my lips had never known.

I loved kissing Rod. Even more, I loved tasting him. He would often squeal and bury his face in the pillow when my tongue hit the right spot. Rod was very verbal. In fact, he would often tell me what he wanted me to do to him, and he would make me beg for what I wanted to do to him.

"Say that word I like to hear," he would insist.

"Please?" I would beg.

In order for me to get what I wanted, I had to look him directly in his eyes and say that one word. Nothing more. I didn't mind. I found his desire to control to be very sexy. However, I knew his weakness. My lips and my tongue got 'im every time!

I took Rod home around the same time as the previous night. Again, he called to make sure I got home okay and we agreed to see each other on Wednesday. It would be our last night together.

✻   ✻   ✻

I spent the entire day thinking about Rod and the unbelievable experience that I was having. I didn't hear from him all day. After I got off of work, I went to the gym. I had a really intense work-out. After the gym, I rushed home hoping to get a call from Rod. As I walked to the building, I noticed a guy sitting on the stoop, but I didn't pay him any attention. When I entered the building, I had this feeling that someone was behind me. When I looked behind me, I realized the guy was Rod!

"What are you doing here?" I asked with a big grin on my face.

"Just thought I'd surprise you. I hope you don't mind," he said.

"Of course not."

All I could do was look at him and laugh. I couldn't believe he did something like this. I was so glad to see him.

We got to the apartment and sat down and started talking like old friends. Our talking led to touching and before I knew it, I was totally naked and Rod was down to a pair of sheer black, sport-cut boxers. He knew he was hot as he stood in front of me adjusting his underwear.

"Do you wanna take a shower?" he asked.

"I'd love it," I said seductively.

Again, Rod turned the lights out. Again we held each other. This time he turned me so that my back was to him. He massaged my back as the stream of water from the shower simultaneously did the same. Rod turned me again. As I faced him, he began to kiss me. He then forced me to my knees and let me take his cock in my mouth. He moaned as I sucked. Rod joined me on my knees and kissed me again. As he kissed me, he gently led me to a seated position. He sat between my legs and I held him as the water beat down on us. As I kissed him on his neck, I ran my hands across his hairy chest.

This night, for some reason, I felt especially close to Rod. Before I knew it, what I was feeling slipped past my lips.

"I love you."

Rod was really quiet. Did he hear me? What had I done?

"How can you love me when we've only known each other for a few days?" he asked.

"I don't know what I meant when I said it, but I only know what I feel at this moment," I said.

Rod snuggled closer in my arms.

We got out of the shower and dried each other off. We were both cold and hurried to the warmth of the bed. I think Rod sensed the sincerity in my confession. He spent a lot of time holding me tight and assuring me that he really cared for me. But he didn't have to say a word. I could read it in his eyes. I couldn't help but think that our feelings were more than either of us had bargained for—especially Rod.

But he was in rare form. Each night he became less and less inhibited. I think he was at a point where he felt free to fully explore his curiosities. He told me that because I was so giving, he was more comfortable doing certain things. He said that he knew I would appreciate these things more because they were "sacrifices."

Rod kissed my lips and began to slowly kiss my neck. He would periodically stop to nibble on my ear, to stick his tongue in my ear. This drove me crazy as did his blowing in my ear. His lips arrived at my chest. He gently kissed my chest and pinched my nipples between his teeth and lips. I loved for him to palm my chest. The more I moaned, the more aggressive he became. Rod worked his way down to my stomach. He loved playing with my navel ring with his tongue. He moved his lips down further and kissed my dick. Could he be thinking about...? Rod stared at my dick and then he stared at me as if contemplating what to do next.

"You want me to suck it, don't you?" he asked.

"Only if you're comfortable," I responded.

"You've been so giving to me that I want to, but I just don't know if I can."

With obvious reluctance, Rod sucked my dick. I was pleasantly shocked. I sat up on my elbows and watched him as he gratified me. His did not seem to be the mouth of innocence.

"Am I doing it right?" he asked.

"Oh, my God," I uttered passionately. "I can't believe you've never done this before."

"I've seen a lot of videos," he said.

No one gets this good by just watching videos. Could Rod have lied to me about this being his first time? What was I thinking? I trusted Rod. He wouldn't lie to me about something like that.

Rod guided me to my backside and his tongue explored my ears, my upper back and the course of my spine. My ass was especially sensitive to his tongue. He could sense it, and he lingered there until proceeding to my thighs.

I rolled over and onto Rod. I straddled him and kissed him.

"Show me how much you want this dick," he said.

I was very detailed in showing Rod how much I wanted it.

"J'son... J'son?" he would call as he tried to pull away.

At times I would have to physically restrain him.

As I came up from a long stroke, he lifted my head.

"Say that word I love to hear."

"Please," I begged.

"That really turns me on... Look at it," he said holding his dick.

He held and stroked it as if it were on display. It looked even bigger and tastier in his hands.

"Is this what you want?" he teased.

"Yeah."

"Say it!"

"Pleeez!"

With this, he allowed me to sample his sweet dick. Rod writhed in physical and mental delight.

"Yeah, man... You want me to come?"

"Yeah."

"You want me to come?"

"Yeah."

"J'son... J'son... "

Rod exploded all over my face. I stroked his dick in his cum as it grew limp. He let out a loud moan and buried his face in the pillows. I think it was more than he could stand. He tried to stop me, but I persisted until his cum was gone. Isn't payback hell?

I went to the bathroom and got a cloth to clean Rod up. As I wiped his dick, it rose again. So, I went for round two. It tasted even better the second time around. Rod was a true stud. He came a second time within minutes of the first. Once again, I cleaned him up. I think he needed a break this time.

While I started the music up on the CD player, Rod grabbed me from behind and held me. I turned around to face him and he stared me directly in my eyes with an unusual seriousness.

"Tomorrow is the last time that we can be together... I don't know when or if we'll ever see each other again, or if we'll be able to remain friends," he said.

This was not what I expected to hear. I tried not to think about Wednesday. The day was inevitable, but I only wanted to enjoy being in the moment. I didn't want to think about the fact that I'd probably never see Rod again.

"J'son, I really do care about you."

The sincerity of his words brought tears to my eyes. I tried to contain them, but was unsuccessful.

"I don't wanna hurt you... I want you to have fond memories of our time together... I'll make tomorrow special, I promise," he said.

With this promise, he held me even tighter. I wanted to hold him forever, but I knew the night had come to an end.

✧　　✧　　✧

I lay in the bed trying to keep my eyes open. This way it would take Wednesday longer to come. However, physiology took over. When I woke up, all I could think about was Rod. Today would be the last day that I'd see him—possibly forever.

All day, I asked myself how Rod could possibly make tonight more special than any of the previous days. You can't top perfection. However, late that afternoon, I got part of the answer. As we talked on the phone, Rod told me that he wanted to come over early and cook dinner for me. There's something to be said for a straight man slaving over a hot stove.

Rod gave me a list of things to pick up from the grocery store. After work, I went to Safeway and picked up the items. I got everything he asked for and one extra item—whipped cream.

I picked Rod up around six o'clock. He had this large duffel bag that clinked every time he moved.

When we got to my place, he unpacked his duffel bag. Inside were dishes, containers, and seasonings. He plugged the boom box up and placed it in the window. Next, he went straight to the kitchen. Oddly, he seemed to know where everything was. This was the first time that I ever felt like we were a couple.

I sat on the sofa and watched TV while Rod cooked. I was curious about what he was cooking, but I stayed out of his way.

I didn't know if Rod had noticed the whipped cream in the refrigerator.

"Rod?"

"Yeah?"

"I bought some whipped cream."

He came into the living room holding a different can of whipped cream.

"I did, too."

We both laughed.

Whatever Rod was preparing smelled really good. Moments later he walked in with a sample of something on a fork.

"Taste this."

"Hum... this is good," I said.

It was beef but very spicy. He came in again with something else for me to taste. It was chicken, and it tasted even better. He finally told me that he was making fajitas.

Rod came into the living room once more and asked if he could turn the TV off. Of course I said yes. He turned off the lamp and lit the two candles that were sitting on the table opposite the sofa. On his way back into the kitchen, he pressed PLAY on the boom box. Sade serenaded us. It was true: What Rod and I had really was "No Ordinary Love."

Rod brought everything into the living room. There were so many dishes. There was a dish with the chicken, a dish with the beef, a dish of diced fresh tomatoes, a dish of rice pilaf, a dish of lettuce, a dish of shredded cheeses, a dish of sour cream, a dish of corn, and a dish of tortillas. He even had a dish of his own very special fajita sauce. All the different colors were beautiful. Everything looked delicious.

I took a tortilla and loaded it with the chicken, lettuce, tomatoes, rice, cheese, and sour cream. I topped it with his special sauce and took a bite.

"You like it?" Rod asked.

"It's delicious," I said.

"I like cooking for people who like to eat and aren't picky. My girl is picky."

"I'm easy to please," I flirted.

Rod and I had our fill of the fajitas.

After we finished eating, Rod cleared away the dishes. He brought out a dish of the biggest strawberries I had ever seen. They were topped with chocolate and whipped cream. This isn't quite what I had in mind for the whipped cream. He fed me my first bite, and I fed him his.

When we were done, Rod took the dish out to the kitchen. I told him that I would wash the dishes later. This was our last night together and I didn't want to waste one moment on good housekeeping.

Rod joined me on the sofa. Neither of us said a word. I didn't want to talk, I just wanted Rod to hold me. He must have heard me thinking.

"Come here," he said.

I leaned over and put my head on his chest. I was in heaven. I asked him to take his shirt off. He obliged, and I laid my head once again on his chest. His heart pumped with great force. I loved to just lie and listen to the beat of his heart.

Rod lifted my head and began to kiss me. I, too, was soon out of my shirt. I savored every moment. As I slowly breathed in and out, I took in Rod's scent. When he was aroused, this scent seemed to intensify, all the while luring me to the source of my ultimate pleasure—his dick.

We created a burning friction. I undressed him and held his dick. I could feel the heat created by our passion. To cool it off, I went into the kitchen and got the whipped cream. I covered his entire dick—all nine inches—in the sweet coolant. His was the perfect sweet course at the end of a delicious meal.

"Damn, baby... damn!" Rod uttered.

I rolled Rod onto his stomach and sprayed the whipped cream from the base of his neck as far down as I could go. As I ate my way down, Rod cringed. His body shook uncontrollably as I got closer and closer to his ass. I ate the cream from between his cheeks. He squealed and grasped for anything that he could get his hands on.

Rod asked me to take my shorts off. As I was undressing, he stood up and kissed me. He guided me to the sofa and laid on top of me. He placed his dick between my thighs. My imagination ran wild. His dick rubbing between my thighs made me feel like if I was being penetrated.

"Fuck me," I said.

Rod simulated the moves of actual penetration. He moved up and down, in and out. With my eyes closed, I pretended we were there. I opened my legs wider, eventually wrapping them around his waist.

"J'son, I am so tempted."

Obviously Rod was enjoying this game, too. In my mind, his dick thrust in and out of me. I called his name.

"Rod... Rod... "

"Yeah, baby... this is all yours... take it all," he said.

It all seemed so real. Rod brought me to an unbelievable climax. I collapsed beneath him and opened my eyes.

"Are you okay?" he asked.

"Yeah... oh, yeah," I responded.

I must have looked disoriented.

We lay there for several moments. Rod went to the bathroom and got a cloth to clean me up. He was so gentle. He got down on the sofa beside me. We began to kiss again. I wanted him to experience an orgasm like the one I had just experienced. My mouth found its way to his dick. My lips performed long, slow strokes.

"That's it," Rod said.

He would always let me know when my mouth was positioned just right. He put one hand on each side of my face and guided the motion and speed. I could feel that he was at that point, but he was trying to savor the feeling.

"Your mouth feels so good," he said.

I wanted to taste those sweet juices for the last time.

"I want you to come for me," I said.

As if granted permission, Rod exploded. With each contraction, the hot cum shot from his dick. As I always did, I rubbed his dick in his cum. This always drove him crazy. He contorted his body in the air and clenched the sofa pillows. Just as he did for me, I went to the bathroom and got a cloth to clean him up for the last time. I wiped his dick with the wet cloth in what seemed like slow motion. I didn't want to lose Rod.

Rod and I fell asleep on the sofa in each others arms. When we woke up it was about four a.m.

"J'son, I have to go."

"I know."

We dressed without saying a word. As we walked to the door to leave, Rod pulled me by the arm and hugged me. He pulled back and kissed me on the lips. I guess this was good-bye.

Neither of us said a word as I drove him home. When we arrived, we sat in the car motionless for a while. Rod broke the silence.

"J'son, you take it easy."

I just nodded my head. He grabbed my hand as he exited the car. He leaned over and looked at me, simultaneously patting his chest. I knew what that meant. When he closed the door, tears streamed down my face.

When I got home, I went to the kitchen to wash the dishes. I couldn't stop crying. I finished the dishes and was walking to my bedroom when I noticed the light blinking on my caller ID box. It had to be a message from Rod.

"Hum, J'son, this is... uh... Rod... Hum... I know you're not home yet, but I wanted to leave this message for you, so you can hear it when you step in... Just wanna remind you yet once again how very special you are to me... hum... I don't have no regrets about what happened... you're very special... hum... and you do have a place in my heart... I don't know when or if we'll ever see each other again... as friends... but just know that I'll never forget the time that we had... I do care about you. I hope you find everything in life that you're looking for, you deserve it... I hope you don't forget me... You take it easy now... All the best... This is your friend Rod signing out... Peace... and one love."

IMPENDING SEX

Lawrence Schimel

I try not to jerk off the night before I plan to have sex. This is a superstition that's developed over the years, from my performance anxiety and the hope that the accumulation of sperm will give me a thicker, splashier cum when I do ejaculate, showing off. As if impressing a man in this fashion could earn his undying love and devotion, or that I'd want him if it could.

I didn't say this was a rational superstition, merely the one I've got. If I know I've got a date scheduled during which I hope to get laid, I'll sometimes plan my entire week to build up to that moment.

Tonight I plan to have sex with two men I have not yet met, and I haven't jerked off for days.

They found me on the Internet.

I've always been a little disdainful of all the Internet sex and dating that one always hears about—from more of my own friends, even, than I at first realized. But in some ways, I passively consented to it, if only because I filled out the Personal Profile form, which is tantamount to writing a personal ad for yourself and giving permission to every stranger on-line to cruise you and chat you up. On one network I have an account with, there's a pull-down menu for "Status" with only three options: Single, Married, Married But Available; can you tell that this is a gay Internet provider, with the presumption that all anyone uses an Internet account for is to trade gifs and JPEGs and meet men?

I filled out my form honestly—a gay taboo—but I'm young enough to get away with this. My profile isn't at all sexual in nature, with regard to me physically or my sexual preferences;

most of the men on this service fill in their stats somewhere in their profile—height, weight, age, dick size, top/bottom, etc.—to avoid having to retype those in as the first "getting to know you" questions when someone sends an Instant Message.

This is standard practice for gay men on most any Internet service. But this little local gay Internet provider I use also has space for little gifs of each member on their personal profile, and I'd put one up of me.

This is what caught Xavier's attention one night when he was cruising the personal profiles of other men on-line. He sent me a private chat message: "U R cute."

I always resent the intrusion of these messages—especially because I usually don't find the men who send them attractive. Which proves I'm just a hypocrite, since even while I'm not using the on-line service as a way for meeting men, if they rank above a certain threshold of sex appeal, I'm interested anyway.

I looked up his profile. It told me he was French, had been living in London, and was now in New York for a few months working for the U.S. office of his firm. But more importantly, it showed me that he was strikingly handsome. I normally prefer dark men: dark skin, dark hair, dark eyes. Xavier was blond, blue-eyed, and fair. But he was square jawed and close-cropped, with bulging arms and pecs. He looked impossibly butch, and I was instantly interested.

I responded to his chat, opening a two-way window, "You're hot, too."

I'm not comfortable using the shorthand (i.e., bad-grammar) of chat conventions; the instincts of a full-time writer and editor, perhaps. I spend so much time in front of a keyboard correcting such mistakes that I can't bear the thought of making them intentionally (and picking up the habit).

Already I felt nervous, because there's something I find so deadeningly routine about cybersex. My friend R. proudly showed me a "scene" he'd done one night in a chat room, insisting that cybersex transcripts were a valid form of pornography to rival any written stories in magazines, such as the ones I wrote. It was one of the most banal and uninteresting sexual texts I'd ever read; clinical descriptions in medical textbooks about venereal disease have more oomph for me.

On-line sex lacks spontaneity because you lack all the sensory clues—sound and smell and taste and touch—that make another person sexy in an infinite variety of ways, so there's an inescapable rote-ness to IM scenarios. They're "literary" (if not always literate), limited to how two people can interact through text.

I, however, am a voyeur. I like the *visual* aspects of sex. I keep the lights on. I don't like mirrors, but I like to watch myself having sex: the sight of my cock as it slides into another man's mouth, of his body laboring over mine as he thrusts inside me.

We did not engage in on-line sex, Xavier and I. We had no intention of engaging in on-line sex. While the on-line community was the venue through which we met, cruised, connected, it was not the arena in which we wished to consummate our brief relationship.

We did talk about sex.

"What R U into?" he asked.

There were so many predictable scripts this could have cued, but I didn't want to use any of them, because what I want might not come in a prepackaged form, I thought.

I reread his profile. I noticed the last line, which I'd overlooked before, pointing readers to his lover's profile as well. Gabriel was Italian, younger than Xavier by two years (they were 28 and 26). He was pictured in a bathing suit, knee-deep in what appeared to be the Mediterranean, sun shining off the bronzed skin of his taut body. He was a hairdresser, something so stereotypically gay it was funny—and yet erotic at the same time because it was not what he looked like at all... and it's uncommon among the men I know.

I asked if he and Gabriel had been together long. Something safe, innocuous, avoiding the topic of sex between me and him— or them.

But I was attracted to both their pictures. I was excited that they had stumbled across me, surprised that I was what they were looking for, since they—and the idea of a threesome—both fit my fantasies.

Would I like to be looked after? he asked.

I wasn't certain what the term "looked after" meant and said so. I was being only slightly disingenuous here; I needed them to be explicit in what we were planning.

He explained it.

I liked the idea of getting fucked by one while sucking off the other. I said so. We began to work out details.

He asked if I slept with a lot of guys.

I said I hadn't been fucked in a while.

He asked if I used my fingers when I masturbated.

He asked if I had a dildo.

He asked lots of variations on the dildo question.

I asked him why he was so curious about my dildo.

He said it turned him on.

He asked me to bring it.

That night, I fucked myself with my dildo.

I was out of practice getting fucked, and wanted to work my way up to the encounter. I had performance anxiety in a new arena.

I kept both their gifs on the screen while I fucked myself.

I have spent days thinking about these two men, who I interact with as flat images on my computer screen and a few typed sentences. I have no idea what their voices sound like. I have no idea how tall they are. What it looks like for either of them to smile suddenly, when pleased or pleasured by something. How either will feel to look at his lover fucking me.

I have spent days discussing my upcoming tryst.

One ex-lover who's now returned to his wife expressed jealousy and said that this made him feel impossibly old. But I felt impossibly young: naive and inexperienced. I've never done anything like this—never had a threesome, never met strangers over the Internet for sex.

Not that I haven't wanted to. I've just never put the energy into making it happen—too nervous and afraid, too passive with making my sex life match my sex fantasies, content to muddle through all the other areas of my life and jerk off each night before bed.

I'd been watching lots of videos of threesomes and group sex. It's something I find an extreme turn-on, to the point where I find the ordinary one-on-one scenes of most commercial gay porn videos tired and dull.

There are often elements of my fantasy life that I don't expect—and sometimes don't even desire—to live out in my actual sex life. I am aware of consciously imagining doing "unsafe" things with men I'm sleeping with, or want to sleep with. I have written before about enjoying rape fantasies and hoping never to be raped.

But the prospect of actually doing something I'd spent so long only dreaming about made my heart flutter. For so many different reasons: Would I be able to do this? As I fucked myself with the dildo that first night we met, I experimented. I pulled it from my ass, wiped it off. I got on my hands and knees, slipped a few lubed fingers in my ass and took the dildo—propped up in front of me with a pillow—into my mouth.

It was nothing like the real thing, I knew, but even still I tried to concentrate on the overload of stimulus, the rhythms of such sex, wondering how I'd react with two real men—two cocks—instead of one silicone one and my hands.

Xavier has described in detail all the things they planned to do to me when we got together.

How could it ever live up to the fantasy? This eager dreadfulness!

I have told practically everyone I know what we plan to do.

There is an element of locker-room bravado in telling my friends and past lovers about the upcoming threesome. I'm bragging about my conquest before it happens.

I am proud of the fact that two men I find extremely handsome find me attractive and want to have sex with me. I am not ashamed to say that I crave the feeling of being desired, and the scenario they plan for me should satisfy this desire, for they will adore and take pleasure in my body. They want to do things to me, things I want them to do to me, but it's the act of doing them to me that makes it erotic for them, and for me.

I've e-mailed their gifs to friends. Phase two of my gloating.

I've gotten many drooling e-mails in response to their images.

There's a practical side to my doing this; I gave one ex-lover and one friend here in New York their e-mail contacts when I sent the gifs, since I'm going into a situation with two men I do not know, so who knows what might happen? Since Xavier and Gabriel have e-mail accounts that require a credit card, I know the on-line provider must have their actual names, addresses, and phone numbers, should something untoward and unhoped-for occur.

But probably the main reason I told so many of my friends was so that I don't wimp out. I am now committed to this choice of action: I must go through with the threeway, or I'll look like a fool to my friends and acquaintances—a loss of face I generally try to avoid whenever possible.

But what happens if we three meet at the coffee shop and it simply doesn't click? I wonder. What if they are discouraged by the goatee I've grown since the photo they saw of me?

One of the writers I've worked with for my anthologies is a well-known porn actor, whose images I've jerked off to many a time, even before I figured out what his name was or followed his career (as porn star or literary figure).

When we met in person, I was expecting to feel an over-whelming sense of erotic tension and was disillusioned when I found it was completely absent. There was something safer about the distance of interacting with him via image—magazine layouts and video—that I was more comfortable with than being con-fronted with him in person, of the fact of having to deal with him as a person, who acted and moved and spoke when he chose to, not when my fantasy of him did. He broke from the script I had for him in my mind.

And now I plan to have sex with two men I've been fantasiz-ing about in this same way. I don't know what will actually hap-pen when we get together, if I will like sex with them, if we'll trick together more than once—or at all. What if it turns out I don't like threesomes after all, I wonder?

Clearly there's only one way to find out.

I put my dildo in a clean plastic bag to bring with me to the coffee shop where we three will meet and place the bundle in my backpack. I go to the bathroom again—the third time I've tried in the last hour—as if I'm preparing for a long car trip and this is my last chance to do so for a long while. I wash my hands, look myself over in the mirror, check my watch, and head out.

JIM THE VIRGIN

D. *Spoiler (pseud.)*

Like it or not, I like virgins. I think of being another man's first sexual contact—and having it be good—as a kind of higher calling. I'm willing to concede that this might be some kind of weird power trip, but to me it seems like the best I can give of myself to another human being in this life. But I don't really care what the motivation is. Erotic wiring is what erotic wiring is.

Over the years, I've run my "Virgin Wanted" ad several times, and I've gotten many responses, but none as uniquely memorable as Jim.

Jim called the ad's voice mail box and said he was curious but unsure. He said if I really want to meet him I should go to a Greenwich Village coffee house the next night between eight and nine o'clock. He told me to be reading a copy of the *Daily News* so he could spot me and, I guess, really make up his mind whether he wanted to meet me. He had a young voice with a pronounced Bronx accent. I canceled other plans, and the next night showed up at Caffé Sha Sha on Hudson near Christopher Street.

Caffé Sha Sha was not one of my usual hangouts, and the *Daily News* seemed to be a rather odd choice of reading material. But there was something about his voice, and I'm such a sucker for virgins. I sat at a sidewalk table and got into Liz Smith. I didn't see him coming, but suddenly someone was pulling up a chair. He stuck out a huge hand and said, "Hi, I'm Jim."

He looked to be in his early twenties, six-two, trim, red hair, freckles, and blue eyes that looked right into mine. He wore a white T-shirt, jeans, work boots, and a black baseball cap that read BRONX. We talked. He said he thought he was bi, but had never had sex with anyone. He had made quite a mess of his life: A high school dropout who had lost himself in a world of drugs and alcohol, he was currently in a half-way house and had a ten o'clock curfew. We seemed to hit it off. I really liked him and was, of course, mad with desire. Just shaking his hand was a turn-on. As I was to find out, there was something about his touch that really mattered to me. I knew if I was patient, I would have him—and he would have me.

"I'd like to see you again," he said as he was leaving to make his curfew, "although I'm not making any promises about sex."

"I like you," I told him, "and I'd like to see you again. How about my place next time? It's not far."

"Okay, but don't try to push me into something I'm not ready for, all right? And how do I just *become ready* anyways? I'm not gonna just decide, 'Well, tonight I'm gonna let someone get my cherry.'"

"Oh, you'll know," I reassured him—and I absolutely meant it. "It's about passion and desire. You'll know you're ready when you're willing to beg for it."

"That'll be the day," the virgin laughed.

I walked him back to Sheridan Square and hugged him good-night. Again I felt a shock from his touch. As I watched him stride away from me, I saw that perfect butt of his for the first time, and I was happy that night. I walked uptown in wonderful summer weather and thought what a kick life can be if you let what you need just come to you at its own pace.

Jim came by a few nights later. We talked, and he said he was nervous. I suggested he let me give him a back rub to help him relax. He shyly took off his shirt, and I got my first look at his well-developed chest and back. His skin was very pale and, typical of redheads, and covered with hundreds of freckles. Despite his size, and all that muscle, it seemed that the slightest touch to this flesh would leave a mark. It was as if he was so shy he would blush just having me touch him. He was innocence personified.

He lay down on the floor and I started on his back, all the time thinking how beautiful he was and how much I wanted my hands on every square inch of him. But then he started telling me how he wanted me to do it.

"Not that way," he instructed, "go down a little. And go in with your thumbs."

"Like this? How come you know so much about this?"

"No, not hard enough. My mother taught me, she's a nurse."

"How's this?"

"No, lemme show you."

And show me he did. He spent an hour on my back and had me take off my pants so he could do my legs. I was in heaven. He might not have been ready for me, but I was ready for him. I started to realize that there was more to Jim than I had thought. But it was time for him to go.

We kept meeting two or three times a week. The rest of my life was becoming of secondary importance. I knew I was falling for him, and it scared me. If nothing else, he was more than twenty years younger than me, was recovering from drugs and alcohol, had nowhere to go after the half-way house, and, of course, had no income. This had never happened to me before, but I had to have him. I decided I would pay any price, accept any consequences. I knew this was madness but I was head over heels in lust. I was going crazy waiting for him to come to me for the sex I was sure was inevitable.

Two months went by. Jim was out of the half-way house and had a room in Queens. He was driving for a fly-by-night moving company. He called often, and we had dinner once a week. He told me a lot more. He was attracted to transvestites, had put an amazing variety of phallic vegetables up his butt, and could give himself a blowjob. He also shared his dreams and aspirations, which started with a high school diploma and continued onto medical school. I kept nurturing and loving him, although we still weren't having sex. In many ways, I was as inexperienced in this kind of relationship as he was.

One time I told him about my own experience with transvestites. You can't be gay in New York all your adult life without running into boys who like to wear women's clothing.

Later that night, sometime after midnight, the bell rang. It was Jim. This was unprecedented. I was already in bed, so I greeted him in a robe.

All he said was, "I'm ready."

"You sure?"

"Yeah. Give me a few minutes in the bathroom."

I noticed he had a bag over his shoulder. While he was in the bathroom I lit some candles and did a few domestic odds and ends to keep myself busy, like getting out the lubricant and unscrewing the top. I finally sat in an easy chair and lit a cigarette. When in doubt: smoke!

Suddenly the bathroom door opened, and there was Jim dressed as a Catholic school girl: white blouse, red plaid pleated skirt, white knee socks, loafers. He'd attached rust-colored pigtails to his own fiery hair with pink bows. He turned his back to me and bent over, pulling up his skirt, showing his white cotton panties.

Rubbing his cheeks, he said, "I'm ready. Really ready. I had to be sure I could trust you and that you'd get off on it. Give it to me! I need it!"

He grabbed me and dragged me to the bed. I was speechless. He knelt in front of me, pulled my robe off, and went down on me. He took all of me into his mouth. I could feel his teeth on my pubic hair. I was close to coming when he pulled away and jumped onto the bed. He was on his knees with his head and shoulders pressed against the bed. His panties were off and he was pulling his cheeks apart, applying the lubricant.

"Come on, do it. *Fuck me!*"

I hesitated. "Are you sure?"

"Of *course* I am. FUCK ME!"

"But... you have to beg and plead for it!"

"Please! Please, PLEASE fuck me!" he whined.

So I did.

And Jim wasn't a virgin anymore.

We settled into an unsettling routine that lasted for several months. The doorbell would ring late at night, unexpectedly, and shortly thereafter I would be introduced to Jim the Nun or Jim the Hooker, the Stewardess, the Nurse, or the Bride. He was wonderfully novel. I never knew what to expect or when to expect it. Once in costume, he was very aggressive, almost manic. He would tear my clothes, devour my cock, make me fuck him all night, screaming for more. Out of role, he would revert to his shy innocence again and tell me about his day moving furniture.

Oh, by the way, I forgot to mention Jim's cock. He would let me feel it, but he wasn't really too interested in having me do anything to it—and so help me, this is true (I can see it now): It was the largest cock I've ever seen on anyone. It was the size of my forearm. It was monstrous. But Jim liked to masturbate alone, while he fantasized about all the things he had and hadn't done in costume. He tried to masturbate with me but said it just wasn't as good. It was too real for him.

Unfortunately, Jim started drinking again and changed. The new Jim got pretty bad. Not only was the virgin fantasy long over, not only was the kinky role-playing erotic charge losing its appeal, but he had become a different and an unappealing person, in costume or out. After several bad incidents, I told him I didn't want to see him when he was drunk. So Jim left my life.

I missed him, but I couldn't think what else I could do. I've had my own issues with alcohol over the years, and I know all about the downward spiral of drinking and drug use. Happily, he reappeared two years later. He was sober, going to school, and had a good job. We stayed friends, although we never had sex again. Jim became a doctor, after all. And he's happily married to a lesbian. Every few months we have coffee at Caffé Sha Sha, and I remember the charm of his lost innocence and somewhat regret my own lost experience. I do have his Bronx baseball cap, which I keep with my collection of hats belonging to virgins. But that is a much longer story.

SHIT HAPPENS

Tim Driscoll

*Layin' back, strokin' my shit, lookin' for a bottom who wants
to sit on some Puerto Rican dick. Wanna dig somebody's back out.
Five-eight, one-sixty, mustache-goatee, nice body, big
uncut cock. Wanna fuck the shit out of someone right now...
Shout me out... Peace.*

Damn, man...!

I woke up in the middle of the night like I always do. It's like 2:15 a.m. on a Sunday morning. I got on "the line"—the Gay Live Network—like I also always do, just reached over for the cordless phone and dialed the number with my thumb in the dark. I use the thumb of the same hand that's holding the phone, because the thumb of my other hand has hold of the waistband of my underpants while the remaining four fingers slide up and down on my dick.

I usually end up just listening to outgoing messages and jerking off to help myself go back to sleep, although sometimes I have phone sex with somebody—or, in rare cases, actually hook up with someone. But he'd have to be really hot for that to happen, especially at two in the morning. Just listening to the voice of this one with the uncut cock could probably get me off. I could probably just keep pressing the # button and listening to it over and over, but I'd like to know how close he is—I mean, where he's calling from. I'm so at the heightened point of my own masturbation now that if a homeboy like him responded to me, it could actually make me go out of my own house, although what I usually say when I'm on the line is that I'm looking for company.

I send him a message, lowering my voice, trying to sound like I'm exciting, but not overly excited.

"Hey, man... five-ten, one-fifty, light brown hair, cut short, green eyes. Very cute face, really, really nice ass. Where you calling from? You like white boys?"

My thumb knows just where to go on the keypad to send the message.

Bleep-bleep.

The perky computerized voice responds to my prompting:

"Your message has been sent."

I listen to the percussive porno-style music that plays while I'm waiting for a response, and just because of the sound of his gruff voice, I'm suddenly feeling like I have to have some dick up my butt *right now.* It's always amazing to me to realize how horniness can thrust me into spontaneous situations so easily. What if he doesn't respond? Am I really gonna leave my nice warm bed at two a.m.? My thoughts drift, my dick softens slightly, I almost fall back asleep, and then...

"You have a message from..."

"Hector."

"Hey, man, I'm in da Bronx... You sound good... Yeah, I like white boys... I like white boy butt... Gimme your digits so I can shout you out."

I let the phone ring twice so that I don't seem too anxious.

"Hello...?"

"Hey man, whassup?"

I like that he doesn't feel any need to identify himself—like the instant familiarity within anonymity. It would actually turn me off if he said, "Hey, this is Hector." His voice is less gruff than it was in his outgoing message, which is comforting to me. It makes him sound like he might be a nice guy as well as a hot top. It's sex that gets me on the line, but there's always that something else that I want to connect with.

"How you doin'?" (That's the best laid-back come-back I have to his "Whassup?")

"Oh, man, I went to this straight party tonight, and I got so fuckin' drunk. And there was this really cute guy there, but we didn't do anything, so now I'm mad horny, layin' here with my dick hard and shit... You wanna come sit on it?"

I try to sound self-assured and definite but, again, not overly excited:

"Sounds good."

"Hey, man, if I pass out, then you'll stay over and get me off in the morning?"

"You mean sleep there with you?"

Omigod, maybe he wants more than just sex.

He responds to the inadvertent blurted-out eagerness in my voice with a dull reply.

"Yeah... You sure you're cute?"

"Yeah, definitely."

"And your butt... you sure it's what you say it is?"

"Hey, man... if you like butt, I'm your boy."

"Git that shit over here."

As I sit on the pot before I get in the shower, my thighs start shaking a little from the nervous realization that I'm really gonna go to the Bronx at three in the morning just to get fucked. I push extra hard, because I know I'm gonna probably get plowed pretty deep, and I don't want to have him pull out his dick and find anything stuck on the condom. Blood, fine, but shit is so embarrassing—and he doesn't sound like the kind of guy who would take well to someone else's shit. I really oughta enema myself, but I used my last Fleet last week when I went to that three-way out in Long Island City. I wasn't really expecting when I went to bed at eleven that four hours later I'd be going out for anal sex, and I don't have a 24-hour Duane Reade in my way-uptown neighborhood, and I can't call him back now and ask if we can hook up some other time. I've learned that if you don't do it in the moment, it's not gonna happen.

I call the Dominican car service that's just around the corner from me. The accented voice on the other end tells me, "Two minute."

I get out to the car and open the door, feeling like the guy behind the wheel somehow knows that I'm on my way to the Bronx to get fucked up the ass. While he drives, leaning comfortably back in the burgundy-colored vinyl seat, I study the reflection of his face in the rear view mirror: the blackness of his mustache-goatee, the smoothness of his caramel-colored skin. He looks into my eyes watching him in the rear view every once in a while, and I look back long enough to see if he'll hold the stare. He just keeps looking away. A rosary hangs off the mirror, and a Virgin Mary statuette with a lonely look on her face stands somehow stuck to the dashboard.

It's winter, and my hands are dry. In my hurry to get out the door, I grabbed a trial-size tube of some lotion and shoved it into my jacket. I squeeze the tube over my open palm between my legs, trying to hide it from the driver's view, but it makes a really obscene-sounding squirt. He looks into the mirror immediately. I'm so embarrassed, but then he says, "I got some too..." and shows me a trial size bottle of some pink stuff from a bath and body shop.

He shakes some out and, as he rubs it on his palms, taking them off of the wheel for just a moment as we go across the bridge, I smell the scent of apple. I lean forward in the seat to show him my brand of lotion and to see if by any chance he has a hard on. No such luck. He's just a straight guy who likes soft skin, and all he's interested in is dropping me off. I sit back and keep to myself the rest of the way.

Hector had told me when he gave me directions to his house to ring the bottom bell (perfect for me, the bottom boy) and then walk down the stairs, and he'd be at the front door of his apartment to let me in. It's a two-family house that he lives in, so I'm really careful to be quiet on the uncarpeted stairs that start squeaking as soon as I take the first step down. But there are, like, three different doors when I get to the bottom of the stairs, and it confuses me, until I see that only one of them has a dead bolt. I knock, trying not to be too loud but also trying to make my knock seem masculine and not too much of a tap. No answer right away. I wait for a few seconds that seem to go on forever and feel my heart beating in the same rhythm as the second more urgent and slightly louder knocking I make next. My legs start to shake. Then my nervousness goes deeper and lower. Sexual anxiety always affects my entire alimentary canal. My mouth gets dry, my throat constricts, I get nauseous, and, worst of all, my colon distends. You'd think it'd constrict like my throat, but no. I was so careful to push every last bit out, but it seems like there's some more shit just dying to drop down. Why now? I knock once more.

Hey, what if *he's* full of shit? What if he made me come all the way over here and this is someone else's house whose bell I just rang and they're gonna call the police or something and catch me inside the hallway of their home? I quickly spring up the squeaky stairs, out the screen door and back out onto the sidewalk. It's weird to be walking in some neighborhood I've never been in, especially on a residential sidewalk alongside of actual lawns and shrubbery. I stupidly think I'll find a pay phone on the corner, but this is the Bronx—I'm not in Manhattan anymore.

After fifteen minutes, I finally do find the pay phone. It's on an embankment next to a chain-link fence, no sidewalk next to it, no building it's attached to—and I see down the street there's a whole pack of homeboys hanging outside of a car, smoke curling, bottles clinking, low voices, goatees, and I'm thinking: *Can they tell I'm a white boy bottom from here?*

I dial Hector's number, thinking that the answering machine's gonna come on, but he answers it in a clear voice, not drunk or groggy at all.

"Yeah?"

"Hey, I rang your doorbell and knocked on your door. Didn't you hear me?

"No." (Not, "Oh, I'm sorry," just "No.")

There's a moment of uncomfortable silence while I wonder if he's even still interested.

"Well, try again, and I'll let you in."

"Well, it'll take me, like, ten minutes to walk back over there... It took me a while to find a pay phone."

"Okay." *Click.*

Well, whatever. I'm a little annoyed, but horniness overwhelms annoyance any day for a non-confrontational bottom. I'm thinking too much about the dick I'll get up my ass to have a bug up my butt. While I'm walking, my legs start shaking again in anticipation and nervousness. I get that feeling in my bowels that I get whenever I'm on my way to do something lascivious. For some reason, it reminds me of the way an engine drops into ignition. I'm still not sure if it's just nervousness or if I need to take another shit.

This time, his apartment door is cracked open, and I don't need to knock. I see that the light in the bathroom is on, and the door right next to it must be his bedroom. I peer in to see a queen-size black-lacquer–framed bed with an enormous shelved and mirrored headboard/display case attached to the back of it—also in black lacquer. Black lacquer seem so Latino... all dark and shiny.

"Whassup?" I hear him say, though I can barely make him out as my eyes adjust to the darkness. Then I see his form. He's wearing boxers. Nothing but. He's got his legs spread open, one hand behind his head, the other offering what's between his legs to me.

I should just jump him right there, fully clothed, start sucking his dick with my boots still laced, but, instead, I feel like I have to say something about how difficult it was to get here.

"You had me scared.... Did you pass out?"

I take off my jacket, planting my feet wide, feeling my ass cheeks spread, again resisting the feeling that my bowels are dropping down. I still can't tell if it's just nervousness or if my body's somehow sabotaging my urges to get plugged by letting go of whatever's down there, preparing the hatch for a dive bomb of embarrassment, punishing me for being such a slut. There's no way I'm gonna ask him right now if I can use the bathroom.

I'll just hope for the best. I've been fucked before with this feeling, and had the tip of the condom have a little bit of shit on it. Top men who fuck ass ought to expect that this is always a possibility.

Hector shoves down his underwear and there they are, his nine uncut inches. He pushes it at the base, and points it at me. Again I think that I ought to just go for it, but I'm still feeling like he should say something nice to me before I blow him, since I had to walk ten blocks to find a pay phone and ten blocks back to get inside his house. Well, who gives a shit? I'm here now, and it is hard—and huge. I bend over to untie my boot laces, never looking away from that thick thing gesturing like it knows exactly where it wants to go. I feel my ignition dropping.

"Yeah, man, suck it... get it nice and hard so I can shove it up your butt... This is what you came here for, right?"

I look up at him, nodding a little and mumbling *mmmhmm* without ever taking my mouth off of it. I don't know why he says to get it hard. It's all the way to the back of my throat. As much as I want to enjoy this, I feel like my body's undermining me. I keep gagging on this thing, unsuccessful at deep-throating because I can't relax the still-constricted *entry* to my alimentary canal while simultaneously tightening the *exit* end to keep it closed. Hector gets impatient and pulls out, then pulls me up onto him, grabbing my ass with both hands.

"You ready?"

I'm not, but I think I'd have to be in the bathroom for half an hour if I was really gonna get myself ready. I figure, what the fuck, just go for it. Hector reaches back towards the headboard, comes back with a single condom between his fingers, rips the package open with his teeth, and hands me the rubbery thing. As I roll the condom over that cock, the way the latex bunches and then stretches, bunches and then stretches makes me think of the peristaltic action of the small intestine. It's not what I want to be thinking.

Now, I usually sit on a dick first to get used to it, and then the guy can push me on my back or flip me over on my belly, pretty much whatever he wants. But after I get that condom over Hector's cock and squirt some lube on him and slide some into me, I roll onto my belly right away (on my belly with my butt up in the air a little is the easiest way for me to get penetrated—plus it's a position where my colon is directed at the least awkward angle).

Hector does this jack-hammer kind of thrusting at my ass-hole—he probably has trouble plunging that thickness into any-one. When it finally goes in, I feel relief and terror at the same time. He starts fucking me so hard that I'm taking short audible inhalations alternated with gasping exhalations.

Suddenly, on one of the short, sharp inhalations, the distinct smell of my own bodily functioning comes into my nostrils. The whole thing is ruined for me now, because all I can do is worry about what kind of mess I'm making on that latex sheath that he's gonna eventually see and whether or when that same smell that I smell is gonna waft up to his nose. He keeps pumping, and I'm just taking it without any pleasure, hoping he'll just shoot soon and get it over with. I'm glad I'm on my belly, because also with all the worrying, my dick's gone down dramatically, and that would only make it worse for me to see the look on the guy's face that's fucking me gazing down at a limp little prick.

"That's it, man... that's all I can do."

Hector slides his piece outta me and pushes himself off me. I'm completely flattened out on my stomach worrying now that somehow I didn't satisfy him and that it's my fault he couldn't come even though he was drunk way before I even got over here. Did he smell something? I reach down in-between my butt cheeks, foolishly hoping that all the slickness I feel down there is just lube. I twist my head back around towards him as he stands up and sways a little with that big dick bobbing up and down in front of him. It's really dark on the side of the bed where he stood up, and he's facing toward the bathroom, so he doesn't see me as I bring my fingers to my nose.

Shit.

"Um... the condom might be a little bit dirty," I say.

He doesn't respond with words, just looks down at his dick, although it's so dark where he's standing that he couldn't see what might be on the end of the condom even if he wasn't inebriated. I watch his hairy ass stumble along the side of the bed, his hands held out in front of him as if his dick is steering him towards the light of the bathroom. He disappears around the door frame.

Shit.

I'm afraid to follow him into the bathroom or even over to the doorway of the bedroom. I don't want to invade his space if he needs some right now. I'm sure he's blaming me for making a mess on his prick. Still, I've gotta see how bad things are between my butt cheeks and wipe myself up before it starts to drip down my thighs. I push myself carefully up onto my knees, and as I do, my hand passes over the hollowed-out place on the bed where my dick was smashed down while he pounded me. There's wetness—a whole circle of wetness that's already seeped down into the sheets—too big a circle of wetness that I could think it's just my own pre-cum.

Shit.

I wiggle my knees over to the edge of the bed, keeping my thighs and butt cheeks pressed together. Bare feet down onto the carpet, I look over the black-lacquer headboard/display case thinking that on one of those shelves there's gotta be a big box of tissues. I see figurines and rosary beads and wine glasses and then, on one shallow shelf, I see what in my hopeful/nervous/anxious-to-clean-myself-off desperation looks like two stacks of paper napkins right next to each other. I could bend over to look closer, to make sure that they're napkins, but I don't want my butt cheeks to slide apart without having something to catch the drip. So I reach my hand in, sliding my slick finger back towards me along the papery surface, like I would if I was in a fast-food restaurant or a diner, thinking that the top napkin is gonna give... and it doesn't. So I guess it's not two stacks of napkins. It's not even two stacks of something else, because the stacks don't seem to separated. But what else would two stacks of papery surfaces that don't separate be?

Shit.

I lean carefully over, feeling my upper inner things sliding along one another, and I see that it's a book that he left open on the shallow shelf, and that on the left side of the book—the side I didn't slide my finger across—there's a heavy metal object in the shape of a cross. Why would he have a cross-shaped object laid across one page of an open book? Unless that book was... oh, my God... The Bible! Jesus Christ, I just touched his *Holy Bible* with my shit-smeared finger!

This time I don't just think it, I actually whisper it out loud... "Shit!"

My quick-witted writer's mind inappropriately starts in on word play involving knowing him now in more than just one Biblical sense, but this really isn't funny right now.

Oh, God, what do I do?

Should I take the book over to the door, where I'll be able to see in better light what kind of damage I've done and risk having him come in suddenly to see me with my slightly shit-smeared hands holding his Holy Bible open?

He comes back into the bedroom in his boxers. I can't tell if he's annoyed, or still just inebriated.

"Um, I think I messed up your sheets."

"I need some privacy right now."

All the homeboy just went out of him, using the word privacy. I really ruined the whole thing. At least having to leave the room for him to strip the sheets give me time to go into the bathroom and clean myself up. I leave the bathroom door open and stand in front of the open toilet, drawing wads of toilet paper off the roll while looking around at more black lacquer: a tissue box cover (no wonder there wasn't a box on the headboard/display case), a dusty toothbrush glass, a squirt bottle for the liquid hand soap. He suddenly comes around the corner and startles me. I've wiped like six times and flushed three. All the shit's gone. Now there's just blood. I'm so glad there's just blood. He sees the bright red on the stark white right before I drop it in the bowl.

"You're bleeding?"

The obvious concern in his voice overshadows all the tense feeling he shot towards me when he asked for privacy.

"It's no big deal."

"I'm gonna drive you home."

"No, that's okay, just call me a car."

I feel a strong, strange need to be completely independent right now. The shock of the shit and the relief of the blood have transcended not only my horniness but also the usual loneliness I feel after promiscuous hook-ups. His sudden concern actually gives me a powerful feeling of not needing to deal with him any longer. I'm not embarrassed anymore. I just want to be back at home in my own bed all alone.

He calls the car on his cordless.

"They'll be here in two minutes."

I apologize again: "I'm really sorry."

"It's okay... (an awkward pause)... it happens."

I swear his hesitation right before he said "it" was because he was half-catching himself from saying—and half-weighing whether or not to say—"shit." I try to see in his facial composure any hint of humor, but if there is one, he hides it well. I feel the urge to make the joke myself, but I'm too tired.

"You sure you're okay?"

This time he sounds like he's hoping I'll just say yes and get the fuck out of his house.

Nonchalantly, I do just say it. "Yes."

I walk slowly up the squeaky stairs, not caring if I make any noise, relieved at not having to squeeze my legs together, feeling a smoothness between my inner thighs, a pleasant lightness in my lower abdomen, a strange heaviness in my head.

As I walk out into the cool morning breeze, I'm wondering what the driver waiting outside is gonna look like, and if he'll look longer at me in the rear view mirror than the last one did. As I get inside the car this time, I see Jesus glued to the dashboard holding out a holy hand. I slam the door shut, wondering how often, if ever, Hector reads the good book.

PLAY PARTY

Doug Harrison

Hot, horny, and hung.

God, *I'm tired of these ads! Isn't anyone average? Is the entire gay population over-endowed and over-sexed? Or do only the over-endowed and over-sexed advertise? But, if they're over-endowed and over-sexed, why do they all need to advertise?*

Yeah, here's the ad I've been looking for:

Private Monthly Parties
*in well equipped South of Market
home dungeon. Experienced players only.
Call 415-869-FUCK.*

I wonder how they define "experienced." Oh, well, here goes. I slowly dialed the provocative number.

"Hi, my name's Doug. I saw your ad in the paper. When's the next party?"

"Hold on! First tell me about yourself."

Shit, I've got to be interviewed to play. But I guess it's good they're particular.

"I'm five foot-eight, blond hair, blue eyes, and I have a light mustache. I'm lean and work out to keep my gymnast's build. And I have a 7½ inch dick that doesn't quit."

"What type of play you into?"

"I like to suck dick, and have the favor returned. I'm into heavy nipple play, and I've been spanked a lot. And I really get off on play piercing."

"What about bondage?"

"Okay, as a bottom. I'm not too good with knots, yet."

"Ever been to a sex club?"

"No."

"Been to play parties?"

"Yeah, a few."

"Which ones?"

"The Leathermen's Club, mostly."

"You know Joel?"

"Yeah, he's spanked me a couple of times, and we jerked each other off. He's hot."

"Well, okay. Our next party's this coming Friday. It's at my apartment at 640 Patrick Street, number 7. Doors open from nine p.m. to midnight. Party lasts till four a.m. Bring your own toys; we have safe sex supplies. Looking forward to meeting you, Doug. My name's Ted."

"Thanks, Ted. See you Friday."

I went to bed and began the string of restless nights that led to Friday.

This is dumb! I'm not very experienced. And there are so many bottoms for every good top. What if a sadistic top gets hold of me? What if nobody gets hold of me? I won't know anybody there. But, maybe, just maybe, I'll have a great time. Oh shit, I haven't had a really good time at any of these play parties. But this is different; it's a private home. And it's different than the bar scene. Or is it? I don't think I'll go. But I should try it out. I'll wonder what I missed if I stay home again. I wish I didn't have to search like this for Mr. Perfect!

Friday arrived, and I left work early to take my obligatory pre-party nap. I showered, douched (a fellow can hope, can't he?), and packed my toybag. At this stage in my budding leatherboy's career, there weren't too many items from which to choose. I included my homemade rope flogger, a small paddle, nipple clamps with adjustable jaws, a black leather jock, and a stainless steel cockring. I also brought my red fanny pack with its collection of safe sex supplies: condoms, a small container of lube, and gloves.

I had planned to wear nothing beneath my tight 501s. But horny impulse led me to retrieve an old white cotton jock buried in my bottom dresser drawer. I put it on, and admired myself in the mirror. *Not bad! Such a cute boy!* I cupped my palm over the pouch and slowly rubbed its frayed cotton. I unpacked the nipple clamps from my toybag, tightened them on my nipples, and twisted my hands through the jock's elastic leg bands. *Boy in bondage!* As I pranced about, small circles of white light danced across my chest, reflected from the crystal beads on my mother's rosary. I had hung it from the mirror's support post after her funeral several months ago. I abruptly turned from the mirror.

I stuffed myself into the 501s, put on a white tank top and black boots, grabbed my leather jacket and toybag, and hurriedly left.

I drove to Patrick Street. Of course, this being San Francisco, I had trouble finding parking. I ended up walking several blocks through a rough neighborhood, my whistle at the ready. Darkened warehouses loomed over three-story, gray, ramshackle clapboard houses that contained far too many apartments. I walked near the edge of the sidewalk, as far away from building fronts and alleys as possible, with a gait I prayed looked more confident than I felt. I welcomed the occasional street lamp.

I made it safely to the address. The large concrete building had a thick wrought-iron gate protecting glass doors. I could see into an elegant foyer that belied the neighborhood.

I rang, identified myself, and was told by a gruff voice to come up to the second floor. He buzzed me through two doors into a large lobby with highly polished black tile floors that reflected a warm glow from several large chandeliers. Ignoring the elevator, I slowly ascended a winding staircase to a hallway with a rich, beige carpet.

I knocked at number 7. A man wearing only gray Calvin Klein shorts opened the door. He said nothing, and I entered into a large kitchen devoid of furniture. Several ice chests of soft drinks and beer sat on the floor in front of a sink that contained a mound of ice cubes. The food was sparse: crackers and cheese, pretzels, and popcorn.

I noticed an unstable mound of overstuffed black garbage bags sealed with tags in the far corner of the room. I took off my jacket, stuffed it in a bag, wrote up a name tag, and threw my small bundle on the heap.

About half a dozen men stood around talking and sipping drinks. No one came forward to introduce himself. Attire ranged from nothing to leather jocks or shorts to the classic leather-man's look: boots, chaps, jock, vest, and hat.

Snippets of conversation wafted through a haze of pot smoke: "This is his third marriage in two years. He should change therapists or listen to himself." "She'd be perfect for the part if she'd only learn how to sing and act." "That was the best blow job I've had in a long time. Definitely has no gag reflex."

Two naked guys, each grasping the other's buns, were kissing in the center of the room, their hard dicks throbbing against hairy bellies. A bald man was on his knees, servicing a skinny kid who was smoking a joint and glancing around the room. I stared at a short body builder, his physique perfect for duplication in marble. He did not return my glance. His vacuous gaze played counterpoint with his rapid hand motions as he alternated an index finger from nostril to nostril and snorted.

There were two exits from the kitchen. Thick black curtains separated it from the remainder of the same level and a stairwell led to a lower floor. I proceeded down the stairs.

I passed through a double set of heavy black curtains into another world. The large family room had been converted into a playroom with thin black plastic lining each wall from ceiling to floor. Dim lighting came from small red bulbs that cast a surrealistic glow. The disco music that sounded faint in the kitchen assailed my ears with Depeche Mode's "Strange Love." The smell of poppers blasted my nostrils. It was like unexpectedly coming upon the odor of a dead skunk while driving along a country road, only I couldn't roll up the car windows.

This looks like a scene from a Fellini movie, but I don't think even his imagination could conjure up all these tableaux.

A couch occupied the space beneath the stairwell. Two men sat intertwined, their tongues lost in each other's throats. A sweaty man knelt before them, sucking one hard cock, then the other, and sporadically trying to simultaneously stuff both into his hungry mouth. He grasped the obligatory small brown bottle in one hand.

Most of the room was occupied by two large metal frames, each supporting a sling made from thick black leather straps. The one on the right contained a naked man with his head thrown back, his eyes closed, and his mouth hanging open as he alternated growls, pants, and screams. A man, clad only in a black cotton jock, was standing at the foot of the sling with his hand and half his forearm up the recumbent's asshole, which was smeared with gobs of Crisco. When the fister periodically removed his hand, it was obvious he was not wearing a glove.

The other sling was wildly gyrating as the bottom tied to it by his wrists, ankles, and waist was getting his brains fucked out. He wore only a tightly laced black leather hood that completely blocked his vision and hearing. His welcome assailant, wearing only a chrome cock ring, was grasping the sling chains and throwing his entire weight behind his unsheathed cock as he pounded the greedy hole.

A jail cell door was anchored to the far wall. A naked man was handcuffed to its high cross bar with his arms stretched above his head. A man dressed in a police uniform was striking his prisoner's hard dick with a black nightstick. Each blow only served to make the dick harder.

The room was jammed with roaming men. A few were leaning against the walls and staring at the varied scenes in progress, while others were offering encouragement to the participants. Most were playing with themselves, eyes focusing on unseen distant objects. I retreated up the stairs to the kitchen.

I took a deep breath and parted the curtains leading from the kitchen into the upper play area. It probably served as a combination living room and dining room under normal circumstances. It was large, dim, and lacked the usual furniture. The walls were covered with familiar black plastic; a few red bulbs cast ambiguous shadows. The Depeche Mode selection had changed to "Can't Get Enough." Several mattresses occupied a corner, and about ten chairs were scattered along various portions of the wall. There was also a large couch. A St. Andrew's cross occupied a portion of the rear wall, and it was lit by a tightly-focused, white spot light. A long table upholstered in black leather was next to the cross; judging by the number of large eyebolts along its perimeter, I conjectured its main function was bondage.

There were only a few men in this large area. A solid wooden chair was bolted to a small platform in the center of the room. It reminded me of an electric chair without any wiring. A thin blond man wearing only a black blindfold was securely strapped to it with thick, white rope. An unattractive gnome squatted on its wide seat. He grabbed a clump of the blond's hair and forced his mouth up and down his short dick.

Four men stood, knelt, and leaned in a pyramidal pile next to the doorway. Dicks, hands, and mouths rapidly changed positions as they searched for novelty. Two men were fucking doggie-style on one of the mattresses. A third joined them to make a monkey-in-the-middle coupling. No condoms were in evidence. I turned to leave.

"It's okay to come in," said a firm, resonant, baritone voice with welcoming authority. It was both a statement and a command.

I turned slightly and tilted my head upward to make contact with sparkling, penetrating brown eyes. The deep brim of the man's black leather cap cast a gray shadow over his smooth forehead. His mustache set off a handsome face that was, well, aristocratic. He wore no shirt and had a finely chiseled torso. A plain, gold crucifix hung from a large-linked gold chain that circled his neck. Circular gold nipple rings accentuated well-developed pecs. His biceps left no doubt that he could easily pick me up. I longed to run my tongue across the fine brown hair that covered his chest and stretched in a narrow line down his flat, hard stomach and spread out to cover his abdomen. Black leather chaps clung to muscular legs. A black leather jock with chrome studs teased me with its bulging pouch. A large hunting knife hung from his right hip, and a coiled whip from his left.

I don't know how long I silently stared at him, shifting my weight from foot to foot and wringing my hands behind my back. *God, he's gorgeous! Is he just being sociable? Does he really want to play with me? Why me? I'm so short. Lord, I am not worthy. Damn, will I ever stop being an altar boy?*

He gestured with his eyes, and I went to him. I stood there, head bowed, feet apart, hands behind my back, waiting.

"This your first time here?"

"Yes, sir," I said in a voice that was close to cracking.

"What brings you here?"

"I wanted to try something different."

"How different?"

I said nothing as my eyes darted around the room.

"Do you trust me?"

"Yes, sir!"

"I want you to be my boy for the next few hours."

"I would be honored, sir."

"Follow me."

He turned. As I had suspected, his chaps framed not a bubble butt, but a firm, muscular ass, the type that could propel a hard dick for hours without hesitation. It was covered with wisps of fine brown hair.

I followed him to a dark space against the far wall where a large black suitcase sat next to an unoccupied chair. He reached inside and pulled out a gleaming, stainless steel collar. It was about two inches tall and had shiny spikes protruding from it.

"When you wear my collar you belong to me, and only me. I expect complete obedience. You give up all control, all sense of identity."

"Yes, sir."

I began to get hard as he reached around my neck to put on the collar. I was completely hard when he snapped the padlock shut.

"You will address me with any combination of 'Daddy' and 'sir' that you find appropriate."

I shuddered at the word "Daddy."

"Yes, sir!"

"That's a good boy. Now, strip, and put your boots back on after you take your jeans off." He leaned against the wall, hand on hip, and watched me undress.

I took off my tank top. *Oh my God! I left the nipple clamps on! Oh shit!* I noticed a slight grin on his face as I sat down to remove my boots. I took off my 501's.

"That's an interesting jock," he observed. "They stopped making that brand years ago. Leave it on!"

I put my boots back on and again stood before him.

"Those nipples of yours look like they've taken a lot of abuse."

"Yes, sir."

"Mostly self-inflicted?"

"No, sir. I mean, Yes, sir. I can take it, sir."

"That's not what's it's about," he snapped.

He used his index fingers to lightly brush the tips of my nipples, just in front of the clamps. I groaned with pleasure. *Alleluia!* He stepped back and looked deep into my eyes.

"You like that, don't you, boy?"

"Yes, sir, thank you, sir." I was getting hard again. I reached for my crotch.

"I didn't tell you to touch yourself!" he hissed. *Mea culpa!* I quickly placed my hands behind my back.

He pulled a leather thong from his toybag, carefully gauged its length, and cut it with his hunting knife. He tied each end to the nipple clamps, and placed its center between my front teeth. He placed the palms of his hands on each side of my face, looked intently into my eyes and whispered, "Hold this in your mouth and don't let go!"

Then he slapped my cheek. Hard. My face jerked to one side and a searing pain ran through my nipple. But I didn't let go of the thong. He abruptly slapped the other cheek. He continued to alternate blows as the tears streamed down my cheeks and my nipples cried out for relief. Just when I was about to drop the thong, he stopped. He ran his hands slowly through my hair.

"Take a deep breath, and we'll get rid of these clamps." He gently removed the clamps on my outbreath. I screamed as they came off. He put his arms around me and lightly stroked my back. His firm smile caressed his next words.

"Worship my boots," he commanded. "I want to feel your tongue through the leather."

He sat on one of the metal folding chairs, his arm resting on his toybag. I knelt before him, hoping my smile was as beatific as my youthful cherubic grin when I knelt before my parish priest. *Oh, sir, my Daddy! Thanks be to God.*

I grabbed the backs of his tall, black leather boots and my long, blond hair completely covered their tips. I pressed my lips as tightly as I could on their shiny surface, feeling the outline of his toes. I ran my tongue over their surface. Tears of joy, of passion, of thanksgiving ran down my cheeks and mixed with my saliva to anoint the leather. I licked the mixture evenly over the smooth surface and used my hair to shine the boots to a sparkling luster. I looked up. I was not the only one with tears in his eyes.

"I have a reward for you," he sighed. He stroked his crotch and slowly removed the cup of his leather jock. A magnificent dick sprang forth, like the man—long and narrow, and firm but beautiful. I approached it slowly. *I will go to the altar of God, to God who gives joy to my youth.*

I put my hands behind my back and leaned over. His scepter was waiting patiently, a drop of pre-cum glistening at its tip. I brushed it off with the tip of my tongue and drew it into my mouth. I took the swollen head between my lips and ran my tongue around the corona. I slowly slid my mouth along the entire length of the shaft, while running my tongue along its underside. He moaned. I sucked voraciously, relaxing my throat and taking it all on the downstroke. He encouraged me by grabbing my hair and rapidly pumping my head up and down. I could hardly breathe. When he was about to come, he gently pushed me away and took a deep breath.

"Good boy," he said as he put his codpiece back on. He put his left boot on my right shoulder. "Such a good boy, I'm going to give you a choice. We can go downstairs and use one of the slings or go over to the cross. Whatever you choose, I still expect complete obedience."

The cross, the cross. Lamb of God. I offer myself to thee. The surge of fire in my stomach was a mixture of lust and fear. I caressed the lust but couldn't suppress the fear.

"The cross, sir, please, the cross, " I whispered.

"Take my bag," he commanded.

I took his bag and followed him to the wooden cross. It was shaped like an X, about seven feet tall and painted black. Four large eyehooks protruded from its top and bottom ends. I placed his toybag about six feet from the cross and turned to him.

"Take the piece of leather from my toybag and spread it out here on the floor. Arrange my whips in a row, tails pointing toward the wall, with what you consider the most gentle whip on the right, increasing in severity to the left."

"Yes, sir." I knelt and rummaged in his bag. There were paddles, crops, and things I had never seen before. I found the piece of leather and spread it out on the floor, careful to smooth out any creases. I saw two large carabiners in the corner of the bag. Each one contained the wrist straps of several whips. I struggled to lift them out and released the whips.

I had always thought that a whipmaster only needed one general-purpose whip. But, as I handled these instruments of pain and pleasure, it was obvious that the sensations from a flat-tailed flogger would be very different from those from a knotted cat-o'-nine-tails.

I had never seen such a collection. They were short, they were long. Some were black, some were red, some were brown, some were green; some were mixtures of colors. They ranged from about a foot and a half to over two feet in length. Some looked soft, some looked fierce. Some had smooth tails, others were braided. Some had tapered ends, others were knotted. And there were two coiled single-tail whips. *These implements are about to kiss my back!*

"Face me," he ordered. He put two padded black leather cuffs on my wrists and two larger ones around my boots.

"Comfortable?" he asked.

"Yes, sir!"

"Good!" He locked all four restraints with small brown padlocks. He kissed me on the forehead and led me to the cross. "Raise your arms." He ran chains through the upper eyebolts and through the D-rings on my wrist cuffs. He ran his hands along my arms, checking that I had enough room to move slightly. Likewise, he secured my feet.

Finally, he looped a thick, soft white rope several times around my waist and tied it to the middle of the cross. He paused, I imagined, to admire his handiwork.

What the hell am I doing here? I just met this man! My hard-on mocked my increasing fear, and I wanted to stroke my dick. Just then I felt his codpiece against my asscheeks and his hand cupped my jock. I began to purr.

"Remember, you're in a cocoon of love," he whispered into my ear. "No safe words are necessary. I can read your body language. And keep your eyes closed," he ordered. His hypnotic command made a blindfold unnecessary. By this time, a small audience of voyeurs had gathered around us. I was disappointed I wouldn't be able to watch their reactions to our scene.

Then it began. He reached around my head with a many-tailed, very soft flogger and drew it languidly across my face. I drank in the overpowering aroma of leather.

He stepped back, and I could feel a gentle breeze on my back as the tails got closer and closer. It turned to a gentle rubbing, tenderly caressing my back like a fluffy summer breeze. *Oh my God, that's sexy.* I sank into it. But, almost imperceptibly, the breeze became warmer and warmer, until it felt like hot, midday equatorial sunlight was pouring down onto my back. And then my back began to feel like it was sunburned. At this point he must have changed to a heavier flogger, because the caresses turned into a dull thudding sensation. It was mesmerizing. *The endorphins must be flowing.* Fear crept in again to replace my curiosity, but it was a welcome fear. I stopped thinking about his choice of floggers and started to float way.

The thudding remained, but the blows became sharper and sharper. The sunlight had turned to raindrops that became razor-sharp hailstones. I wasn't conscious of the restraints, or my body, or, for that matter, my mind. I existed only in the now.

I was writhing, screaming, crying. As anchored as I was, I was floating. Floating in plethora of swirling colors—reds, greens, and blues. I was a fleck of dust swirling in a kaleidoscope. The swirling motion became more intense until I was spinning in a dark whirlpool. The black water coalesced into a drab dress.

"Why those beads, Mommy?"

"Because I'm talking to God about Daddy."

"Why won't Daddy come home?"

"Because he's with God."

"I want Daddy! I hate God!"

"Don't ever say that!" she screams as she smacks the boy's cheek. "Oh God, I'm sorry, I'm sorry." She clutches the boy to her breast as her tears trickle onto his forehead.

The boy's sobs metamorphose into whimpers. "I don't want to live with Granny. I want Daddy to come home."

"So do I, angel, so do I."

I shot out of the whirlpool, riding waves of cold water in a narrow stream. One bank was pain, the opposite pleasure. I reached out and touched one, then the other, then both simultaneously. The pain was excruciating, biting into my back like a dull saw blade. Yet I looked forward to the next blow. It opened doors to unknown worlds, like being on acid. When I finally felt I couldn't take anymore, he backed off slightly, paused, and then we began to crescendo to yet another, and higher crest. I rode these undulating waves like a jellyfish in warm, turbulent water. I'm hanging from this cross, Daddy. Oh, yes, sir... flog me, Daddy. Scourge me, Daddy, please, Daddy, sir!

"We're climbing higher, boy. Go to the top of the building. Reach for it!"

I scaled a tall building, arms and legs reaching over windows, striving to touch the distant, azure sky. Each lash of the flogger propelled me higher. The brick facing turned into white wooden siding on a shabby farmhouse. I stopped at a third floor attic window and looked through the dirty pane into the past.

The teenage boy brushes cobwebs from an old wooden trunk. He opens the lid and rummages through the collection of musty clothes. He picks up a picture and stares at it intently. A young man in a gymnast's uniform stares back at him with a youthful grin. *Dad.* He looks at the clothes: dungarees, T-shirts, a warm-up suit, a uniform, shirts, jackets, socks, and tattered shoes. He finds a jock and holds it up. Looking at the picture, he sniffs the jock. *I can feel you, Dad, I can feel you.* He lowers his shorts and puts on the jock. He lies on the dirty floor, the uniform over his face, and grabs his cock. He cautiously beats off, coming on his stomach. He wears the jock the remainder of the day, and wears it to bed that warm summer night, dreaming of his father.

Take me, Daddy, take me. This is my body.

I felt a hand on my wrist. He was checking my circulation.

"Water?" he asked. I nodded and drank from the bottle that touched my lips. My eyes remained closed.

"You're beautiful, boy. We're almost done. I'm going to use the single tail now."

He stepped back, and the crack of the whip stung my ears as he warmed up. I soon felt a light brushing on my back that evolved into a series of sharp mosquito bites. I clenched my fists. The next strike was like a searing knife cut. I screamed and thrashed as I shook the cross.

"Can you take five of those, boy?"

"Yes, sir."

"Count them out for me!"

"Yes, sir."

Whack!

"One, sir!" This stroke was like a punch from a red-hot lance, and it knocked the breath from me. He waited until I recovered.

Whack!

"Two, sir!" I let go off all tension, hanging as limp as my bondage would allow.

Whack!

"Aaaah! Three, sir!" The pain left me nowhere to go except outside my body.

Whack!

"Oh, oh, oh! Four, sir!" I was trying to fly over the pain like clouds below, but occasionally a puff would billow up and touch me, slicing me in two.

Whack!

"Fi-fi-five, sir!" *Am I bleeding? I'm offering my blood to Daddy.* I swallowed my sobs.

"It's okay for boys to cry," he said. He stood behind the cross, placed my head on his shoulder, and held me tightly around the waist.

"Let it all out," he said. "Let the good come in. I'm here. You're beautiful. You're loved." I wept as I had never cried before. Years of anger, hurt, and repression rose to the surface, trying to choke me as they were forced aside and replaced by the warm glow of compassion and love that soon engulfed me.

His arms left me and I felt a momentary, warm pressure on my upper back.

"Slowly open your eyes," he said. I did. He had dimmed the spotlight, and stood facing me. He held a large paper towel in front of my face. It had two, reddish-brown, disjointed x's imprinted on it.

"This is the pattern your blood left," he said. *This is my blood.* I began to whimper softly as he unshackled my hands and feet and freed my waist. And then I felt something cool on my back. He must have been blowing his warm breath on me, but it felt refreshingly cold after the sting of the whips.

"I'm going to fuck you." The words floated through my sobs and hung there like a perfect landscape on a clear morning.

He took my hands and placed them at the center of the cross. I was now leaning over, my back parallel to the floor. I waited patiently as he put on a condom and a glove. I soon felt a lubed finger gently probing my asshole. I began to move my butt back and forth and arched my back like a cat in heat. His finger massaged the exterior of my rectum and then went inside with a slow, circular motion, cautiously expanding me. His other hand reached around me. It was wide enough so that the nails of his thumb and forefinger could dig into a nipple each. I moaned with pleasure. The swollen head of his dick pushed against my asshole, and I relaxed to allow him easy entry. Only it wasn't that easy, as it turned out. I hadn't been fucked that much, and his dick was long. I had to move back and forth with his pumping and breathe deeply to get past the pain. The intense sensations in my butt, the pain in my nipples, and the warmth of my back converged into a total experience where separate body parts ceased to exist.

"Yes, sir! Fuck me, sir. Please fuck me hard, sir!"

He grabbed the sides of my jock like the reins of a horse and pumped furiously, his hips slamming against my butt.

"Is this what you want, boy?"

"Yes, sir!" *Dad, Dad, Dad.*

He reached around, pulled my hard dick from its pouch, and smeared it with lube.

"Let's see you come, boy!"

"Yes, sir!" I grabbed my dick with my right hand, while still holding onto the cross with my left. I stroked furiously.

"I'm coming," he shouted.

"Oh, yes, sir, come in me, come in your boy!" He reared back, still in me, but pulling the jock to the point of breaking. I could feel the spasms in his dick.

"Oh, God... oh God... oooh!" he roared.

"Daddy, Daddy, Daddy." I closed my eyes and saw my father's face. I could feel the orgasm building within me, pushing aside all reality except itself. I shuddered violently and squirted my load onto the cross. My father's image disappeared.

He pulled his cock out of me, the end of the condom bulging with his seed. *I hope I can get a mouthful of that someday.* He took his hunting knife and cut the waistband and leg straps of my jock. *Not my jock, not Dad's jock. No!*

"Oh, please don't cut my jock, sir. Oh, God, whatever you want, sir!" He wiped away my tears with the jock and threw it in a wastebasket. He led me to the wall, lay against it, and guided me into a fetal position with my head in his lap. He brushed my hair back from my eyes.

"Welcome back, boy. My name's Brad. I'm taking you home tonight."

"Yes, Daddy." *I offer myself entirely to you. Keep me, guard me as your property and possession. Amen.*

FLAME

Tom Bacchus

To:custserv@netbud.com
X– Originating-IP:[206.170.1.232]
From:"cuir_dude"@hotmail.com>
To: custserv@netbud.com
Subject: Re:Cancellation of Account
Date:Mon,23Feb199818:32:34PST
NetBuddiesCustomerService@netbud.com

Dear Sirs:

In what I hope will be your last e-mail to me, you wanted to know why. Why am I breaking it off? Where did you go wrong?

Well... not only are your visuals nothing but a bunch of racist ageist muscle fascist bullshit, but I can't download the pictures!

But why I am really canceling my account with Net Buddies is:

cubandick

The guy never showed up.
Do you know how long I waited?
I don't even like cappuccino.

dachs_hund

Yes, your own little chat host. Our little repartee went something like this. Actually, it went exactly like this, since I logged our conversation. It would come in handy in someone's... psychological profile... don't-cha think?

By the way, is it true that your company is connected to Scientologists?

dachs_hund: dude you have a great profile
cuir_dude: thanks
dachs_hund: want to talk?
cuir_dude: about...?
dachs_hund: i dunno... what all you into?
cuir_dude: pumping eating sleeping
cuir_dude: hehe
cuir_dude: you?
dachs_hund: same as me, except my order would be sleeping, pumping, and eating <grin>
cuir_dude: sounds like a better schedule
dachs_hund: thanks... what's your name mean>?
cuir_dude: what do you think?
dachs_hund: dunno. But you would have to be pretty into it to have that be your name. Uh, medicine?
cuir_dude: it's got nothing to do with medicine. Lemme give you a clue. I used to be pup_boy.
dachs_hund: pups could be boys too
cuir_dude: pups
cuir_dude: yup
cuir_dude: I was in this 'zine called Pup a while back
dachs_hund: gotcha
dachs_hund: cool
cuir_dude: this guy who writes stuff for the web site got me a freebie membership
dachs_hund: yeah? what about him?
cuir_dude: it's worth every penny.
dachs_hund: talked to him before
cuir_dude: yeah? He's funny
dachs_hund: yeah... huh?
cuir_dude: wrote a story about me
dachs_hund: he did? Where? What site?
cuir_dude:.......in....a....book.
dachs_hund: .;~~~~~~~
cuir_dude:
dachs_hund: oh.
dachs_hund: so, you in hunt mode?
cuir_dude: me?
dachs_hund: see anyone else in this room?
cuir_dude: I'm... well, I'm looking for a younger guy

cuir_dude: into some fun light stuff
cuir_dude: but maybe something intense
cuir_dude: you?
dachs_hund: light stuff... intense? like smbd?
cuir_dude: Duh!
cuir_dude: but none of that Eagle chaps crap ;)
dachs_hund: ahhhhhh, i see... I knew there was a reason you seemed cool
cuir_dude: wrestling, ropes, playing games
dachs_hund: I'm totally into that
cuir_dude: really?
dachs_hund: yeah... i have the sockets in my ceiling to prove it
cuir_dude: HAHA
dachs_hund: <grin>
cuir_dude: what hangs from the ceiling? or should i say who?
dachs_hund: you, me... could be anyone.
cuir_dude: huh
cuir_dude: profile sez looking for friends only
dachs_hund: you want to hang from my ceiling?
cuir_dude: hehe
dachs_hund: well, friends have to share the same interests...
cuir_dude: I like Spidey. He hangs.
cuir_dude: you have a boyfriend?
dachs_hund: and besides I got tired of all these freaks messaging me
cuir_dude: i know
cuir_dude: they should call it Freak.Net!
dachs_hund: but your profile peeked my interest
cuir_dude: LOL!
dachs_hund: not everyone is a freak... a few really cool people
cuir_dude: such as...?
dachs_hund: ever talk to crew_cut?
cuir_dude: nope
cuir_dude: couple in DC that have nude shots
dachs_hund: he's cool
cuir_dude: talked w/ his pup, who made a vid w/ Donnie Russo.
dachs_hund: really? who?
cuir_dude: dc_boat something
cuir_dude: i forget
dachs_hund: no prob

dachs_hund: where you located? sf?
cuir_dude: lower haight
dachs_hund: really? cool... mission area here
cuir_dude: so, ya got pix of you hanging from the ceiling you could send me?
dachs_hund: heh, i wish
cuir_dude: no?
dachs_hund: i have videos... <smile>
cuir_dude: really?
cuir_dude: are you in pron?
dachs_hund: huh? oh, yeah... no not really. mostly just amateur stuff "home movies" but I have been an extra before
cuir_dude: that is too funny
dachs_hund: what? home movies? haven't you ever done that before?
cuir_dude: I posed for a guy.
dachs_hund: oh really?
cuir_dude: but just for his 'zine
dachs_hund: nude?
cuir_dude: oh yeah
cuir_dude: we dated for a while
dachs_hund: cool... what's he like?
cuir_dude: brilliant, funny, wild
dachs_hund: cool
cuir_dude: once he tied me up and wouldn't let me come for hours
dachs_hund: how sweet!
cuir_dude: yes, it showed that he cared
cuir_dude: hehe
dachs_hund: yup
cuir_dude: so, did you say you got a boyfriend?
dachs_hund: yeah i do
cuir_dude: so, you do 3-ways?
dachs_hund: yeah, can do that
dachs_hund: you into that?
cuir_dude: depends on the boyfriend
dachs_hund: check out the profile for sf_muscl
cuir_dude: ok
dachs_hund: you like it?
cuir_dude: <in a stewardess voice> One moment, puh-lease.

cuir_dude: woah! scary!
dachs_hund: what?
cuir_dude: what's with the naked alien?
dachs_hund: huh?
cuir_dude: the blurry face effect
cuir_dude: weird!
cuir_dude: is that your boyfriend?
dachs_hund: no me. oh, sorry about that... you can see the original if you want
cuir_dude: ok
dachs_hund: you want me to send you the unblurred shot?
cuir_dude: pronto!
dachs_hund: gotcha
cuir_dude: so sf_muscl is your boyfriend?
dachs_hund: the top pic is
cuir_dude: oh
dachs_hund: bottom pic is me
cuir_dude: well
cuir_dude: oh!!
dachs_hund: oh?
cuir_dude: now i am confused
<invalid command>
cuir_dude: now i am confused
dachs_hund: that's okay
cuir_dude: so yeah, so...
dachs_hund: i sent you the pic
cuir_dude: oh, i will look for it
cuir_dude: thanks
cuir_dude: i got an underwear shot of me somewhere
cuir_dude: I'll send it to you
cuir_dude: where's best?
dachs_hund: cool... docks_hound@netbud.com
cuir_dude: ok
cuir_dude: well, i should go. Gotta movie date
cuir_dude: then eat then sleep then...?
dachs_hund: <grin>
cuir_dude: later stud

He sent a nude picture that assured it.
Replicant.

He had the body of a guy who would be an extra in a pron video. Not porn. *Pron.* Imagine *Deep Space Niner.*

Our meeting, had I bothered:
Since I don't drink booze and he doesn't do coffee, we would have protein smoothies. He would tolerate the entire seated chat, but I know it to be hopeless. I will tell by the controlled way he keeps his chin at a certain angle, perpetually.

He would look at me in a way that would remind me of a Damon Knight short story/*Twilight Zone* episode, "To Serve Man," because he would be feeling my arm for muscle texture.

I knew that, because I saw it in the picture. There was this soullessness, a strange look in his eyes. I anticipated, had I been accepted, being bitten.

The last dog that bit me was sent to the pound.

But I should not blame you for your hiring practices!
Why am I canceling my membership?
Mostly:

topboy8!
As if.
Do you have an Exaggerator Button in Photoshop somewhere on that web site?
Not a top, not a boy, and no way 8.

In his profile, his cock resembled a blessing of flesh, an orchestra of suckable cock.

We chatted a bit on-line, but I cut through it. I was hungry too now, I guess. It was a full moon.

cuir_dude: So, ya wanna get together?

When he answered the phone (later I would realize I had never given him mine, and was sooooooooooooooooo glad) his voice reminded me of the glass coffee table of an auto salesman in Fort Lauderdale. Like that guy in *Fargo.*

All the time I thought, hang up now. Hang up now.

I didn't. I wanted to suck a dick. I didn't care if he had the inevitable single teddy bear in the middle of the bed. I didn't care if he had *Martha Stewart's Living* as bathroom reading. I wanted a dick in my mouth, and besides, he lived in Fox Plaza, and I hadn't been in that *Logan's Run* job in years. A view too? Fab.

As I walked down the hall of his floor, I remembered living in such a structure, and the torment. I was put off by the very obvious way a white-haired man walked right in front of me and entered the apartment next door to my Mystery Date.

The moon was full, I was a scruffy surf dude ready for action.

He wasn't.

He was Donald Duck.

No, he was a guy who was Donald Duck for a summer job, and considered it an honor.

We made, or I made, some chat.

I rubbed his back. I nibbled his crewcut, the only part of his body that I recall being the least bit erotic to me, because it reminded me of someone else.

As I perhaps too eagerly nestled myself between his legs, I wrapped my lips—oh, so delicately around his growing cock. Please grow, I wished, please make it bloat in my mouth, big as a balloon, just fill my mouth.

He yanked it out. Damn! I should have had that crooked tooth taken out.

I watched him hustle off to the bathroom to inspect his cock for abrasions, spores, whatever.

Upon his return, the announcement: "I'm sorry, but this isn't going to work out."

I was already putting my pants back on.

The walk home was a glorious slap in the face.

He, of all people. This little rat-toad of a saggy-ass queen from bumfuck. If he had any idea the men I fucked, on bulldozers, in vans at Gay Pride, in hotels in Washington, D.C., while hundreds of pals Stormed the NIH a few blocks away!

I fucked the world, twice already.

He had all those mirrors. One entire wall of mirror. What the fuck is with that? How could there *not* be someone on the other side?

I was probably the only person to go this far with him—ever. I felt sorry for his next guest.

Yesterday, he showed up at my gym.

I took one long stare at him, turned away, and proceeded to press sixty pounds more than he had on the machine a moment before.

In the showers, he almost got to see it—what he never saw before. I teased my towel shut like a small curtain. Closing time for you.

"I wrapped my towel around me like a Dorothy L'Amour sarong," as Joni says, and did not even turn to see topboy8 again. I would quit this gym today, if not only for the assurance of not having to ever see that pathetic rubber dog of a face that made me even bother, made me rely on the crap shoot of an electronic jack-on-line machine, that I would allow the placement of an ad, and not the stars, or my instinct, or my nose to determine my next affair.

Because, long after you've done it with Mister Net Buddy, the best ones disappear. The lousy ones, and the less than lousy ones, hang around your life like lichen.

GETTING PERSONAL

David Harrison

I had been consistently perceived as male for at least nine months, after a year and a half on hormones, and hadn't had any surgery yet, when I decided it was time to check out sex with my new body and place my first personal ad. I'd been a lesbian for fifteen years before my transition. Now I was coming out of a long-term relationship and finding myself looking at men. It was during my four-and-a-half-year relationship with none other than the lovely Kate Bornstein, who years earlier had undergone her own gender change, that I transitioned. Kate made it safe for me to face the gender issues that had been chasing me for so long. It was the relationship I had wanted all my life and now, almost as a cruel joke, it too was changing. I was starting to be attracted to men.

Kate saw it coming long before I did. She said: "I have a feeling that if you decide to go through with a gender change, you'll want to be with men and not want to be with me." It was one of her biggest fears, and of course I hotly denied the possibility. But gender changes have their own agendas. Although it took me a long time to actually admit it (because it was such a painful realization), I found myself not attracted to her in the way I used to be. I was not able to give her what she needed, because I was so self-involved. And her attraction for me had shifted also. The chemistry had literally changed.

"Is it the hormones?" people ask. In my opinion they likely play a large role, but more in facilitating the blossoming of the seed that was there in the first place. I'd had a male homoerotic sensibility as a small child. My first sexual fantasies, at age five, were going to bed at night as Paul and George of the Beatles and taking turns fucking each other.

Anyhow, there I was, shell-shocked, coming out of my relationship (not to mention dealing with my own transition), and really needing to explore sex with men. I was horny as hell, and after some encouragement from a couple of friends, I made my first foray into the world of the personals. I started out by answering other people's ads, and it was with one of these encounters that I had my first experience as a transsexual man being with a man. It remains one of my best experiences because we had a great verbal rapport, shared interests, and mutual respect, as well as fun in the sack. We still keep in touch.

When I first started out being sexual as David, I decided that, although I knew I wanted to get top surgery done, I didn't want my anatomy getting in the way of my feeling pleasure. I wanted to be sexual and still feel I could be a man—perhaps stretch the definition of what a man is, in other people's minds—instead of conforming my mind and body to fit someone else's idea. So while I still had breasts, I wore a T-shirt during sex, so I didn't experience dysphoria by being visually reminded of their presence. Different men dealt with me in different ways, depending on how limited or open their own conception of gender was.

But before meeting any of them, I had to screen messages left on the voice mail. Let's get real—at the beginning I talked to almost everyone, because I really wanted to get laid. And I wasn't as picky as I am now. I was an adolescent—it was time to experiment! Despite seeing hundreds of male clients while working as a professional dominatrix over a span of two years, my experience with men as partners up to that point had been somewhat limited: I had never had a boyfriend in my life and had had sex with only three men (once with each) before I came out as a lesbian when I was 19. How would it be different now? And what kinds of men would be interested in me?

At that time I couldn't conceive that a gay man would want to be with me because of what is and isn't between my legs. Some of that was confirmed initially. I placed my ads in the "Men Seeking Men," "Bi," "Trans," and "Other" sections, and I never got a response from "Men Seeking Men." For the most part, female-to-male transsexuals are still unknown to mainstream culture. When most people hear or use the word "transsexual" it is understood to mean male-to-female. And there is certainly no pornography (that I've seen) about us.

After I had been approached about being part of a slick "out-there" show on sex by one of the cable networks and asked if I would possibly model nude, the show was dropped. I asked the researcher (who was quite hip and initially enthusiastic) to tell me the truth. She said that the two producers were a couple of straight guys who couldn't see how they could make an FTM transsexual be sexy. Sexy to them. While MTF transsexuals are fetishized in pornography (as part of someone else's fantasy, not their own), FTM's have been invisible. And so it follows that most guys answering my ads would be uninformed.

Bruce left only his name and number on my personals voice mail. I called him back.

"Your ad sounded tantalizing."

"Umm hm..."

"So... how long ago did you begin your sex change?"

"I started hormones a year and a half ago."

"Hmmm... I don't mean to be disrespectful—but what does your body look like?"

"I have what resembles female anatomy, but otherwise I look like a man."

"But with your clothes off...?"

"Are you mostly interested in men, or women, or both?"

"I'm heterosexual," he says.

"Well, I doubt that you'd find me attractive, then."

"I'm attracted to masculine-looking women."

"I'm not a woman. People tell me I look like a gay man. Have you been with transsexuals before?"

"Yeah, once. It was a really interesting experience. I'll never forget it."

"Male-to-female or female-to-male?"

"Uhhh... male-to-female. I played with her cock... What kinds of things do you like to do in bed?"

"It depends on who I'm with."

"Maybe we can get together..."

"Look—I did not place this ad to be an exotic experience for someone else. Besides, the kind of men I'm attracted to are mostly gay men or gay-identified bisexuals. Do you understand?"

"Yes. Maybe we can get together."
"I don't think so. It wouldn't work."

Sometimes the sex has been great, and I've had a lot of fun. The times it hasn't clicked have mostly been with men who described themselves as bisexual, but essentially lead straight lifestyles. It usually worked up to a point, and then they lost their erections. After having a whole string of those, I asked one guy: "Is it the chemistry, my body, or what?" thinking that because this was happening with such frequency, I must be a lousy lay. He said it was partly chemistry, but also guys sometimes lose erections in new and unfamiliar situations. I guess I'd qualify for that. Then he said to me: "You responded like a woman when I was fucking you." And I wish I'd said to him: "Have you ever fucked a man? Do you know how a man responds?"

I'm not typical of most transsexual men, in that I enjoy being fucked in my vagina with a penis. The whole point of my gender transition was to free myself up. If something feels good to me, I'm not going to stop doing it because it doesn't fit someone else's notion of what a man is. And as much as I can show bravado about the whole thing, sometimes I feel very shy—that, first of all, I was a boy born with a vagina and, second, that I actually enjoy using it. Although I'd like my genitals to be different, for right now I can deal with what I have.

A guy named Carl left a message saying he'd like to talk.
"I'm looking for a new experience."
"Are you attracted to men?"
"No. I'm straight."
"You should know then, that even though I still have the plumbing I was born with, I'd look like any other guy to you."
"But you have female genitals, right?"
"Sort of... My clitoris has grown a lot. It's about two inches long when erect. It looks like a very small penis."
He wanted to come over and meet me anyway. As he walked in and sat down, he barely looked me in the eye.
"Aren't you supposed to like women?"
"My gender identity, which is who I feel I am inside, is a different issue than sexual orientation, which is who I'm attracted to."

He was already overloaded, and this tipped him over the edge.

"You know, a lot of guys have a hard time with this. It brings up a lot—like thinking that if they're turned on to me, maybe they're gay."

His eyes flashed with recognition, and he laughed nervously. As I showed him out through my narrow hallway, he walked past making sure that no part of him touched me.

It's a common expectation of men I meet through the ads that I look like a masculine woman or a butch dyke. I have explained again ad nauseam that I have sideburns, a goatee, a hairy belly—hair all over. That if they saw me on the street they would think I was like any other guy. Is that emphasis enough? But many are still surprised when they meet me. Another assumption is that now that I'm a "man" I should want to be with women and that I would automatically want to assume the "male-dominant" role in sex—in other words, to act out the traditional hetero dynamic.

I get a message from a cross dresser named Annabelle, who said:

"It sounds like we'd be perfect for each other."

"What are you interested in?"

"Everything."

"What specifically do you like?"

"Role-reversal."

"I can't imagine what that would be for me."

"Well, you know... I'm looking for someone to escort me. Someone to 'augment' my femininity."

"I don't think we're compatible."

Then I talk to Steve—or Sandra.

"Have you been with guys before?" I ask.

"No."

"Are you attracted to guys?"

"No."

"Then why did you call me?"

"I have this fantasy. Me dressed as Sandra going out with you. You're dressed as a man but really a woman."

"This is not about dressing up, for me."

"Oh, I understand."
"No, you really don't."

I really try to be forgiving, because I know most people just don't have the information. I can't blame them for their ignorance—but sometimes I get so angry. I burn out from constantly having to explain myself. Fortunately some guys just innately get it, and those are the ones with whom I end up having a great time.

I've always felt an inherent power imbalance in hetero relationships. It's unavoidable because of the culture's implicit (and explicit) expectations of gender roles and behavior. It feels quite alien to the way I'm wired. Which is probably why I have always been queer no matter what gender I am. Aside from all I have yet to understand about my own desire, I do know that a relationship starting out with an equal power balance has always been important to me. That can be a safe springboard to exploring erotic power-exchange in a more conscious way.

What I've learned through doing the personals has been crucial in forming my new identity. By putting myself out there, I got to find out how I want to be related to and also what is unacceptable. That aside—I love sex and that's really why I do it! Most of the men I've met and/or with whom I've had sex, have been very personable. Some guys, even though I am a totally new phenomenon to them, have treated me with great respect and made the adjustment very well. These are usually guys whose main interest is men. It's with them that I've had the hottest sex. I would guess this is because in being conceived as gay out in the world, one is confronted by society's views of homosexuals as "less than men" and "like women." And this can lead to questioning one's own gender in a way that most heterosexual men never have to. So, in finding a place in the world as a man on one's own terms, often it is less of a leap on a visceral level to experience me as just another type of man.

As much as others have had assumptions about me, I have also had to challenge my own preconceptions about men—particularly having been raised as female. I assumed that all gay men were size-queens and that none would want to be with me because I have a pussy and a tiny dick. I'm discovering that there are plenty of queers out there to whom that's not important. For many, it's about masculinity in all its possible expressions, a dick being only one aspect of that.

I also had this idea that a gay man (or any man for that matter) would automatically have a more positive body image and comfort with their sexuality than me, because they have the "right equipment." I was wrong. If anything, it's shown me that I'm not doing too badly at all and that most people have something about their body they're not quite satisfied with and would like to change.

My sexuality has shifted enormously since my transition. At first when I started having sex with people I met through the ads, old programming would creep in. I was raised to be a nice girl. As a woman, I would have been called a slut if I were working the sex ads the way I've been doing. But as a gay man, being told you're a slut is frequently considered a compliment! There were times (early on) when I played with guys I wasn't really attracted to or didn't even like that much. After they'd leave I'd think: "I can't believe I did that." It was partly horniness and partly not knowing my boundaries yet. Nowadays I am more confident that I'm desirable. Every transsexual I know wonders at some time—usually when they're in the first year or two of transition—if they are ever going to have a lover again and if anyone is going to be attracted to them. I went through that—and sometimes I still do.

So how is sex different now? I actually feel like I'm in my body, which helps. I enjoy sex as recreation more than I did before, and I'm able to distinguish between sex and romance—whereas in my former incarnation, the lines frequently blurred. Definitely hormones. Since I began my second adolescence, I've evolved into being a lot less dick-focused and more into the whole person—which is, after all, how I want people to relate to me.

Recently I have taken to posting ads on-line and have been (for the most part) getting better responses :

Hi David:
I'm a 39 yo Gay man living in SF. I'm 5'9", 190 lbs, bear-type. I have bright blue eyes and brown fur (including a full beard, which I wear short). I'm sexually adventurous, although more top than not, and male identified (e.g., I

don't care what's between your legs, as long as you are a man inside). I had many friends in the TS/TV community in Chicago and have been looking for friends (as well as playmates) since I moved to SF 2 yrs ago. I'm HIV negative, and plan to stay that way. My interests include music, both playing and listening, motorcycles, photography, art in general, and roller coasters. I don't smoke or drink. I have been told I have a healthy amount of boy left in me.

Please drop me a line—I'd love to get to know you, and I look forward to hearing from you.

Greg

When I first started doing the personals, I was telling a friend about it and reading her my ads. She asked:

"So, do you have gay sex with these guys?"

"What do you mean by gay sex?"

"You know, fucking in the ass."

So... if two women are fucking each other in the ass, are they having gay sex, or are they just fucking each other in the ass? What about when a woman is fucking a man in the ass? And what is it when a dyke and a fag have sex with each other? Or, when a man is fucking a man in the vagina? Is that heterosexual? As my friend James said to me after we had played for the first time: "Sex is not about body parts. It's about the erotic energy that happens between two people."

TO BE LOVED

David Pratt

I decided I had to be like this to be loved:
Upbeat and kind.
Fun.
Myself, but not too much. Not so much myself that they'd get nervous. I had to be sweet in a world of privately enraged men and in spite of my own private rage.

I placed an ad in the *Village Voice* the Wednesday before Thanksgiving 1995, and again the Wednesday after. I said I liked long walks and long talks. It's sappy and conventional. It raises the awful prospect that after all our manic self-invention, we'll have to face our need for the same trite stuff They pushed all along, in their numbing world of washer-dryers and highboys.

The world that bred us, then cut us off. After all the fabulous outfits and nights at the opera, after all the *Mandate* centerfolds, will all roads lead back there, where we'll be strapped into a mini-van?

But I do like long walks and long talks. Judging from the responses I got, a lot of other men do. Or want to. Or would like to think they do.

For a touch of individuality I mentioned my love of Irish traditional music. The *Voice* typo'd that; I forget just how. The typo became a point of conversation with my respondents.

For "fun"—because I longed to believe that I was not so serious (as one man had said) or uptight (another's word)—I mentioned that I love to ride the Cyclone at Coney Island. Most of the men who responded said everything sounded good, except the Cyclone. They said I could ride the Cyclone by myself.

I think I said I liked arts. All gay male personals say that. Or the not-much-more-specific "music and movies." (Though I did once see a personal placed by a self-confessed Philip Glass fanatic.)

I did not say that I like sports, because I don't. So many gay male personals say they like sports that I wonder what became of the soft, silent boys who, like me, dreaded and flunked weekly gym classes? Where are my comrades who, when they stepped to the softball plate, drew groans and pleas to let others pinch hit, who were laughed at uproariously for their attempts at wrestling, inevitably with one another? Where in the personals is Clarence Dawes, absent from school every Tuesday, the day we had PE? Is Clarence absent from the personals, too? Or has he placed an ad that claims he likes sports? Because if he said he hated sports, he knows the reader would picture... well... him, just as he is. And move on, to someone who said they liked sports.

Someone maybe like Richie Blank. Strapping Richie excelled at PE, was always chosen first for teams. He had plenty of girlfriends. He finally married, just a couple of years ago. Yes, someone like Richie Blank, only queer.

My ad said nothing about my body (there is little to say, one way or the other). As far as the other guy, I said little. I did not feel comfortable specifying in shape, straight-acting, or even nonsmoker. I phoned my ad in a week or so before Thanksgiving.

Ah, those unknowns, out there! Those mystery men whose strings I could now pull!

I waited.

❖   ❖   ❖

That October, my AIDS buddy, a 36-year-old mother of two, had died after a harrowing seven-month struggle. I wasn't with her; I was on my way back from my first stay at a writers colony in southern Vermont.

After leaving Lisa's funeral, walking up Seventh Avenue South in a dour, purple dusk coming to night, I cruised a wide-eyed, 19-year-old student from Staten Island. We exchanged numbers.

Nineteen. O-o-okay. One more and I would get serious. I would begin to settle.

Frank, the 19-year-old, didn't know what he wanted, but he wanted it now and lots of it. He felt abashed about every aspect of himself—his youth, his ethnically mixed face with its big nose and its zits—and he couldn't stop grinning and blushing and rolling or batting his eyes. I can't remember what we did the November weeknight he came over. Shortly after we finished, I asked him to go. I decided I had to stop looking for love in the wrong places. My therapist had asked, why not place an ad? So I did.

❧   ❧   ❧

Perhaps due to the busy time of year, I received only twenty-some responses. When you reach someone through a personal, you first make chat around your histories with ads, and I spoke to men who'd advertised at other times and received seventy or eighty responses. Yet the couple dozen that left me voice-mails were more than enough, because one aspect of this endeavor had taken me by surprise:

Blind dates.

I had never been on a blind date. When you place a personal, though, you set yourself up for nothing but blind dates, one after another. I managed four: two coffees and two dinners through which I and another nice fellow labored to piece together conversation, though I and perhaps he knew there was no click. This is a sad realization, no matter that the man and I are strangers. It's hard to sip coffee and chat about job, family, rent, and hobbies while the weltschmerz of that realization sinks in.

On a more pragmatic level, the whole thing feels like a waste of time—an exercise, a prolonged slide down from hello. I felt bad for the guy, bad for myself, bad for all gay men, and I also knew I could be cleaning out my closet or polishing my latest short story. (Anyone who comes to this city has more than domesticity on their mind to begin with.) Or I could be curling on the couch, hot mug and novel in hand, putting the novel down a long moment to dream of the next man.

And yet I could not refuse a man who'd just walked through a restaurant door. I mean, he might turn out... Well, no, maybe not. And yet even at the end of the evening I couldn't just say no. A clean, up-front rejection is no better than an understood one. This is why the phrase, "I'll call you" must exist in every language.

Herewith, then, my four blind dates:

Randy—a radio traffic announcer in his late thirties—portly, balding, sweet, recently out and a bit self-conscious about it. He conversed in the tidy, generic phrases of an announcer—except when he spoke of his ex, Chris, whose love had brought him out. Then a wistfulness entered his voice and passed quickly. I might have loved Randy. I tried picturing it. He certainly was kind. But I feared a man who neither looked nor acted like anyone I had ever pictured loving. I conceived a relationship as handing my life over, and I couldn't hand my life over to that. Or, as it would turn out, to various other things.

Randy and I went on two dates. After the second, a matinee of *Persuasion,* I said, "Good movie," and Randy said, "Good movie, good company." I smiled and nodded and agreed that I would call him. I honestly thought I might. But I didn't. And he never called me.

Max wanted to know, ten minutes into our meeting over coffee, whether I was a top or a bottom. Max was a top. He felt it was never too soon to establish such preferences. I agreed, to be friendly, and told him I could switch hit. Toward the end of our coffee date, Max announced that with exams coming up (he was a law student) and then his Christmas break (in the Philippines), he would have no time to get together and would even be unreachable by phone for the next five weeks. Maybe six, he wasn't sure. But I could leave a message, if I liked.

On the sidewalk in front of the NYU law library, we said a goodnight that I hoped Max knew I knew was a good-bye.

I think I sound as though I felt superior to these men. I thought I couldn't help that. I had put out a call; they had answered. But relationships don't happen because one participant sits and awards points to the other. Relationships choose their participants. I wanted to scream at my dates in all their self-consciousness, "No! I have no power! This makes me nervous and self-doubting, too!" Still, the dating game scared me, so if an audition dynamic did hold itself out to me, I would go with it. With Randy I felt closer to a balance in this respect, though he often felt a need to apologize and explain his coming out late. I reassured him, meanwhile taking some pleasure in how I might look to him: He came out young, he's got it all together. After all, I had never felt much admired by anyone for anything. I'd get it where I could.

Max had turned the tables. He took charge with that top-bottom question. Yet that did not manage to allay his fears. The next man, Barry, put me in complete charge, and the date was a disaster.

Barry and I met at a café on Forty-ninth Street. I sensed early that there would be no spark. We ordered cappuccinos. Barry had just come from work, so we talked about work.

As Barry talked, he blushed, covered his mouth or the whole lower half of his face. I find it hard to discuss my work situation—part-time office job, part-time not-so-renowned author. Barry's embarrassment reached its peak when he discussed his job. He lowered his eyes, stammered, covered his mouth, confessed that he held an administrative/caretaking kind of position in show business, and blushed. I sensed that, like me, he felt embarrassment at not having followed through with a creative theater career. I had neither the skills, nor the courage, to open that discussion: "How do you feel about assisting an agent? How and when did you make The Decision? How do you feel when the agent yells at you for making the coffee wrong, and you stand with the pot in your hand, remembering the spring you did *Guys and Dolls?* I feel I killed myself off young. I wonder if you feel what I felt working in the ticket office, placating irate subscribers? Is it like what I felt, assistant stage managing at twenty-three, when so long ago, at twenty-two, I'd acted in *The Three Sisters* and *Tartuffe* and had refused to believe it would end?"

My history was too much like Barry's for me to bear. Plus—no spark. I had no curiosity to see Barry naked. Well, on some level I have that curiosity about any man once he is offered as a possibility for intimacy. If he is kind and attentive and is also a personal archetype, he will stir my blood. If he fits no personal archetype, his unlikeliness may stir my curiosity. Or his attentiveness alone may stir me. Randy's attentiveness made me look at his obesity as cuddliness. But I could not stop seeing obesity. I am not shallow, really. I suppose when the spark is not there, or I am not willing to take the chance of striking it, the surface features become the only considerations. Perhaps on this occasion I placed the wrong kind of ad.

Dan, the last of my blind dates, came the closest to being an intellectual match. I'm not talking about IQ, but about interest. Some kids take apart their toys and want to invent new ones. As a writer, I suppose I take apart reality and make new realities. Dan was a psychologist and a teacher, and so he, too, did both of those. Dan had become close to a sweet, introverted student who had Tourette Syndrome. Dan explained that such people do not, as pop entertainment would have us believe, blurt out streams of random obscenities; rather, most sufferers have particular words. Dan's pupil's word was *nigger.*

"And since he is white," Dan explained over dinner with me on the Upper West Side, "and since he weighs about 135 pounds, you can imagine he gets into a lot of fights. He comes in with bruises all the time and says, 'Oh, I got beat up again.'"

Tourette sufferers may have unusual physical tics as well. Dan's pupil licked things. "On the first day," Dan said, "he came up to me and said, 'Just so you know, before I hand any paper in to you I'm going to lick it. I don't have any control over it.'" Dan described all this with energy, equanimity, compassion, and a touch of wonder. How could I not go for someone who told that story that way on the first date? How could I not go for someone who accepted licked papers?

The naked thing, is how. Dan was good-looking and well-groomed. He was attractive. But no matter the angle from which I studied him, he was not especially attractive to me. Although I loved that Tourette story. Imagine: "SWM, 19, with Tourette Syndrome, seeks SWF 18-21 for companionship and possibly more. I say 'nigger' frequently for no reason at all and often lick things. I can't help it. But I have a good heart and am considered a fun person by my friends."

Wouldn't you want to caress his bruises?

Wouldn't you prefer him to Randy, Max, Barry, Dan, or to moi?

Isn't that the ultimate personal ad?

Isn't that also one ad we know we will never, ever see?

In the clamor of the Christmas holidays, I abandoned the personals. Setting up and going on those four dates had frightened the part of me that clung to certainty, had saddened the part that sought mystery and intrigue, had exhausted the part that guarded the part I held most sacred, most secret. I had felt a wave of anxiety when I crossed the orbit of each of those men. I blamed them—carefully. I slogged to therapy in January snow, head hung, convinced I was unmarriageable. For the next eighteen months,

I went for the quick, intense highs of fuck-buddy improvisations. When those no longer satisfied, I returned to the measured rituals of dating. A succession of men proved tantalizing but unavailable. When a match at last happened, it happened effortlessly. Yet to stay the course and make the most of the opportunity I have been offered, I have had to marshal every resource I have.

I am writing this at the end of March 1998, at the end of an unseasonably warm week.

The sun has been a constant presence, and the trees on Ninth Avenue have burst heedlessly into blossom. I met a man last June at a Gay Pride spirituality workshop. I can not think how to talk about him. He resists summing up, as does our experience together, so simple and so complex.

He is seven years younger than me, from the south of Brazil, has lived in the U.S. the past eleven years, has an undergraduate degree in biological science, was a hairdresser for several years when he first came here, received his masters in social work last spring, now trains high school kids in the Bronx as HIV/AIDS peer educators, smokes, and calls me *Gatinho,* which is Portuguese for kitten. We have had wonderful times and difficult ones and ones in-between.

We have sensed something larger at work. We go out, and I see myself, seated alone across the room, watching the two of us and wondering how in the world people get to do what we are doing. I come back to myself, and the unimaginable feels so small and right, and yet so big, so beyond either of us, like trying to imagine what's beyond the edge of the universe. Early on I told him that, with him, I felt as though I didn't have to do anything. He said I was right.

Neither one of us has conducted himself perfectly. We have each done some of those things that the dating tips in gay magazines say not to do—we are, in other words, ourselves, sometimes too much so—but a deeper sense of partnership and intellectual vibration drives the relationship (and I love seeing him naked). So we talk about or just get over one another's little obsessions or once-in-a-while thoughtless moments. I have discovered what it means to love someone not just in spite of their flaws but because of them, and to receive the same love in return. And each of us has done so much that has turned out to be so right—often without trying, sometimes by trying especially hard.

"Baby," he tells me, "you have no idea what a blessing it is to have someone I can talk to about these things. Not everyone is willing to do that." No they're not. I could not talk to very many men in the ways I talk to him—about insecurities, my past, my ideas for the future. I feel accepted by him. It all feels kind of normal and kind of other-worldly and kind of serene and grown-up.

Truly, I don't know what I did to deserve this, and I can honestly say I was not looking for what I found. I didn't think it would feel like this. I didn't imagine myself in an evolving and deepening partnership. I knew the buzz words—intimacy, growth, sharing—and I mouthed them and claimed to want them, but like a child, I had no idea what I was saying. My four blind dates showed a failure of imagination compared to the little, quotidian ways in which I have been required to stretch by real relatedness, by someone who really wants to know every evening how I am and what I've been doing and thinking and feeling. By someone who will examine what I say, look inside it and inside me, and who will show me his insides. Lying in bed he asks, "You're not afraid any more, are you Gatinho?" And I hug him and say, "No, Babe, not as much."

Of course, I always will be. A little.

We have both felt even better the past week with the coming of spring. His friend told us when the weather turned warm we should drive out to Brighton Beach, eat at one of the Russian restaurants, and stroll on the boardwalk.

We'll have a long talk. As darkness falls, we will look down the beach to see the lights of the Wonder Wheel at Coney Island. Maybe I can convince him to ride with me on the Cyclone. I won't go alone. But if he'll ride with me, I will promise to protect and take care of him.

To seal my promise, I will lick these pages, all over, and present them to him.

ABOUT THE AUTHORS

JAMES JOSEPH ARNOLD has written for *Frontiers, Daily Variety,* and *Prime Health and Fitness* and is the author of the screenplays *Me and Mamie O'Rourke, Lovelines,* and *The Lourdes Kelly Story* and a one-act play, *Bookends.* Jim has also torn what's left of his hair out working in movie business public relations for the last ten years. Raised in Milwaukee and taught by the Jesuits, the School Sisters of St. Francis, and the School Sisters of Notre Dame, he credits his midwestern, Irish Catholic upbringing for the tasteful prose you find in front of you. After 17 years in Los Angeles, Jim recently moved north and began terrorizing San Francisco. His e-mail address is: *jjarnold@primenet.com.*

TOM BACCHUS has never been arrested for public indecency. His hand-painted 'zine, *PUP* (for men who need to be on a leash), is now a collector's item—if you collect that kind of thing. His novella, *Tony Saturday,* can be found on www.gay.net. His two books of stories, *Bone* and *Rahm* (both published by Masquerade) have recently received their first, richly deserved royalty checks. His work is also included in such anthologies as: *Happily Ever After: Erotic Fairy Tales for Men; Stallions and Other Studs;* and *Best Gay Erotica 1998* (Cleis). His safe sex short, *Scenic Route,* can be rented at San Francisco's Superstar Video.

FRED BERNSTEIN grew up in shouting distance of the Long Island Expressway. (That, and everything else in his story, is true.) After graduating from Princeton, he found work as a newspaper reporter *(Newark Star-Ledger)* and magazine editor *(People,*

Metropolitan Home). Convinced he needed to do something more serious with his life, he went to law school (NYU '94). He has clerked for two federal judges and written on gay/lesbian legal issues (particularly the problems facing gay men who have children). He has published articles in *The Advocate, The New York Times,* and *The Washington Post.* An inveterate traveler (and travel writer), he lives on an island conveniently situated between Newark, LaGuardia, and Kennedy airports. He is still friends with his college roommate, Andrew, but has not seen Stuart since their date. He can be reached via e-mail at *FABnyny@aol.com.*

ROY CAMERON was born in 1949 in Okinawa, Japan, the son of U.S. Air Force parents. He was raised in Louisiana, Mississippi, and California (Los Angeles). In 1985, after spending almost 20 years in the design industry, he suffered a heart attack and decided to refocus his career. He was hired as a case manager for the Long Beach Center AIDS Project and soon became its acting director. In 1988, he moved to San Francisco, where he opened Your Personal Best, an exercise facility that specialized in working with persons who suffer from "gym fear." In 1996, after complications following major surgery, he moved to Palm Springs to recuperate. Today he is fulfilling a lifelong dream of creating a holistic fitness resort, The Renewal Center. He remains single and receives correspondence at *BearInBoot@aol.com.*

JAMESON CURRIER is the author of *Dancing on the Moon: Short Stories about AIDS* (Viking, 1993) and of the documentary film *Living Proof: HIV and the Pursuit of Happiness* (1993). His novel, *Where The Rainbow Ends,* was published by Overlook Press in October 1998. His short fiction has appeared in *Art & Understanding, Evergreen Chronicles, The Minnesota Review, Lisp, Backspace, Genre, Christopher Street, LGNY,* and in such anthologies as *Certain Voices, Ex-Lover Weird Shit, Men on Men 5, The Mammoth Book of Gay Erotica,* and *Best Gay Erotica.* A member of the National Book Critics Circle, Currier's writings on AIDS and the gay community have appeared in numerous national mainstream and community publications from *The Washington Post, The Los Angeles Times,* and *Newsday* to *Lambda Book Report, The Harvard Gay and Lesbian Review,* and *Body Positive Magazine.* He can be reached at *JCurrier1@aol.com.*

PATRICK ARTHUR DAKIN is a student at Goddard College in Vermont, where he is studying writing. This is his first published work. He would like to dedicate the piece to his close friend Lee, for helping him find the courage to actually tell the story. He gets his e-mail at *pdakin1@hotmail.com*.

J.R.G. de MARCO has written extensively for the gay/lesbian press, from *The Advocate* and *In Touch* to *The New York Native* and *Philadelphia Gay News* (PGN). In 1983, his article "Gay Racism" was awarded the prize for excellence in feature writing by the Gay Press Association and was anthologized in *Black Men, White Men* (Gay Sunshine Press, 1984), *Men's Lives* (Macmillan, 1989), and *We Are Everywhere* (Routledge, 1997). His work has appeared in such additional anthologies as *Gay Life (Doubleday,* 1986), *Quickies* (Arsenal Pulp Press, 1998), and the forthcoming *Angie Loves Mary, Vinnie Loves Sal* (Guernica, 1999), a collection of gay and lesbian Italian-American writing. A number of his plays have won awards and competitions with productions and staged readings. He lives in Philadelphia, where he is working on a non-fiction book as well as a novel. Interruptions are welcome at *jrgdemar@aol.com*.

TIM DRISCOLL is a writer and an actor who has developed and produced three solo performance plays in the past three years: *Genders Collide Inside My Dance Belt; My Hole Life;* and *Creative Fluid. My Hole Life* was also recently published in *The Evergreen Chronicles.* His work has been broadcast several times on WKCR out of Columbia University, and he reads regularly at the Cornelia Street Café in Greenwich Village as the newest member of a collective of gay and lesbian writers called Three Hots and a Cot.

ERASMO GUERRA was born and raised in the Rio Grande valley of south Texas. He has been published in the anthologies *New World: Young Latino Writers,* edited by Ilan Stavans (Delta, 1997), and *Gay Travels: A Literary Companion,* edited by Lucy Jane Bledsoe (Whereabouts Press, 1998). He now lives in New York City, where he is at work on a novel.

JESSIE McHALLON HALL is a pseudonym for a writer and editor who wishes for unspecified reasons to remain anonymous. He has been widely published in gay anthologies and in the mainstream press. He gets his e-mail at *EditWriter@aol.com*.

DAVID HARRISON is an actor and playwright who has contributed to a number of anthologies, including: *Beyond Definition: New Writing from Gay and Lesbian San Francisco* (Manic D Press, 1994); *Assaults on Convention: Lessons from Lesbian Transgressors* (Cassell, 1996), and *Out in All Directions: A Treasury of Gay & Lesbian America* (Warner Books, 1997). As well as acting in other people's plays, he continues to internationally tour his own solo piece, *FTM*. "Getting Personal"—which was first published as "The Personals" in *Pomosexuals: Challenging Assumptions About Gender and Sexuality* (Cleis, 1997)—was originally written as a performance piece for the May 1995 opening of Loren Cameron's photo exhibit, "Body Alchemy." David's e-mail address is *peterpants@earthlink.net*.

DOUG HARRISON, Ph.D., is an engineering manager who does "weird things" on weekends. He has been an active member of the San Francisco leather community and a modern primitive for over ten years. He identifies as a bisexual top/bottom and seeks transcendence through meditation, music, and intense physical experiences. He has led workshops and organized retreats dealing with consensual S/M for the last ten years. Doug has published several technical papers and two collections of technical proceedings. His erotic writing includes reviews, essays, and short stories that have appeared in *Body Play* and the humorous sex 'zine *Black Sheets*. He is currently working on several short stories for various anthologies and a book on erotic whipping to be published by Daedalus Publishing Company. Doug was chosen Mr. June for the AIDS Emergency Fund's 1999 South of Market Bare Chest Calendar. He also appears in porn videos. Doug and his domestic partner, Bill, live in San Francisco. They have an open relationship. Doug can be reached at *puma@dnai.com*.

MARC J. HEFT is a native New Yorker who now resides in Greenwich Village. Although he was born in New York, his family decided to move to New Jersey when he was only three years old. At the time he had no choice but to accompany them and hopes one day to be able to forgive them for this. He is the executive vice president of a public relations consulting firm. He enjoys film, theater, traveling, and adventures of all kinds. This is his first published piece, and—for those who are wondering— he remains single, yet hopeful. He can be found at *hudsonmarc @aol.com.*

NELS P. HIGHBERG has had work published in *A Loving Testimony: Remembering Loved Ones Lost to AIDS* (Crossing Press, 1995) and *Generation Q* (Alyson Publications, 1996), and he often contributes to the *Gay People's Chronicle* in Cleveland. He has earned masters degrees in women's studies and comparative studies at Ohio State University and is currently working towards a Ph.D. in English at the University of Illinois at Chicago. His academic work focuses on representations of AIDS.

WAYNE HOFFMAN is a journalist whose work has appeared in dozens of publications, including *The Advocate, XY,* and *Torso.* He is co-editor of *Policing Public Sex: Queer Politics and the Future of AIDS Activism* (South End Press, 1996) and a contributor to the anthology *Generation Q* (Alyson, 1996). He currently lives in New York, where he is the arts editor of *The New York Blade.*

ERIC LATZKY is the author of a novel titled *Three Views from Vertical Cliffs* (Amethyst Press, 1992). He has also written about culture and the arts for various publications in New York and Los Angeles. He was born in New York and has lived in Paris and Los Angeles. Since returning to New York in 1990, he has been employed as the communications director of a multi-media performing arts center and as a public relations agency vice-president. He currently works at home representing clients in the arts and culture to the media. He is 35 years old and at work on a second novel. E-mail may be sent to *ECharlesNY@aol.com.*

J'SON M. LEE, though born in Brooklyn, NY, is essentially a North Carolinian and a graduate of the University of North Carolina at Chapel Hill. He is 28 years old and currently resides in our nation's capital, where he works in commercial real estate. An avid fan of the arts, he recently discovered a passion for writing, which he finds both therapeutic and revelatory. He dedicates this first published piece to E. Banks. (Now I know it would have been a mistake if I hadn't allowed myself the chance to feel your love. We'll meet again.)

OWEN LEVY is the author of the best-selling 1980s novel *A Brother's Touch*. A native New Yorker and Stonewall survivor, he lived in Berlin from the mid-1980s until recently. He has received residency fellowships from the Helene Wurlitzer Foundation in Taos, New Mexico, and the MacDowell Colony in Peterborough, New Hampshire. As a freelancer, his reviews, entertainment stories, and profiles have appeared in various gay and mainstream publications. His e-mail contact address is *110213.1664@compuserve.com*.

BARRY LOWE lives in Sydney, Australia. He summarizes himself as follows: "GM Taurus in long-term relationship (Capricorn) seeking interesting playmates as fodder for his writing. Compatibility essential: You must believe that Mamie Van Doren, Annette Funicello, Doris Day, and porn star Kevin Kramer are god!" His latest play is *Homme Fatale: The Joey Stefano Story* (1998). Others include *The Death of Peter Pan* (1994), *Seeing Things* (1994), *Dutch Courage* (1997), *The Extraordinary Annual General Meeting of the Size-Queen Club* (1996), and *Rehearsing the Shower Scene from "Psycho"* (1995). His short stories have appeared (in the U.S.) in *The James White Review,* the first volume of *Flesh and the Word,* and *The Mammoth Book of Gay Erotica,* among others. You can e-mail him at: *barrylowe@wr.com.au.*

GLENN MILLS's entry in this anthology represents the first publication of his creative work (unless you count the two personal ads mentioned in his story). Upon giving up his fast-track to a corner office in 1995, he realized his fantasy of working at the Corner (restaurant, that is) with some of Kansas City's most artistically (and sexually) diverse biscuit-and-gravy slingers. Between stints of trying to convince his co-workers and customers that he was not Opie Taylor, he played around at bank consulting in New York and stapling things as a Kelly Girl at Hallmark. In 1997, he finally became poor enough to afford a return to school and is currently a graduate student in creative writing at University of Missouri–Kansas City. He recently completed his first screenplay, and is presently working on a second screenplay and a longer memoir. He can be contacted via e-mail at: *gnrlmills@aol.com.*

ACHIM NOWAK is a native of Germany who now lives in Manhattan. Excerpts from his forthcoming memoir, *Graham Greene Is Dead,* appear in the anthologies *Men on Men 6* and *Gay Travels: A Literary Companion.* Another excerpt won a PEN Syndicated Fiction Award and was broadcast on National Public Radio. His writing has also appeared in the *James White Review* and *Washington Review.* His performance work, created with choreographer/director Wendy Woodson and other collaborators, has been presented in venues throughout the U.S., Canada, and Europe. Recognition for his work includes a fellowship from the NEA and a 1997 fellowship in nonfiction literature from the New York Foundation for the Arts. He is a founding member of Three Hots and a Cot, a collective of queer writers in New York City. He can be reached at *AchimOne@aol.com.*

ROBERT E. PENN is a community organizer, educator, author, consultant, and survivor. He is the author of *The Gay Men's Wellness Guide: The National Lesbian and Gay Health Association's Complete Book of Physical, Emotional and Mental Health and Well-Being for Every Gay Male* (Holt, 1998). For five years he managed the Gay Men's Health Crisis HIV Prevention programs, and he continues to lecture across the U.S. and in Europe and South America on such subjects as health and wellness, heterosexism, racism, homophobia, safer sex, living well with HIV, and the design of culturally appropriate public health and disease-prevention programs. His poetry and prose appear in such anthologies as *Shade, We Are Everywhere, Milking Black Bull, Sojourner,* and *The Road Before Us;* magazines and journal appearances include *Essence, Shooting Star Review, Thing* and *COLORLife,* as well as *The Portable Lower East Side* and *Art & Understanding.* In addition to writing new prose, fiction and dramatic pieces, he serves as the treasurer of Other Countries: Black Gay Expression, the writing, performance, and publishing group. Contact him at *REPenn@juno.com.*

NEIL PLAKCY received his MFA in creative writing from Florida International University. His fiction and nonfiction have been published in many local and national magazines, including *The Miami Herald, Computoredge,* and *Florida Architecture.* He lives in Miami, where he tries to avoid gawking too much at the boys on South Beach. He has written two mystery novels—starring a gay police detective in Honolulu—that he hopes will someday be published. Though he swears he recently met a great kisser, he can be reached at *kimofl@juno.com.*

DAVID PRATT has published short fiction, poetry, and essays in *Christopher Street, Art & Understanding, The James White Review, Genre, Excess Compassion, The Chiron Review,* and other periodicals. He was the winner of the 1996 fiction competition conducted by In Our Own Write in New York City. He belongs to the New York literary collective, Three Hots and a Cot. He is currently completing his first novel and starting his second. Address e-mail to David to *DWP152@aol.com.*

TOM REILLY is a New York School realist painter. Represented in many collections, he is the winner of the Smith-Wellman Award. He is currently artist-in-residence at Instituto de Zulia, Maracaibo, Venezuela.

DAVID SANDERS was born in Manhasset, New York, and educated at Georgetown, George Washington, and New York universities. He resides in New York City and works in the entertainment industry. His interests include painting, composing, and, most of all, writing. He has written two novels, a collection of poetry, and a series of children's books. "DHEA, Testosterone, Minoxidil, Fruition, and Eye Zone" is his first published work.

LAWRENCE SCHIMEL is the author of *The Drag Queen of Elfland* (Circlet Press, 1997) and the editor of more than twenty anthologies, including *Two Hearts Desire: Gay Couples on Their Love* (with Michael Lassell; St. Martin's Press, 1997), *The Mammoth Book of Gay Erotica* (Carroll & Graf, 1998), *Switch Hitters: Lesbians Write Gay Male Erotica and Gay Men Write Lesbian Erotica* (with Carol Queen; Cleis Press, 1996), and *Things Invisible to See: Gay and Lesbian tales of Magic Realism* (Circlet Press, 1998), among others. He is the immediate past co-chair of the Publishing Triangle, the organization of gay men and lesbians in publishing, and was the co-programmer (with Cecilia Tan) of OutWrite™ 1998, the national gay, lesbian, bi- and transsexual writers' conference. His *Pomosexuals: Challenging Assumptions About Gender and Sexuality* (with Carol Queen, Cleis Press, 1997) was a recipient of a Lambda Literary Award. He currently lives in New York City, where he writes and edits full-time, and can be reached at P.O. Box 528, New York, NY 10011.

D. SPOILER (pseud.) did not wish to offer any information about himself other than that which appears in his story.

ABOUT THE EDITOR

MICHAEL LASSELL is the prize-winning author of three collections of poetry: *Poems for Lost and Un-lost Boys* (Amelia, 1985), winner of the first Amelia book award; *Decade Dance* (Alyson, 1990), winner of a Lambda Literary Award and a finalist in the Gregory Kolovakos Award for Writing about AIDS; and *A Flame for the Touch That Matters* (Painted Leaf Press, 1998). He is also the author of *The Hard Way* (A Richard Kasak Book, 1995), a collection of poetry, short stories, and essays. He is also the editor of three pocket anthologies: *The Hard Way: Classic Gay Love Poems* (St. Martin's Press, 1995); *Eros in Boystown: Contemporary Gay Poems About Sex* (Crown, 1996), a Lammy finalist; and, with Lawrence Schimel, *Two Hearts Desire: Gay Couples on Their Love* (St. Martin's, 1997).

His writing has appeared in numerous anthologies, including *Men on Men, Flesh and the Word, High Risk, Hometowns, Gay & Lesbian Poetry in Our Time, Best Gay Erotica, The Mammoth Book of Gay Erotica, The Columbia Anthology of Gay Literature*, and *W.W. Norton's New Worlds of Literature*. His fiction, poetry, and essays have appeared in scores of literary anthologies (from *Fag Rag* and the *James White Review* to the *Portable Lower East Side* and the *Kansas Quarterly*), newspapers (ranging from *The New York Times* to *Frontiers* and *New York Native*), and magazines (*Out, The Advocate, Movieline, Dance, Mirabella, Westways, Live!*). His work has been translated into French, German, and Dutch.

Lassell holds degrees from Colgate University, the Yale School of Drama, and California Institute of the Arts, where he has taught in the Division of Critical Studies as well as in the School of Theater. He has worked as a critic (for the *L.A. Weekly* and the *Los Angeles Herald Examiner*) and as the managing editor of *L.A. Style* and *Interview* magazines. He lives in New York City, where he is the features editor of *Metropolitan Home* magazine. He can be reached at *MJLassell@aol.com*.

OTHER BOOKS FROM PAINTED LEAF PRESS

POETRY

My Night With▪Mi Noche Con
Federico García Lorca
Jaime Manrique
0-96515583-8
Bilingual Edition

Night Life
Paul Schmidt
0-9651-5580-3

Winter Solstice
Paul Schmidt
0-9651-5582-X

October for Idas
Star Black
09651-5581-1

Cold River
Joan Larkin
0-9651-5585-4

Desire
Tom Carey
09651558-4-6

Sor Juana's Love Poems
Sor Juana Inez de la Cruz
Translated By Jaime Manrique and Joan Larkin
0-9651558-6-2
Bilingual Edition

In the Open
Beatrix Gates
0-9651-5585-4

Island Light
Eugene Richie
0-9651558-8-9

A Flame for the Touch That Matters
Michael Lassell
0-9651558-9-7

Fiction

Bad Sex Is Good
Jane DeLynn
1-891305-00-X

Colombian Gold
Jaime Manrique
1-891305-01-8

New York Sex: Stories
Edited by Jane DeLynn
1-891305-03-4

Please visit our Website at
www.paintedleaf.com